DATA BANK ON
INDIAN POLITY

DATA BANK
ON
INDIAN POLITY

Compiled and Edited by

Arvind M. Dwivedi

ANMOL PUBLICATIONS PVT. LTD.

NEW DELHI - 110 002 (INDIA)

ANMOL PUBLICATIONS PVT. LTD.
4374/4B, Ansari Road, Daryaganj
New Delhi-110 002
www.anmolbooks.com

Data Bank on Indian Polity

First Edition 2001
ISBN 81-261-1002-3

PRINTED IN INDIA

Published by J. L. Kumar for Anmol Publications Pvt. Ltd., New Delhi-110 002 and Printed at Tarun Offset Press, Delhi.

CONTENTS

PREFACE

In the present complex society, due to increased number of aspirants for rare opportunities, competition has become acute and the situation of 'survival of fittest' has come. Gone are the days when the degrees were enough to get a job. Now the thorough study of any subject is required to get through in any competitive examination. The objective multiple choice type questions are asked almost in all the competitions. In order to meet the increasing demand of the aspirants to equip them with ready and uptodate knowledge, we have prepared the Data Bank on Indian Polity. It is concise, comprehensive and dependable which has a wide coverage of the syllabus.

The proportion, of questions from Politics in General Study has get tremendous increase in the recent past. Near about 15% questions are asked from this portion. In the present data bank we have touched all the corners of syllabus as well as the latest pattern of questions asked in UPSC, SSC, LIC, GIC, CDS, NDA and other examinations. We have taken utmost care in preparing the questions with particular gradation and level of the various examination.

The readers can send us their valuable comments for further improvements in the subsequent edition of the book.

—Arvind M. Dwivedi

1
CONSTITUTIONAL DEVELOPMENT

1. The first attempt to regulate the affairs of the English East India Company was made by
   (a) The Regulating Act of 1773
   (b) Pitts India Act of 1784
   (c) The Charter Act of 1861
   (d) Dundas Bill of 1783.

2. Which of the following acts created the Supreme Court of judicature at Fort William?
   (a) Regulating Act of 1773
   (b) Montague Chelmsford Reforms Act 1919
   (c) Minto-Morley Reforms Act 1909
   (d) None of the above.

3. The office of the Governor General was for the first time created under
   (a) The Regulating Act of 1773
   (b) Indian Councils Act 1861
   (c) Dundas Bill of 1783
   (d) None of the above.

4. The Pitts India Act of 1784 was largely based on
   (a) Dundas Bill of 1783
   (b) Fox India Bill of 1783
   (c) Regulating Act of 1773
   (d) None of the above.

5. Under which of the following Charter Act was the general Indian trade thrown to the British subjects?
   (a) 1813 (b) 1853
   (c) 1793 (d) None of the above.

6. The East India Company was deprived of monopoly of trade with India except for tea under
   (a) The Charter Act of 1813
   (b) The Charter Act of 1835
   (c) The Charter Act of 1853
   (d) None of the above.

7. The East India Company directed to maintain two separate accounts for its commercial transactions and territorial possessions under
   (a) The Charter Act of 1861
   (b) Pitt's India Act 1784
   (c) Charter Act of 1813
   (d) None of the above.

8. Under which of the following Acts the British missionaries permitted to go and settle in India?
   (a) The Charter Act of 1773
   (b) The Charter Act of 1813
   (c) The Charter Act of 1833
   (d) None of the above.

9. Which one of the following provisions was made in the Charter Act of 1833?
   (a) Government services in India were thrown open to all Indians
   (b) The designation of the Governor General of Bengal was changed as the Governor General of British India
   (c) The commercial functions of the East India Company came to an end and now it had only political functions
   (d) All of the above.

10. Under which of the following Acts was the President of the board of control made the minister for Indian Affairs?
    (a) Pitts India Act of 1784
    (b) The Charter Act of 1833
    (c) The Charter Aact of 1835
    (d) None of the Above.
11. The Governor-General of Fort William was redesignated as the Governor-General of India under
    (a) The Charter Act of 1833
    (b) Dundas Bill of 1783
    (c) The Charter Act of 1793
    (d) None of the above.
12. Which of the following Acts added a Law member to the Governor-General's Council?
    (a) Regulating Act of 1773
    (b) Indian Councils Act 1861
    (c) The Charter Act of 1833
    (d) None of the above.
13. Under which of the following Acts was a bid to bring about centralisation in legislative field made for the first time?
    (a) The Government of India Act 1919
    (b) Regulating Act of 1773
    (c) The Charter Act of 1833
    (d) None of the above.
14. Under which of the following Acts was the office or employment under the company thrown open to all residents and subjects of His Majesty without any distinction of religion, place of birth, descent, colour etc?
    (a) The Charter Act of 1833
    (b) Regulating Act of 1773
    (c) Indian Councils Act of 1909
    (d) None of the above.

15. The system of recruitment on the basis of merit was introduced by
    (a) The Charter Act of 1813
    (b) Indian Councils Act of 1909
    (c) The Charter Act of 1833
    (d) None of the above.

16. Under which of the following Acts was a separation in the commercial and political functions of the East India Company made?
    (a) Indian Councils Act, 1909
    (b) Indian Councils Act, 1892
    (c) The Charter Act of 1833
    (d) None of the above.

17. Under which of the following Acts were all the services thrown open to the competitive examination during British Rule?
    (a) Regulating Act of 1773
    (b) Indian Councils Acts 1892
    (c) The Charter Act of 1853
    (d) None of the above.

18. Under which of the following Acts was the Governor General's council enlarged for the purpose of legislaton by addition of six new legislative members?
    (a) The Charter Act of 1853
    (b) Indian Councils Act 1861
    (c) Regulating Act 1773
    (d) None of the above.

19. Which one of the following was not included in the Charter Act of 1853?
    (a) Governor-General was given the power to veto the bills passed by the legislative council
    (b) A provision was made for an open competitive examination for recruitment to the Indian Civil Service

(c) The Bill passed by the legislative council could not be vetoed by the Governor-General

(d) Under this Act a legislative council for India was created.

20. By which of the following Acts was the Governor General redesignated as Viceroy

(a) The Act of 1858

(b) Indian Councils Act 1909

(c) Indian Councils Act 1892

(d) None of the above.

21. According to the Act of 1858 the territory was divided into

(a) Provinces (b) States

(c) Zones (d) None of the above.

22. Under which of the following Acts was Indian Councils created?

(a) The Act of 1858 (b) The Act of 1935

(c) The Act of 1909 (d) None of the above.

23. By which of the following Acts were the military and naval forces of the East India Company transferred to the services of the Crown?

(a) Indian Councils Act 1909

(b) Indian Councils Act 1892

(c) The Act of 1858

(d) None of the above.

24. Under which of the following Acts were the powers of the Court of Directors and the Board of Control abolished and their powers vested in the Secretary of State for India?

(a) Indian Councils Act, 1892

(b) Indian Councils Act, 1909

(c) The Act of 1858

(d) None of the above.

25. The system of double government was done away by
    (a) The Act of 1858 (b) The Act of 1909
    (c) The Act of 1935 (d) None of the above.

26. The administration of the East India Company's Empire in India was formally taken over by the Crown of England under
    (a) The Regulating Act of 1773
    (b) The Charter Act of 1813
    (c) Pitts' India Act 1784
    (d) None of the above.

27. According to the Government of India Act, 1858 the Governor General-in-council was responsible to
    (a) Secretary of State
    (b) British Crown
    (c) British Parliament
    (d) None of the above.

28. Under which of the following Acts was the Government of India transferred from the Company to the Crown?
    (a) Regulating Act 1773
    (b) The Act of 1858
    (c) Indian Councils Act 1892
    (d) None of the above.

29. When did the British Crown assume sovereignty over India from the East India Company ?
    (a) 1858 (b) 1885
    (c) 1853 (d) 1847.

30. Which one of the following was not among the provisions of the Act of 1858?
    (a) The East India Company was abolished.
    (b) The administration of India and the Indian territories was transferred to the Crown
    (c) The Governor-General of India was to be known as the Viceroy of India

(d) The administrative power of India was to be shared between the East India Company and the Crown of England.

31. Which Act was the first statute enacted by Parliament for the Governance of India under the direct rule of British Government?

(a) Government of India Act , 1858
(b) Indian Councils Act 1861
(c) Indian Councils Act 1892
(d) None of the above.

32. When was the Proclamation of Queen made which outlined the principles which were to form the basis of future Government in India?

(a) 26 January,1858 (b) 1 November, 1858
(c) 15 August, 1858 (d) None of the above.

33. By Government of India Act 1858, the powers of the Crown were to be exercised by the

(a) Secretary of State for India assisted by a council of fifteen members
(b) Council of India
(c) Secretary of State for India
(d) None of the above.

34. Under which of the following Acts was the ordinance making power of the Governor-General granted for the first time?

(a) The Indian Councils Act, 1861
(b) The Indian Councils Act 1892
(c) The Indian Councils Act 1909
(d) None of the above.

35. By which of the following Acts was the Governor General's Legislative Council enlarged and given purely Legislative functions?

(a) The Regulating Act 1773
(b) The Indian Councils Act 1909

(c) The Indian Councils Act 1861
(d) None of the above.

36. Which of the following Act initiated the policy of legislation resolution?
(a) The Indian Councils Act 1861
(b) Regulating Act 1773
(c) The Act of 1858
(d) None of the above.

37. By which of the following Acts were the foundations of the system of administration in India laid which lasted till the end of British Rule?
(a) The Indian Councils Act 1861
(b) The Indian Councils Act 1892
(c) The Indian Councils Act 1909
(d) None of the above.

38. By which of the following Acts were the law making powers which were taken away from the presidencies of Bombay and Madras by the Act of 1833 restored to them?
(a) The Indian Councils Act 1861
(b) Regulating Act 1773
(c) The Indian Councils Act 1909
(d) None of the above.

39. Under which of the following Acts were the members of the Legislative Councils for the first time given right to ask questions from the government and seek other information?
(a) The Indian Councils Act, 1909
(b) The Indian Councils Act, 1892
(c) The Indian Councils Act, 1861
(d) None of the above.

40. By which of the following Acts was the Governor General given Absolute Veto in matters pertaining to legslation?

(a) Regulating Act, 1773
(b) The Indian Councils Act, 1861
(c) The Indian Councils Act, 1909
(d) None of the above.

41. Morley-Minto Reforms were implemented by
(a) The Indian Councils Act, 1861
(b) The Indian Councils Act, 1909
(c) The Indian Councils Act, 1892
(d) None of the above.

42. Which of the following Acts provided for the first time for separate representation to the Muslim community?
(a) The Indian Councils Act, 1892
(b) The Indian Councils Act, 1909
(c) The Indian Councils Act, 1861
(d) None of the above.

43. Under which of the following Acts was the federal court provided?
(a) Act of 1909 (b) Act of 1892
(c) Act of 1858 (d) None of the above.

44. Under which of the following Acts was the Communal Electorate system introduced by the British in India for the first time?
(a) The Indian Councils Act, 1909
(b) The Indian Councils Act, 1861
(c) Government of India Act, 1919
(d) The Indian Councils Act, 1892.

45. Which one of the following first initiated the idea of Provincial Autonomy?
(a) Despatch of Lord Hardings in 1911
(b) Morley-Minto Reforms Act, 1909
(c) Montague-Chelmsford Reform Act, 1919
(d) None of the above.

46. Which of the following is also known as the Act of 1919?
   (a) Montague-Chelmsford Reform Act
   (b) Regulating Act
   (c) Montague-Morley Reforms Act
   (d) None of the above.

47. Under which of the following Acts was the office of the High Commissioner created?
   (a) 1919 (b) 1910
   (c) 1935 (d) None of the above.

48. The system of dyarchy was introduced by the British in India under the
   (a) Government of India Act, 1909
   (b) Indian Councils Act, 1892
   (c) Government of India Act 1935
   (d) None of the above.

49. Dyarchy in the provinces was introduced by the
   (a) Government of India Act, 1919
   (b) Indian Councils Act, 1861
   (c) Indian Councils Act, 1909
   (d) None of the above.

50. Montague-Chelmsford Reform led to the inactment of the
   (a) Government of India Act, 1919
   (b) Indian Councils Act, 1909
   (c) Indian Councils Act, 1861
   (d) None of the above.

51. Which of the following is not the main feature of the governmental system prescribed by the Act of 1935?
   (a) Dyarchy at the Centre
   (b) Federation and provisional autonomy
   (c) Dyarchy in the provinces
   (d) None of the above.

52. Dyarchy was replaced with autonomy by
    (a) The Act of 1919
    (b) The Act of 1935
    (c) The Act of 1909
    (d) None of the above.

53. Under which of the following Acts was the Indian councils abolished which had been in existence 1858?
    (a) 1867 (b) 1909
    (c) 1935 (d) None of the above.

54. Under which of the following Acts was the Federal Public Service Commission created?
    (a) Government of India Act, 1935
    (b) Indian Councils Act, 1861
    (c) Indian Councils Act, 1909
    (d) None of the above.

55. Provincial Autonomy was introduced on
    (a) Jan. 30, 1937 (b) Jan. 30, 1936
    (c) April 1937 (d) None of the above.

56. Under which of the following Acts was provincial autonomy introduced in India?
    (a) Indian Councils Act, 1861
    (b) Indian Councils Act, 1882
    (c) Indian Councils Act, 1909
    (d) Government of Indian Act, 1935.

57. When did Cripps Mission come to India?
    (a) 1942 (b) 1943
    (c) 1944 (d) None of the above.

58. Who of the following suggested Rajaji formula in 1944 with a view to resolve the political deadlock in the country?
    (a) C. Rajagopalachari (b) Mahatma Gandhi
    (c) J.L Nehru (d) None of the these.

59. The appointment of a Governor-General in each Dominion was provided by
    (a) Indian Councils Act, 1861
    (b) Mountbatten Plan
    (c) Indian Councils Act, 1909
    (d) Indian Independence Act, 1947.

60. Which of the following Acts abolished the office of the Secretary of State for India?
    (a) The Act of 1919 (b) The Act of 1935
    (c) The Act of 1947 (d) None of the above.

ANSWERS

1.	(a)	2.	(a)	3.	(a)	4.	(b)
5.	(a)	6.	(a)	7.	(c)	8.	(b)
9.	(d)	10.	(b)	11.	(a)	12.	(c)
13.	(c)	14.	(a)	15.	(d)	16.	(c)
17.	(c)	18.	(a)	19.	(c)	20.	(a)
21.	(a)	22.	(a)	23.	(c)	24.	(c)
25.	(a)	26.	(d)	27.	(a)	28.	(b)
29.	(a)	30.	(d)	31.	(a)	32.	(b)
33.	(a)	34.	(a)	35.	(c)	36.	(a)
37.	(a)	38.	(a)	39.	(b)	40.	(b)
41.	(b)	42.	(b)	43.	(d)	44.	(a)
45.	(a)	46.	(a)	47.	(a)	48.	(d)
49.	(a)	50.	(a)	51.	(c)	52.	(b)
53.	(d)	54.	(a)	55.	(c)	56.	(d)
57.	(a)	58.	(a)	59.	(a)	60.	(c)

2
MAKING OF CONSTITUTION

1. A constitution is
   (a) a set of ordinary laws
   (b) a set of financial laws
   (c) a set of official laws
   (d) the basic structure which defines the powers of the state and the rights and duties of its citizens.

2. "All constitutions are the heirs of the past as well as the testators of the future" Among the following who made the above observation?
   (a) A.B. Kiete (b) A.C. Diecy
   (c) Sir Iver Jennings (d) V.N. Shukla.

3. Who made the Constitution of India?
   (a) The King of England
   (b) The British Parliament
   (c) The Indian Parliament
   (d) The Constituent Assembly.

4. A Constituent Assembly is
   (a) Convened to change ordinary law
   (b) Convened to make ordinary laws
   (c) Specially convened to frame the constitution of the country
   (d) Convened to pass the budget of a country.

5. The demand for eastablishment of the Constituent Assembly was first made by the Indian National Congress in 1936 in its session held at
   (a) Bombay (b) Lucknow
   (c) Lahore (d) Faizpur.

6. The Constituent Assembly was set up under the
   (a) Cabinet Mission Plan of 1946
   (b) Government of India Act, 1919
   (c) Government of India Act, 1935
   (d) Indian Independence Act, 1947.

7. The Cabinet Mission plan was announced on
   (a) April 16, 1946 (b) May 16, 1946
   (c) June 16, 1948 (d) July 17, 1946.

8. When was the Constituent Assembly eastablished to form a Constitution of India
   (a) 26th November 1949 (b) 10th June 1946
   (c) 26th December 1949 (d) 6th December 1946.

9. The Constituent Assembly met for the first time on
   (a) December 9, 1947 (b) December 9, 1946
   (c) December 10, 1946 (d) December 7, 1949.

10. The Constituent Assembly was not a sovereign body in the beginning but it became a sovereign body after
   (a) July 1946 (b) 15 August 1947
   (c) 26th January 1950 (d) December 2, 1946.

11. The chairman of the Drafting Committee to prepare a Draft Constitution of India was
   (a) Dr. Rajendra Prasad (b) Shri J.L. Nehru
   (c) Dr. B.R. Ambedkar (d) Dr. RadhaKrishnan.

12. The president of the Constituent Assembly was
   (a) Dr. B.R. Ambedkar
   (b) Dr. Rajendra Prasad
   (c) Shri J.L. Nehru
   (d) Sardar Vallabhbhai Patel.

13. The Constitution of India was passed on
   (a) 26th January 1950 (b) 26th January 1949
   (c) 26th January 1951 (d) 26th November 1949.

14. The Constitution of India was promulgated on
   (a) 26th January 1950 (b) 26th January 1951
   (c) 26th February 1950 (d) 26th January 1952.

15. Under the Cabinet Mission Plan the Constituent Assembly was to consist of
   (a) 379 members (b) 369 members
   (c) 500 members (d) 400 members.

16. Why was the Constitution of India promulgated on January 26, 1950?
   (a) Because January 26, 1950 was an auspicious day
   (b) Because Dr. Ambedkar wanted it to be promulgated on this day
   (c) Because January 26, 1950 was an inauspicous day
   (d) Because in 1929 the Indian National Congress had passed a resolution under the presidentship of Pandit J.L. Nehru in its Lahore session to observe January 26 every year as "Purna Swaraj" or Independent Day.

17. Who among the following was not a member of the Drafting Committee of the constitution?
   (a) Shri N. Gopalachari Ayangar
   (b) Dr. Rajendra Prasad
   (c) Dr. B.R. Ambedkar
   (d) Shri Alladi Krishnaswami Ayyar.

18. The Drafting Committee of the constitution did not have as its member
   (a) Alladi Krishnaswami
   (b) K.M. Munshi
   (c) N. Gopalaswami Ayyangar
   (d) Sardar Vallabhbhai Patel.

19. How much time did the Constituent Assembly take to prepare the Constitution of India?
    (a) 2 years 11 months and 18 days
    (b) 5 years 11 months and 19 days
    (c) 3 years 10 months and 7 days
    (d) 4 years 11 months and 17 days.

20. Who is called the Father of the Indian Constitution?
    (a) Shri J.L. Nehru
    (b) Mahatma Gandhi
    (c) Dr. B.R. Ambedkar
    (d) Shri K.M. Munshi.

21. Who had given the idea of a Constitution for India of all?
    (a) Mahatma Gandhi
    (b) Shri M.N. Roy
    (c) Shri J.L. Nehru
    (d) None of the above.

22. June 3 plan was also known as the
    (a) Mountbatten Plan (b) Cabinet Mission Plan
    (c) Wavell Plan (d) None of the above.

23. Which of the following was the original due date announced by Mr. Attlee, Prime Minister of England for transfer of power to the Indians?
    (a) August 15, 1947 (b) February 20, 1947
    (c) June 1948 (d) June 1949.

24. Which one of the following was not a provision of the Indian Independence Act 1947?
    (a) India was no more under the British Crown
    (b) The Power of Paramountcy of the British over the Indian states was not to lapse
    (c) The British India was Partioned into two independent dominions India and Pakistan
    (d) The Indian states were given the option to join India or Pakistan or to remain independent.

25. The formation of an Interim Government set up on September 2, 1946 was first envisaged by
    (a) Wavell Plan (b) Cripps Mission
    (c) Cabinet Mission Plan (d) None of the above.

26. The objectives of resolution which formed the basis of the preamble of the constitution was moved in the Constituent Assembly on Decembr 13, 1946 by
    (a) Sardar Patel
    (b) Pt. Jawahar Lal Nehru
    (c) Dr. Rajendra Prasad
    (d) Dr. B.R. Ambedkar.

27. The Constitution of India was ordained by
    (a) The people of India directly
    (b) The British govenrment before transferring powers to Indians
    (c) The people of India through their representatives in the Constituent Assembly
    (d) None of the above.

28. Indian Constitution envisages
    (a) a democratic system
    (b) a presidential government
    (c) a bicameral system
    (d) a unicameral system.

29. The constitution of India was inacted by a constituent Assembly set up
    (a) by the Indian congress
    (b) by the British Governor General
    (c) under the Indian Independence Act 1947
    (d) under the Cabinet Mission plan 1946.

30. The Constitution of India was adopted and came into force on
    (a) January 26, 1949/ January 26, 1950
    (b) August 15, 1947/ January 30, 1950
    (c) November 26, 1949/ January 26, 1950
    (d) January 26, 1949/ November 26, 1950.

31. The members of the constituent Assembly were
    (a) Directly elected by people
    (b) Nominated by Governor-General
    (c) Elected by the Provincial Assemblies
    (d) Nominated by Indian National Congress.

32. The Parliamentary System of government in India is based on the pattern of parliamentary government
    (a) Germany (b) Canada
    (c) Britain (d) France.

33. The Indian Constitution is
    (a) Flexible
    (b) Very rigid
    (c) Partly rigid and partly flexible
    (d) Rigid.

34. The spirit of the Constitution of India is unitary because
    (a) Under some circumstances, the parliament can make laws
    (b) All India Services have been provided
    (c) Only parliament has the power to amend the constitution
    (d) All of these are true.

35. The first meeting of the Constitution Assembly of India was held on
    (a) August 15, 1947 (b) November 26, 1949
    (c) December 9, 1946 (d) January 26, 1948.

36. According to the constitution , India is a Secular State which means
    (a) There will be no religion
    (b) Religious worship is banned
    (c) The state regards religion as a private affair of its citizen and there is no discrimination on the basis of regilion
    (d) State patronises the religions.

37. The Constitution of India contains

(a) 280 Articles (b) 305 Articles

(c) Over 400 Articles (d) 260 Articles.

38. A preamble is a

(a) Name

(b) Slogan

(c) Preface or an introduction especially of an Act of parliament giving its meanings and purposes

(d) Poem.

39. Which of the following is described as the soul of the Constitution?

(a) Directive Principles of State Policy

(b) Fundamental rights

(c) Power of judicial review enjoyed by the Supreme Court

(d) Preamble.

40. How many times, the preamble has been amended so far

(a) Never (b) Thrice

(c) Once (d) Twice.

41. The preamble of the Constitution of India was amended by

(a) 42nd amendment

(b) 24th amendment

(c) 39th amendment

(d) None of these.

42. The preamble of the Indian Constitution reads

(a) We, the people of Constituent Assembly adopt, enact and give to ourselves this constitution

(b) We the people of India in our Constituent Assembly adopt, enact and give to ourselves this constitution

(c) We the citizens of the Constituent Assembly of India adopt, enact and give to ourselves this constitution

(d) None of the above.

43. From which of the following constitutions we have borrowed the idea of the preamble
    (a) Constitution of U.S.A.
    (b) Constitution of France
    (c) Constitution of Canada
    (d) Constitution of U.K.

44. Which of the following is not correct?
    (a) A Preamble is a part of the constitution
    (b) The Preamble of our constitution is not justiciable
    (c) A Preamble is not a part of the constitution
    (d) None of the above.

45. According to constitution, India is
    (a) Quasi-Federal
    (b) A unitary state
    (c) A union of states
    (d) A federation of states and union territories.

46. According to the preamble of the constitution, India is a
    (a) sovereign, democratic republic
    (b) socialist, democratic republic
    (c) sovereign, socialist, secular, democratic republic
    (d) None of the above.

47. Which of the following is not among the sources of the Constitution of India?
    (a) Opinions of the constitutional jurists
    (b) Enactments of the Indian Parliament
    (c) Debates of the British Parliament
    (d) Debates of the Constituent Assembly.

48. Which of the following is not a feature of the Indian federation?
    (a) Division of powers
    (b) Partly rigid constitution
    (c) Written and Supreme constitution
    (d) Committed judiciary.

49. The following does not come under the union list
    (a) Currency and Coinage
    (b) Insurance
    (c) Prisons
    (d) Banking.

50. The chief source of Political Power in India is
    (a) the parliament and state legislatures
    (b) the constitution
    (c) the people
    (d) the President.

51. Which type of citizenship is provided by the Constitution of India?
    (a) Double citizenship (b) Multiple citizenship
    (c) Single citizenship (d) None of above.

52. Which one of the following rights is available only to the citizens within the territory of India?
    (1) Freedom of speech
    (2) Right to form Associations or Unions
    (3) Equality before Law
    (4) Freedom to assemble peacefully without arms
    Select the correct answer using the codes given below:
    (a) 1, 2 and 4 (b) 1, 2 and 3
    (c) 2, 3 and 4 (d) 1, 3 and 4.

53. How many articles and schedules did the Indian Constitution contain when it was originally passed
    (a) 395 articles and 8 schedules
    (b) 397 articles and 9 schedules
    (c) 398 articles and 10 schedules
    (d) 399 articles and 12 schedules.

54. In how many parts, the Constitution of India has been divided
    (a) 21 (b) 11
    (c) 2 (d) 9.

55. Which of the following is a feature of the Indian Constitution?
   (a) Protection of minorities and backward classes.
   (b) Presidential Government
   (c) Unitary Government
   (d) Double citizenship.

56. Our constitution grants universal adult franchise to all those men and women who have attained the age of
   (a) 20 years (b) 25 years
   (c) 18 years (d) 21 years.

57. The word 'Federation' is used in which part of the Indian Constitution?
   (a) Part III
   (b) Schedule 3
   (c) Article 395
   (d) Indian Constitution does not use the term 'Federation'.

58. The citizenship of a person can be lost through
   (a) termination (b) deprivation
   (c) renunciation (d) all of these.

59. The first session of the constituent assembly was held in
   (a) Calcutta (b) Bombay
   (c) New Delhi (d) None of the above.

60. How many schedules are there in the present Indian Constitution?
   (a) 7 (b) 5
   (c) 9 (d) 12.

61. The Muslim League decided to boycott the Constituent Assembly because
   (a) they wanted Muslims in majority
   (b) they wanted Islamic rule
   (c) they thought, they have been inadequately represented
   (d) they wanted a separate Constituent Assembly.

62. The two words, added in the preamble of the constitution through the 42nd amendment are
    (a) socialist and democratic
    (b) socialist and secular
    (c) socialist and Republic
    (d) democratic and republic.

63. The Constituent Assembly adopted our National Flag on
    (a) August 15, 1947
    (b) January 26, 1950
    (c) July 22, 1947
    (d) January 30, 1951.

ANSWERS

1.	(d)	2.	(b)	3.	(d)	4.	(c)
5.	(d)	6.	(a)	7.	(b)	8.	(d)
9.	(b)	10.	(b)	11.	(c)	12.	(b)
13.	(d)	14.	(a)	15.	(b)	16.	(d)
17.	(b)	18.	(d)	19.	(a)	20.	(c)
21.	(b)	22.	(a)	23.	(c)	24.	(b)
25.	(c)	26.	(b)	27.	(c)	28.	(c)
29.	(d)	30.	(c)	31.	(c)	32.	(c)
33.	(c)	34.	(d)	35.	(c)	36.	(c)
37.	(c)	38.	(c)	39.	(d)	40.	(c)
41.	(a)	42.	(b)	43.	(a)	44.	(a)
45.	(c)	46.	(c)	47.	(c)	48.	(d)
49.	(c)	50.	(c)	51.	(c)	52.	(a)
53.	(a)	54	(c)	55.	(a)	56.	(c)
57.	(d)	58.	(d)	59.	(c)	60.	(d)
61.	(d)	62.	(b)	63.	(c)		

3

FUNDAMENTAL RIGHTS AND FUNDAMENTAL DUTIES

1. Fundamental Rights are inshrined in the constitution in
   (a) Part V
   (b) Part III
   (c) Part II
   (d) Part IV.

2. Fundamental Rights are
   (a) Those basic conditions of social life without which a citizen cannot be at his best self
   (b) The rights of the Police
   (c) The rights of the rulers
   (d) None of the above.

3. The idea of incorporating Fundamental Rights in the Constitution of India has been borrowed from
   (a) The Constitution of France
   (b) The Constitution of Germany
   (c) The Constitution of U.S.A.
   (d) The Constitution of Britain.

4. How many Freédoms were originally provided under Article 19?
   (a) 6
   (b) 4
   (c) 7
   (d) 8.

5. The following has ceased to be a Fundamental Right in the Indian Constitution
   (a) Right to Property
   (b) Right to Religion

(c) Right to equality
(d) Right to constitutional remedies.

6. Which of the following is not guranteed by the Indian Consitution?
(a) The right to religious freedom
(b) The right to equality
(c) The right to constitutional remedies
(d) The right to free education upto the age of 14.

7. The Fundamental Rights ensure protection of
(a) People against exploitation by traders
(b) The pride of citizens
(c) Citizens against arbitrary rule
(d) Law and order in the country.

8. The Fundamental Rights have the sanction of
(a) The Supreme Court (b) The Constitution
(c) The Government (d) None of the above.

9. The Right to Constitutional Remedies has been granted under Article
(a) 31 (b) 35
(c) 32 (d) 30.

10. Which one of the following rights was described as the "heart and soul of the constitution" by Dr. Ambedkar?
(a) Right to freedom of religion
(b) Right to freedome
(c) Right to equality
(d) Right to constitutional remedies.

11. The Fundamental Rights of the citizens of India
(a) can be suspended by the President with the prior approval of Supreme Court
(b) cannot be suspended under any conditions
(c) can be suspended by the President during national emergency
(d) can be suspended by the council of ministers.

12. Which one of the following courts is responsible for the enforcement of Fundamental Rights
    (a) High Courts
    (b) Supreme Court
    (c) District and Session Courts
    (d) (a) and (b) both.

13. Our Constitution grants to the citizens
    (a) Five Fundamental Rights
    (b) Six Fundamental Rights
    (c) Nine Fundamental Rights
    (d) Seven Fundamental Rights.

14. Right to equality has been granted under Articles
    (a) 18 to 22 (b) 29 to 30
    (c) 24 to 26 (d) 14 to 18.

15. The Fundamental Rights granted to the Indian citizens are
    (a) Always absolute (b) Absolute
    (c) Not absolute (d) None of the above.

16. The Fundamental Rights of the Indian citizens were
    (a) added by 42nd amendment
    (b) incorporated in the constitution by 44th amendment
    (c) enshrined in the original constitution
    (d) None of the above.

17. Which can issue writs for the enforcement of Fundamental Rights?
    (a) The Parliament
    (b) The President
    (c) The Supreme Court
    (d) The Council of Ministers.

18. The Fundamental Rights granted to the Indian citizens are
    (a) Justiciable
    (b) Sometimes justiciable and sometimes non-justiciable
    (c) Non-justiciable
    (d) None of the above.

19. Which Fundamental Rights cannot be suspended during an emergency under aticle 352 of the Constitution?
    (a) Right to constitutional remedies
    (b) Right to equality
    (c) Right of life
    (d) Right to freedome of speech.

20. Cultural and Educational rights have been dealt with under Articles?
    (a) 30 and 31 (b) 31 and 32
    (c) 29 and 30 (d) 33 and 34.

21. The Right to Freedom can be restricted
    (a) in the interest of Nation's secruity
    (b) in the interest of public order
    (c) in the interest of friendly relation with foreign countries
    (d) in all the above grounds.

22. Fundamental Rights are justiciable means that a citizen can seek the assistance of
    (a) President of India to enforce his Fundamental Rights
    (b) Courts for the inforcement of his Fundamental Rights
    (c) Ministry of Law for the enforement of his rights
    (d) None of the above.

23. A socialist ideology is reflected by
    (a) Free and compulsory education of children upto 14 years of age
    (b) Equitable distribution of material resources to prevent concentration of wealth
    (c) promotion of cottage industries
    (d) None of the above.

24. What is the objective behind the cultural and educational rights in the chapter on Fundamental Rights?
    (a) To preserve Indian culture
    (b) To evolve a single culture
    (c) To eradicate illiteracy
    (d) None of the above.

25. Right to freedom of religion has been granted under Articles
    (a) 29 to 31 (b) 25 and 26
    (c) 25 to 28 (d) 25 to 47.

26. Traffic in human beings and forced labour have been prohibited under article
    (a) 23 (b) 25
    (c) 24 (d) 26.

27. Which Article has prohibited the employment of children under fourteen years of age in factories, etc
    (a) 25 (b) 23
    (c) 24 (d) 22.

28. The Fundamental Duties are added to the Constitution
    (a) by the Constitutent Assembly itself
    (b) by the 44th Amendement
    (c) by the 42nd Amendment
    (d) by the 24th Amendment.

29. In which part of the Constitution, the Fundamental Duties are contained?
    (a) Part V of the Constitution
    (b) Throughout the Coustitution
    (c) Schedule XI of the Constitution
    (d) Part IV-A of the Constitution.

30. Following is the bulwark of personal freedom
    (a) Mandamus
    (b) Certiorari
    (c) Hebeas Corpus
    (d) Quo-warranto.

31. The right to impose reasonable restrictions on the Fundamental Rights of Indian citizens is vested in
    (a) The Council of Minister
    (b) The Supreme Court
    (c) The President
    (d) The Parliament.

32. The basic conditions imposed on the citizen's Right to assemble, is that the assembly should be
    (a) Peaceful
    (b) Unarmed
    (c) Non-violent
    (d) Peaceful and unarmed.

33. Which of the following articles guarantees to all persons equality before the law and equal protection of law as within the territory of India?
    (a) Article 14 (b) Article 16
    (c) Article 15 (d) Article 17.

34. In which one of the following Constitutions no duties have been imposed on the citizens?
    (a) Constitution of Japan
    (b) Constitution of Former U.S.S.R
    (c) Constitution of U.S.A
    (d) Constitution of India.

35. Which of the following articles states that no person shall be deprived of his life or personal libety except according to procedure establised by law?
    (a) Article 21 (b) Article 20
    (c) Article 22 (d) None of the above.

36. In which of the following points is the Indian Constitution similar to that of U.S.A?
    (a) Rigid Constitution
    (b) Fundamental Rights
    (c) Rule of Law
    (d) Directive Principles of State Policy.

37. Which one of the following rights has only been granted to the citizens of India and denied to non-citizens?
    (a) Protection of life and personal liberty
    (b) Freedom of speech, assembly and association
    (c) Equality before law
    (d) Right to constitutional remedies.

38. Which of the following Fundamental Duties have been enumerated in our Constitution for the citizens?
   (a) To uphold and protect the sovereignty, unity and integrity of India
   (b) To cherish and follow the noble ideals which inspired our national struggle for freedom
   (c) To defend the country and render national services which called upon to do so
   (d) All of the above.

39. The granting of Fundamental Rights to citizens aims at ensuring
   (a) Socialistic government
   (b) An independent judiciary
   (c) Individual liberty
   (d) None of the above.

40. Does our Constitution provide for the Natural Rights?
   (a) Yes (b) No
   (c) Sometimes (d) None of the above.

41. How many Fundamental Duties have been mentioned in our Constitution?
   (a) Eight (b) Fifteen
   (c) Ten (d) Nine.

42. Which one of the follwoing has not been enumerated in our Constitution among the Fundamental Duties for the Citizens?
   (a) To value and preserve the rich heritage of our culture
   (b) To help the poor
   (c) To safeguard public property and to abjure violence
   (d) None of the above.

43. The Fundamental Rights of the citizens of India have been criticised on the grounds that
   (a) They are the absolute authority
   (b) They are hemmed in by too many restrictions
   (c) They are covered in language beyond the comprehension of ordinary citizen
   (d) Both (b) and (c).

44. Which of the following is not included in the right to equality?
   (a) Equality before law
   (b) Equal pay for equal work
   (c) Right against discrimination on the grounds of race, caste and religion etc.
   (d) None of the above.

45. The Right to Freedom of Religion granted by the Indian Constitution implies that the Indian citizens
   (a) Have to follow the religion of the state
   (b) Are free to have faith in a religion other than the state religion
   (c) Have the freedom to profess, practise or propagate a religion of their choice
   (d) None of the above.

46. The idea of fundamental duties is derived from
   (a) British Constitution (b) American Constitution
   (c) Russian Constitution (d) None of the above.

47. Equality of opportunity in matters of public employment has been provided under the article
   (a) 16 (b) 17
   (c) 15 (d) None of the above.

48. Which one of the following statement is correct?
   (a) Directive Principles are superior to fundamental Rights
   (b) There is no relationship between Fundamental Rights and Directive Principles
   (c) Fundamental Rights are superior to the Directive princples
   (d) None of the above.

49. The Fundamental Rights granted by the Constitution of India are not enforceable through Article 32 against
   (a) District Boards (b) State Government
   (c) Central Government (d) Private Individuals.

50. Under which Article the Freedom to establish and maintain institutions for religious and charitable purposes has been granted

(a) 26 (b) 29
(c) 27 (d) 28.

51. What does the phrase "equality before the law" used in Article 14, mean?

(a) That all laws are the same for everybody
(b) That all individuals are equal
(c) That all individuals are equally subjected to the ordinary law of the land
(d) None of the above.

52. The rights granted by Part III of the Constitution are restricted in respect of militay and police personnel by virtue of

(a) Article 20 (b) Article 13
(c) Article 21 (d) Article 33.

53. Can the Parliament of India amend the Fundamental Rights?

(a) Yes
(b) No
(c) Never
(d) None of the above.

54. Which has been the most controversial Fundamental Right?

(a) Right to Fredom of Religion
(b) Right to cultural and educational rights
(c) Right to freedom
(d) Right to property.

55. Who of the following does not constitute an exception to the provision of Article 14 (equality before the law)

(a) The Governor
(b) The President
(c) The Prime Minister
(d) The Foreign diplomates.

56. Untouchability in any form has been declared as unconstitutional under
    (a) Article 16 (b) Article 17
    (c) Article 15 (d) Article 18.

57. The Chapter III on Fundamental Rights contains four articles from
    (a) Article 16 to 39 (b) Article 10 to 33
    (c) Article 12 to 35 (d) Article 14 to 37.

58. Right to property was eliminated from the list of Fundamtnetal Rights during the tenure of
    (a) Ch. Charan Singh (b) Smt. Indira Gandhi
    (c) Sh. Rajiv Gandhi (d) Sh. Morarji Desai.

59. The Fundamental Rights granted to the Indian citizens
    (a) Can never be suspended under any circumsantaces
    (b) Can be suspended
    (c) Can not be suspended
    (d) None of the above.

60. The provision for abolition of titles comes under article
    (a) 17 (b) 18
    (c) 20 (d) 19.

61. Which one of the following statement is correct?
    (a) The right to property was never a fundamental right
    (b) The Right to Private Property was granted by the original constitution but it has since been moved from the list of Fundamental Rights
    (c) The Right to Private Property was removed from the Constiution by the 42nd Amendment
    (d) None of the above.

62. Fundamental Rights are binding
    (a) On Central Government only
    (b) On local government only
    (c) On provisional government only
    (d) On all central, local and provincial government.

63. The right against exploitation prohibits
   (a) Begar
   (b) Traffic in human beings
   (c) Employment of Children below 14 years in factories, mines etc.
   (d) All of the above.

64. Article 16 says about the equality of opportunity in matters of public employment the state shall not discriminate on grounds only of
   (a) Caste. sex
   (b) Religion, race
   (c) Descent, place of birth or residence
   (d) All of the above.

65. The right of work has
   (a) been included in our Constitution in Part III
   (b) not been granted to the citizens in Indian Constitution
   (c) been granted to the citizens in our Constitution
   (d) None of the above.

66. The right enumerated under the heading "Right to Freedom" does not include
   (a) Protection of life and personal liberty
   (b) Freedom of speech and expresion
   (c) Freedom of conscience
   (d) None of the above.

67. Which of the following is called the *Magna Carta* of Indian liberties?
   (a) The Regulating Act
   (b) Queen Victoria's Proclamation
   (c) The Pitts' India Act
   (d) None of the above.

68. Contempt of court places a restriction on
   (a) Right to freedom of religion
   (b) Right against exploitation

(c) Right to freedom
(d) Right to equality.

69. The Fundamental Rights can be protected by a citizen
(a) Executives inform the courts
(b) Parliament can take up the matter
(c) It is automatically protected
(d) By approaching the Supreme Court which will issue appropirate writs against the concerned authority.

70. Under which one of the following Articles have the High Courts beeen empowered to issue writs for protecting Fundamental Rights?
(a) Article 126
(b) Article 226
(c) Article 32
(d) None of the above.

71. Which one of the following is not included as a fundamental duty?
(a) To safeguard public property and to abjure violence
(b) To uphod and protect the sovereignity, unity and integerity of India
(c) To ensure rule of law in the country
(d) None of the above.

72. In which part of the Constitution, the right to property as Article 300A is now found?
(a) Part V
(b) Part IV A
(c) Part XII
(d) Part III.

73. Which Fundamental Right is concerned with abolition of social distinctions?
(a) Right to equality
(b) Right to life and liberty
(c) Cultural and vocational rights
(d) None of the above.

74. The Fundamental Duties of a citizen include
(a) Respect for the government
(b) Respect for the President

(c) Respect for the Constitution, the National Flag and the National Anthem
(d) All of the above.

75. The Fundamental Rights of the Indian citizens
(a) Formed a part of original constitutions
(b) Are inumerated in Part IV
(c) Were removed by 42nd Amendment Act
(d) Were added by the Ist Amendment Act.

76. The Fundamental Rights can be suspended during an emergency by the President of India under Article
(a) 358 of the Indian Constitution
(b) 360 of the Indian Constitution
(c) 361 of the Indian Constitution
(d) 359 of the Indian Constituion.

77. The Fundamental Right which prohibits traffic in human beings is
(a) Right to equality
(b) Right to freedom
(c) Right to property
(d) Right against exploitation.

78. For enforcing the Fundamental Rights, the courts can issue
(a) Warrants (b) Summons
(c) Writs (d) Notifications.

79. The Right to Property was removed from the list of Fundamental Rights during the tenure of
(a) Smt. Indira Gandhi (b) Ch. Charan Singh
(c) Shri L.B. Shastri (d) Shri Morarji Desai.

ANSWERS

1.	(b)	2.	(a)	3.	(c)	4.	(c)
5.	(a)	6.	(d)	7.	(c)	8.	(b)
9.	(c)	10.	(d)	11.	(c)	12.	(b)
13.	(b)	14.	(d)	15.	(c)	16.	(c)

17.	(c)	18.	(a)	19.	(c)	20.	(c)
21.	(d)	22.	(b)	23.	(b)	24.	(d)
25.	(c)	26.	(a)	27.	(c)	28.	(c)
29.	(d)	30.	(c)	31.	(d)	32.	(d)
33.	(a)	34.	(c)	35.	(a)	36.	(b)
37.	(b)	38.	(d)	39.	(c)	40.	(b)
41.	(c)	42.	(b)	43.	(d)	44.	(b)
45.	(c)	46.	(c)	47.	(a)	48.	(c)
49.	(d)	50.	(a)	51.	(c)	52.	(d)
53.	(a)	54.	(d)	55.	(c)	56.	(b)
57.	(c)	58.	(d)	59.	(b)	60.	(b)
61.	(b)	62.	(d)	63.	(d)	64.	(d)
65.	(b)	66.	(c)	67.	(b)	68.	(d)
69.	(d)	70.	(c)	71.	(c)	72.	(a)
73.	(c)	74.	(d)	75.	(d)	76.	(d)
77.	(c)	78.	(d)	79.	(a)		

IV
DIRECTIVE PRINCIPLES OF STATE POLICY

1. In Which Part of the Constitution, the Directive Principles are inshrind
   - (a) Part III
   - (b) Part II
   - (c) Part I
   - (d) Part IV.

2. The Directive Principles of State policy are included in our Constitution from Articles
   - (a) 37 to 52
   - (b) 38 to 53
   - (c) 36 to 51
   - (d) 39 to 54.

3. Provision for free and compulsory education for children has been made by Article?
   - (a) 48
   - (b) 45
   - (c) 50
   - (d) 41.

4. The Directive Principles of State Policy are
   - (a) Justiciale
   - (b) Always justiciable
   - (c) Non justiciable
   - (d) Sometimes justiciable.

5. Who stated in the Constitutent Assembly that the Directive Principles of State Policy aim at establishment of economic democracy?
   - (a) Dr. K.M.Munshi
   - (b) Pt. J.L.Nehru
   - (c) Dr. B.R. Ambedakar
   - (d) Dr. Radhakrishnan.

6. The Directive Principles of State Policy seek
   (a) To curb the authoritarian rule
   (b) To establish supermacy of the Constitution
   (c) Strengthen judiciary
   (d) To make the Constitution an instrument of social change.
7. The concept of Directive Principles was borrowed from
   (a) The Costitution of U.K
   (b) The Constitution of France
   (c) The Constitution of Irish Republic
   (d) The Constitution of U.S.A.
8. Which article has directed the state to promote international peace and security
   (a) 50 (b) 51
   (c) 53 (d) None of the above.
9. Directive Principles of State Policy are
   (a) Those moral principles which are fundamental in the foreign affairs of the country
   (b) The instruments of instructions from the guidance of the rulers both at the Centre and the state levels for the establishment of just and egalitarian
   (c) The instruments of instructions for the guidance of the policy
   (d) None of the above.
10. Under which article has the state been directed to provide equal justice and free legal aid
    (a) 39 A (b) 41
    (c) 40 (d) None of the above.
11. Who said " The Directive Principles of State Policy do not matter"
    (a) Mr. Diecy
    (b) Mr. Glednill
    (c) Sir Ivor Jennings
    (d) Dr. Ambedkar.

12. The main difference between the Directive Principles and Fundamental Rights is
    (a) Directive Principles are binding upon the citizens whereas Fundamental Rights are not
    (b) Directive Principles have negative sense whereas Fundamental Rights have positive
    (c) Directive Principles are non-justiciable whereas Fundamental Rights are justiciable
    (d) None of the above.

13. The Directive Principles of State Policy were given an overriding position over the Fundamental Rights under certain circumstances by the
    (a) Twenty Fouth Amendment
    (b) Forty First Amendement
    (c) Forty Second Amendment
    (d) Twenty Fifth Amendment.

14. Under which Article has the state been directed to organise agriculrue and animal husbandry on modern and scientific lines?
    (a) 48 (b) 60
    (c) 57 (d) None of the above.

15. Under which Article has the provision for just and humane conditions of work and maternity relief been mentioned?
    (a) 40 (b) 42
    (c) 43 (d) 41.

16. The aim of the Directive Principles of State Policy is to establish
    (a) Communist state in our country
    (b) Welfare state in our country
    (c) Capitalist state in our country
    (d) None of the above.

17. The State has been directed to secure the participation of workers in the management of industries under the article
    (a) 42 (b) 41
    (c) 40 (d) 43 A.

18. Who said "The Principles (Directive Principles) should be made the basis of all future legislation:?
    (a) Dr. B.N. Rao (b) Sh. M.K. Gandhi
    (c) Dr. B.R. Ambedkar (d) Pt. J.L. Nehru.

19. "The Directive Principles at State Policy are like a cheque on a bank payable at the convenience of the bank: who said this in the Constituent Assemble ?
    (a) Dr. Rajendra Prasad (b) Dr. B.R. Ambedkar
    (c) Pt. J.L. Nehru (d) K.T. Shah.

20. The Constitution of India makes a special reference to local government in the part on
    (a) Fundamental Rights
    (b) Directive Principles of State Policy
    (c) The 38th Amendment after the B.R. Mehta Report
    (d) Part II seventh schedule of the Constitution.

21. Directive Principles of State Policy are not privided in the Constitution of
    (a) India (b) Ireland
    (c) Burma (d) U.S.A.

22. Which one of the following is Gandhian Principle?
    (a) The State shall take steps to separate the judiciary from the executive
    (b) The state shall protect every monument or place or object of artistic or historic interest
    (c) The state shall protect the educational and economic interests of the weaker sections of the people and in particular of the scheduled castes and scheduled tribes
    (d) None of the above.

23. The Directive Principles aim at
    (a) Ensuring strengthening of the country's independence
    (b) Ensuring individual liberty
    (c) Providing a social and economic base for a genuine democracy in the country
    (d) The achievement of all these objectives.

24. Our Constitution draws a lot from the Indian Act of 1935, which of the following statement is not correct?
    (a) The concept of Education owes its origin to this Act
    (b) Almost 2/3 of the Indian Constituion owes its origin to this Act
    (c) The legislative assembly as to sit for five years but the legislative council was to be a permanent body
    (d) The Directive Principles are derived from it.

25. Which one of the following articles of the Constitution of India directs state governments to organise village panchayats?
    (a) 40
    (b) 48
    (c) 32
    (d) 51.

26. The enforcement of the Directive Principles of State Policy depends on
    (a) The judiciary
    (b) The will of the government in Power
    (c) The resources available with the government
    (d) All the above.

27. The forty second Amendment of Constitution is a landmark in respect of Directive Principles of State Policy, which of the following was not provided by it?
    (a) Participation of workers in management
    (b) Removal of inequality
    (c) Free legal aid
    (d) Protection of children against exploitation.

28. The Directive Principles of State Policy were included in the Indian Constitution with a purpose of
    (a) Establishing a welfare state
    (b) Establishing a Socialist republic
    (c) Monitoring the governments actions
    (d) Establishing secularism

29. Which one of the following is a Directive Principle?
   (a) Raising of standard of living of the people
   (b) Giving equal rights to all people
   (c) Giving Freedom to all people
   (d) Giving political rights to the people.

30. The Directive Principles may be classified into
   (a) Liberals and Communists
   (b) Socialistic, Gandhians and liberate
   (c) Socialists and Communists
   (d) Gandhians, Liberals and Communists.

31. The Directive Principles of State Policy are directly concerned with
   (a) Fundamental Duties
   (b) Gandhian Principles
   (c) Preamble
   (d) Fundamental Rights.

32. Under which article has it been stated that it is the duty of the state to raise the level of nutrition and the standard of living and to improve public health
   (a) 47 (b) 48
   (c) 46 (d) None of the above.

33. The state shall take steps to separate the Judiciary from the executive in the public services of the state" has been stated under the article
   (a) 50 (b) 52
   (c) 53 (d) 51.

34. Which of the following is not a principle of Panchsheel?
   (a) Non-interference in each others internal affairs
   (b) Non-alignment
   (c) Peaceful co-existence
   (d) Mutual respect for each others territory and sovereignity.

35. Which of the following reflects a socialist ideology?
    (a) Ban on cow sloughter
    (b) Prohibition
    (c) The state being directed to strive for equal pay for equal work
    (d) None of the above.

36. Which one of the following has been wrongly listed as a duty of citizens as outlined in Article 51 A?
    (a) To protect and preseve the natural environment
    (b) To promote harmony and spirit of common brotherhood among the pople of India
    (c) To practise family planning and control population
    (d) To uphold and protect the sovereignity unity and integrity of India.

37. Which one of the Following Directive Principles is a soicalistic principle?
    (a) Equal pay for equal work to all
    (b) Protection of the health of workers
    (c) Prevention of concentration of wealth and means of production
    (d) All of the above.

38. Which amendment reduced the initial period of preventive detention from three months to two months?
    (a) 42nd (b) 44th
    (c) 43rd (d) None of the above.

39. Article Subject matter

    46 (A) Promotion of educational and economic interests of scheduled castes, scheduled tribes and other weaker sections

    47 (B) organisation of agriculture and animal husbandary

    48 (C) Protection of monuments and places and objects of national importance

49 (D) Duty of the state to raise the level of nutrition and the standard of living and to improve public health

Select the correct answer using the codes given below

	46	47	48	49
(a)	C	A	B	D
(b)	A	D	B	C
(c)	A	B	C	D
(d)	D	B	C	A

40. The Directive Principles of State Policy are accorded precedence over the fundamental rights as per the
    (a) 36th amendment (b) 32nd amendment
    (c) 42nd amendment (d) 46th amendment.

41. The enforcement of the Directive Principles depends on
    (a) An effective opposition
    (b) Resources at the disposal of the government
    (c) Independent judiciary
    (d) The whims of the government.

42. "The state shall endeavour to protect and improve the environment and to safeguard the forest and wild life of the country", this has been mentioned under Article
    (a) 80 (b) 50
    (c) 48 A (d) 70.

43. Under which Article has the state been directed to secure for the citizens a uniform civil code throughout the territory of India ?
    (a) 44 (b) 47
    (c) 45 (d) 46.

44. India follows the policy of non-alignment which basically implies
    (a) Being a third world power
    (b) Bringing peaceful amity to the world
    (c) Neutrality towards power blocs
    (d) None of the above.

45. Which Article makes it obligatory for the state to protect monuments, place or objects of artistic or historical interest from disfigurement, destruction, removal disposal or export?
   (a) Article 59 (b) Article 49
   (c) Article 54 (d) Article 39.

46. "The state shall, in particular direct its policy towards securing that there is equal pay for equal work for both men and women", under which article has this been mentioned?
   (a) 40 (b) 38
   (c) 39 (d) 42.

47. Which of the following directives has been included in the Constitution with regard to conduct of international relations?
   (a) Show respect for international law and treaty obligations
   (b) Work for the maintenance of just and honourable relations between nations
   (c) Encourage settlement of internationnal disputes through arbitration
   (d) Work for disarmament.

48. The Constitution enjoins the state to provide a living wage to workers by virtue of
   (a) Article 39 (d) (b) Article 41
   (c) Article 43 (d) Article 38.

49. Which article has directed the state to take steps for promotion of educational and economic interests of scheduled castes, scheduled tribes and other weaker sections?
   (a) 46 (b) 49
   (c) 47 (d) 48.

50. Which one of the following statement is wrong?
   (a) Panchayati Raj has been introduced by most of the states
   (b) In many states of India education has been made compulsory and free upto the age of 14 years

(c) Cow slaughter has been banned all over the country
(d) None of the above.

51. "The state shall strive to promote the welfare of the people by securing and protecting as effectively as it may a social order in which justice-social, economic and political—shall inform all the institutions of the national life", has been mentioned under article
(a) 40 (b) 39
(c) 37 (d) 38.

52. A Socialist ideology is reflected in the Directive Principle which calls for
(a) Securing equitable distribution of material resources of the country to prevent the concentration of wealth
(b) Free and compulsory education for children upto 14 years of age
(c) Promotion of cottage industries
(d) All the above.

53. Which one of the following Directive Principles is not a liberal principle
(a) The state shall protect every monument or place or object of artistic or historic interest
(b) The state shall try to raise the level of nutrition and the standard of living of its people and the improvement of public health
(c) The state shall take steps to separate the judiciary from the executive
(d) None of the above.

54. Regarding Directive Principles of State Policy, it is not correct to say that
(a) They are Fundamental in the governance of the country
(b) It is the duty of the state to apply these principle in making laws
(c) They impose a legal duty upon the state
(d) They are merely instructions or directions issued to legislature and the executive of the coutnry.

55. Which one of the following Directive Principles is not a Gandhian Principle?

(a) The state shall endeavour to promote cottage industries

(b) The state shall endeavour to secure a uniform civil code throughout the territory of India

(c) The state shall take steps to organise village Panchayats

(d) None of the above.

ANSWERS

1.	(d)	2.	(c)	3.	(b)	4.	(c)
5.	(c)	6.	(d)	7.	(c)	8.	(b)
9.	(b)	10.	(a)	11.	(c)	12.	(c)
13.	(c)	14.	(a)	15.	(b)	16.	(b)
17.	(d)	18.	(c)	19.	(d)	20.	(b)
21.	(d)	22.	(c)	23.	(c)	24.	(d)
25.	(a)	26.	(c)	27.	(b)	28.	(a)
29.	(a)	30.	(b)	31.	(c)	32.	(a)
33.	(a)	34.	(b)	35.	(c)	36.	(a)
37.	(d)	38.	(b)	39.	(b)	40.	(c)
41.	(b)	42.	(c)	43.	(a)	44.	(c)
45.	(b)	46.	(c)	47.	(d)	48.	(c)
49.	(a)	50.	(c)	51.	(d)	52.	(d)
53.	(b)	54.	(c)	55.	(b)		

5
UNION EXECUTIVE

1. The Constitution of India vests the executive powers of the Union Government in
   (a) The Prime Minister
   (b) The Parliament
   (c) The Council of Miisters
   (d) The President.

2. The President of India is
   (a) the Head of government
   (b) the Head of state
   (c) the Head of the state as well as the government
   (d) None of the above.

3. The Head of the Indian Republic according to Article 52 of the Constitution is the
   (a) Prime Minister (b) President
   (c) Vice President (d) None of the these.

4. The President of India is elected by the electoral body consisting of
   (a) The members of the Lok Sabha and the State Legislative Assemblies
   (b) The members of both the Houses of Parliament
   (c) The members of Parliament and the State legislative Councils
   (d) The members of both the Houses of Parliament and State Legislative Assemblies.

5. The term of office of the President of India is
   (a) Four years (b) Six years
   (c) Five years (d) Seven years.

6. Qualification for election to President has been stated under Article
   (a) 50 (b) 58
   (c) 57 (d) 60.

7. The oath of office to the President is administered by
   (a) The Vice-President of India
   (b) The Chief Justice of India
   (c) The Prime Minister
   (d) The Speaker of the Lok Sabha.

8. The manner of the election of the President has been mentioned under Article
   (a) 54 (b) 51
   (c) 53 (d) 55.

9. The election to the office of the President is conducted by
   (a) Speaker of Lok Sabha
   (b) Chairman of Rajya Sabha
   (c) Election Commission
   (d) None of the above.

10. The minimum age prescribed for the election of the President of India is
   (a) 35 years
   (b) 40 years
   (c) 30 years
   (d) there is no minimum age.

11. Under Article 56 (a) the President by writing under his hand addressed to the
   (a) Prime Minister may resign his office
   (b) Speaker of the Lok Sabha may resign his office
   (c) Vice-President may resign his office
   (d) None of the above.

12. The provision for oath or affirmation by the President before entering upon his office has been mentioned in the article

(a) 61 (b) 59

(c) 60 (d) 58.

13. The disputes regarding the election of the President are decided by

(a) The Lok Sabha (b) The Supreme Court

(c) The Rajya Sabha (d) None of the above.

14. Which of the following is not appointed by the President?

(a) Judges of the High Court

(b) Vice President

(c) Lt. Governors of the Union Territories

(d) All are appointed by the President.

15. The President can be removed from office

(a) Cannot be removed

(b) When the both Houses of Parliament impeach him

(c) When Supreme Court gives verdict against him

(d) When the Council of Ministers impeach him.

16. The President of India

(a) Can be elected for only two terms

(b) Can not be elected for the second term

(c) Can be re-elected for any number of terms

(d) None of the above is correct.

17. Which one of the following statement is wrong?

(a) The members of the electoral college mark their preferences like first, second etc.

(b) The election of the President is held in accordance with the system of proportional representation by means of a single transferable vote

(c) Nominated members of both Houses of Parliament also participated in the election of the President

(d) All are true.

18. Under which Article has the President power to grant pardons and to remit or commute sentences in certain cases been provided ?

(a) 72 (b) 70
(c) 73 (d) 71.

19. Can the election of the President be held if one or more state assemblies stand dissolved ?

(a) No
(b) Yes
(c) It depends upon the election commission
(d) Only under certain circumstances.

20. The members of all India services are appointed under the signatures of

(a) President of India
(b) The Vice-President of India
(c) The Union Home Minister
(d) The Chairman of the U.P.S.C.

21. Who is legally competent to declare war or conclude peace ?

(a) The Parliament
(b) The Union Council of Ministers
(c) The President
(d) The Chief Justice of India.

22. How many members of Rajya Sabha are nominated by the President from amongst the persons distinguished in art,literature and social service etc.?

(a) 10 (b) 12
(c) 6 (d) 4.

23. Which one of the following legal authority is not appointed by the President?

(a) Solicitor General
(b) Judges of High Court
(c) Judges of Supreme Court
(d) District Judge.

24. Who officiates as President after the resignation of the President of India?
    (a) Chief Justice of the Supreme Court
    (b) Prime Minister
    (c) Vice President
    (d) Speaker of the Lok Sabha.

25. Under which article has this been mentioned that the emoluments and allowances of the President shall not be diminished during his term of office ?
    (a) 57 (b) 60
    (c) 58 (d) 59.

26. The President can promulgate Presidential Rule in a state under
    (a) Article 356 (b) Article 256
    (c) Article 360 (d) Artcle 400.

27. If there is a vacancy in the office of the President it must be filled up within a period of
    (a) One year (b) Three years
    (c) Six months (d) Two years.

28. Which President held office for two consecutive terms?
    (a) Dr. Rajendra Prasad (b) Dr.Zakir Hussain
    (c) Dr.S.Radhakrishnan (d) Both (a) and (b).

29. How many types of emergencies are envisaged by the Constitution
    (a) 4 (b) 3
    (c) 2 (d) None.

30. The final authority to make a proclamation of emergency rests with .
    (a) The Prime Minister
    (b) The Parliament
    (c) The President
    (d) The Council of Ministers.

31. Which one of the following is not a qualification for election of a President of India ?
(a) Should be a Graduate
(b) Citizen of India
(c) Thirty five years of age
(d) Qualified for election as a member of the House of the people.

32. Under which of the following articles can President call a joint meeting of both hHouses when the views of the both houses on a particular bill are diverse ?
(a) 107 (b) 108
(c) 105 (d) 106.

33. When can the President pass an ordinance?
(a) If the Parliament is not in session and the Prime Minister advises it
(b) If parliament is not likely to pass it
(c) If the Nation is in danger
(d) If the Prime Minister advised it.

34. The President
(a) Cannot transfer the Governor of a state
(b) Can transfer the Governor of a state
(c) Cannot always transfer
(d) None of the above.

35. Which state had not come under President rule till 1980 ?
(a) Rajasthan (b) Haryana
(c) Andhra Pradesh (d) None of these.

36. The President of India is not a member of parliament because
(a) He has to be impartial
(b) It is against the dignity of his post
(c) He holds an office of the profit under the government
(d) His status is above all Parliament.

37. Which one of the following was elected President of India unopposed?

(a) Dr. Zakir Hussain (b) N.Sanjiva Reddy
(c) Dr. Rajendra Prasad (d) All of the above.

38. "That the President shall hold office for a term of five years from the date on which he enters upon his office", has been mentioned under article

(a) 76 (b) 54
(c) 56 (d) 66.

39. Procedure for impeachement of the President has been mentioned in article

(a) 61 (b) 64
(c) 62 (d) 63.

40. The President can declare financial emergency in the country under

(a) Article 350 (b) Article 365
(c) Article 355 (d) Article 360.

41. All the Ministers including Prime Minister hold their office during the pleasure of

(a) Supreme Court (b) President
(c) Parliament (d) Vice-President.

42. The President of India has the same constitutional authority as the

(a) President of France
(b) President of U.S.A.
(c) British Monarch
(d) President of former U.S.S.R.

43. The President's address is prepared by

(a) The Speaker of the Lok Sabha
(b) The President's House
(c) The Prime Minister and approved by the Cabinet
(d) The Minister for Parliamentry Affairs.

44. The President cannot issue a Proclamation of Emergency under Article 352 unless it is recommended in writing by
    (a) Defence Minister
    (b) Prime Minister
    (c) Home Minister
    (d) Union Cabinet including Prime Minister.

45. What is the maximum age of President
    (a) 65 years (b) 70 years
    (c) 60 years (d) There is no age limit.

46. The President of India has the power
    (a) to destroy a bill
    (b) to amend a bill
    (c) to send a bill back to the Parliament for reconsideration
    (d) None of the above.

47. Power of President to make regulations for certain Union Territories has been mentioned under article
    (a) 240 (b) 140
    (c) 160 (d) 340.

48. The salary of the President of India is
    (a) Not liable to income tax
    (b) Liable to income tax
    (c) Taxed at a concessional rates
    (d) None of the above.

49. President's rule at the Centre can be imposed
    (a) During Internal Emergency
    (b) During External Emergency
    (c) During External and Internal Emergency
    (d) At no time.

50. Which of the following parts deal with emergency provisions?
    (a) Part XVII (b) Part XVIII
    (c) Part XII (d) None of the above.

51. Which one of the following statements is not correct?
   (a) The President is not a part of the Parliament
   (b) The President can send message to Parliament
   (c) The President can summon each House of the Parliament
   (d) The President can dissolve the Lok Sabha.

52. A candidate for the office of President must be sponsored and seconded by at least
   (a) 2 members of electoral college
   (b) 5 members of electoral college
   (c) 8 members of electoral college
   (d) 10 members of electoral college.

53. In which of the following articles has Power of President to Promulgate ordinances duirng recess of Parliament been stated?
   (a) 125 (b) 121
   (c) 123 (d) 127.

54. When the President declares an emergency in the country, unless approved by the Parliament it remains in force for a period of
   (a) One month (b) One year
   (c) Six months (d) Indefinitely.

55. Which one of the following is not appointed by the President on the advice of Prime Minister?
   (a) Governors of the State
   (b) Chairman and Members of the Union Public Service Commission
   (c) Speaker of Lok Sabha
   (d) Chief Justice and other judges of the Supreme Court.

56. Which one of the following is wrong?
   The President of India appoints the
   (a) Governors of the states
   (b) Chief Ministers of the states
   (c) Prime Minister of India
   (d) Chief Justice of the Supreme Court.

57. When a Bill is presented to the President, he
   (a) may refuse to sign it
   (b) may change certain clauses of the bill
   (c) may send it back for reconsideration
   (d) has to sign it ultimately.

58. Which of the following articles mentions that the President is eligible for re-election to that office
   (a) 60 (b) 57
   (c) 58 (d) 59.

59. The Chiefs of three Defence Forces are appointed by
   (a) Prime Minister
   (b) Parliament
   (c) President
   (d) Cabinet.

60. Which of the following type of emergency has not been promulgated in our country so far?
   (a) Emergency due to internal clashes
   (b) Financial emergency
   (c) Emergency due to internal disturbances
   (d) Presidential Rule.

61. President's Rule can be imposed in a state for a maximum period of
   (a) 6 months (b) 2 years
   (c) 3 years (d) 1 year.

62. For the election to the post of the President
   (a) Each elected M.P or M.L.A has an equal number of votes
   (b) All M.Ps and M.L.As have one vote each
   (c) M.L.As of different states have different number of votes
   (d) M.Ps and M.L.As of a state have the same number of votes.

63. Who are not the members of the electoral college electing the President?
   (a) Members of the Assemblies of Union Territories
   (b) Elected members of Rajya Sabha
   (c) Elected members of state assemblies
   (d) Elected members of Lok Sabha.

64. The President of India declares a state of emergency in the country when
   (a) The Parliament advices him in this regard
   (b) The Vice President advises him
   (c) He is convinced that the situation in the country demands so
   (d) The Prime Minister recommends in this regard.

65. The President cannot issue a proclamation of Emergency under article 352 unless it is recommended in written by
   (a) Prime Minister
   (b) Home Minister
   (c) Union Cabinet including Prime Minister
   (d) Defence Minister.

66. Which of the following is not the requisite qualification for a candidate to be eligible for election as the President of India?
   (a) Must be a member of either House of Parliament
   (b) Not less than 35 years of age
   (c) Must not hold office of profit
   (d) Must be eligible to become a member of Lok Sabha.

67. Procedure for impeachment of the President has been mentioned in Article
   (a) 64 (b) 63
   (c) 62 (d) 61.

68. Can the President remove an individual Minister?
   (a) Only when the Prime Minister advises it
   (b) No, never

(c) Yes, if he thinks the minister unfit
(d) It is not clear whether he can do so or not.

69. Which of the following statement is correct?
(a) The President of India is the real head of the state
(b) The President of India is the nominal head of the state
(c) The President of India does not exercise his powers on the advice of the Prime Minister
(d) None of the above.

70. The final authority to make a proclamation of emergency rests with
(a) The Parliament
(b) The President
(c) The Council of Ministers
(d) The Prime Minister.

71. A national emergency can remain in operation with the approval of Parliament
(a) For an indefinite period
(b) For a maximum period of six months
(c) For a maximum period of one year
(d) For a maximum period of three years.

72. The Law officers who hold office at the pleasure of the President are
(a) The Attorney General and the Law Minister
(b) The Chief Justice of the Supreme Court and the Attorney General
(c) The Attorney General and the Solicitor General
(d) The Law Minister and any judge of the Supreme Court or of a High court.

73. How many members the President can nominate of Anglo Indian Community to the Parliament?
(a) 1 (b) 2
(c) 6 (d) 8.

74. How may times the national emergency has been declared in the country by the President?
   (a) Never
   (b) Ten times
   (c) Once
   (d) Thrice.

75. Which one of the following is not a financial power of the President of India?
   (a) No money bill can be introduced in the Lok Sabha without the prior approval of the President
   (b) The President can pass the budget when the Lok Sabha has been dissolved
   (c) The President appoints the Finance Commission
   (d) The President calls the budget to be laid before the Parliament.

76. The President of India may seek the advice of the Supreme Court on any question of law or fact of public importance under the Supreme Court's
   (a) Original jurisdiction
   (b) Appellate jurisdiction
   (c) Advisory jurisdiction
   (d) None of the above.

77. The President of India holds office for a term of five years from
   (a) the date given by the Parliament
   (b) the date on which he is elected
   (c) the date on which he enters upon his office
   (d) the date notified by the election commission.

78. The President of India can make laws through ordinances
   (a) during the recess of Parliament
   (b) Under no circumstances
   (c) On the subjects contained in the Union list
   (d) None of the above.

79. Before the expiry of his normal term the President of India can send his resignation letter addressed to
   (a) The Speaker of Lok Sabha
   (b) The Chief Justice of Supreme Court
   (c) The Vice President
   (d) The Prime Minister.

80. A Financial emergency can be declared by the President
   (a) When the Parliament recommends so
   (b) When there is a threat to the Financial stability or credit of India
   (c) When the Council of Ministers recommends
   (d) None of the above.

81. The Parliament has been given the power to make such provision as it thinks fit for the discharge of the functions of the President in any contingency not provided for in the Constitution under Article
   (a) 70 (b) 72
   (c) 71 (d) 73.

82. A proclamation of emergency must be placed before the Parliament for its approval within a period of
   (a) Three months (b) One month
   (c) Four months (d) Six months.

83. When the President refers a question of law or fact to the Supreme Court for its opinion
   (a) The court may report its opinion to the President
   (b) The Court has to express its opinion
   (c) The court may decline to consider the matter
   (d) The court should do as directed by the President.

84. Regarding his power of pardon the President can employ it in
   (a) Pardoning a sentence of death
   (b) Offences against laws in the union and concurrent lists
   (c) All the cases of punishment by a court martial
   (d) All the above.

85. Which of the following parts deal with emergency provisions?

(a) Part XII (b) Part XVII

(c) XVIII (d) None of the above.

86. Which one of the following three types of emergencies has been declared the maximum number of times

(a) Financial emergency

(b) Constitutional emergency

(c) National emergency

(d) All three equal number of times.

87. The President gets a salary of

(a) Rs. 50,000 per month

(b) Rs. 10,000 per month

(c) Rs. 15,000 per month

(d) Rs. 20,000 per month.

88. All executive action of the Government of India shall be expressed to be taken on the name of the President", in which article has this been mentioned ?

(a) 76 (b) 77

(c) 79 (d) 78.

89. The President has the power to reduce the salaries or allowences of all government servants during the

(a) Presidential Rule in a state

(b) Financial emergency in the country

(c) Emergency in the country due to an external aggression

(d) Emergency in the country due to internal disturbnaces.

90. The President in India generally has

(a) A great deal of choice in the apppointment of Prime Minister

(b) No Power to refuse the appointment of a certain person as Prime Minister

(c) Some choice in the appointment of the Prime Minister

(d) No choice in the appointment of the Prime Minister.

91. The President can be removed from his office only on the grounds of
   (a) violation of the Constitution
   (b) clashing with his cabinet
   (c) showing favours to the members of his family
   (d) disobedience of the orders of the Supreme Court.

92. Can the President nominate any one of the Lok Sabha?
   (a) He cannot do so as it is an elected body
   (b) He can nominate two members of the Anglo-Indian Community if he thinks that the community is not properly represented in the House
   (c) He can nominate 12 members distinguished in various activities like literature, science, music etc.
   (d) He can nominate two members from depressed classes if they are not properly represented.

93. When the President transfers a judge from one High Court to another High Court, he is bound to consult by virtue of article 222 of Constitution
   (a) Governors of States
   (b) Union Law Minister
   (c) Chief Justice of India
   (d) Attorney General of India.

94. Which one of the following is not a judical power of the President of India?
   (a) He can remove the judges of the Supreme Court on grounds of misconduct
   (b) He appoints the Chief Justice and other judges of the Supreme Court
   (c) He can consult the Supreme court on any question of law or fact which is a public importance
   (d) He can grant pardon, repriclies and respites to persons.

95. How much pension does the President get after his retirement
   (a) Rs. 20,000 per annum
   (b) Rs. 25,000 per annum

(c) Rs.

(d) Rs. 30,000 per annum.

96. The dispute regarding the election of President can be filed and settled in
   (a) the Supreme Court
   (b) the Election Commission
   (c) the Parliament
   (d) none of the above.

97. The authority to proclaim emergency vests in
   (a) The Prime Minister
   (b) The Parliament
   (c) The Council of Ministers
   (d) The President.

98. The President can declare emergency in the country either due to an armed rebellion or due to an external agression under
   (a) Article 356 (b) Article 360
   (c) Article 352 (d) Article 359.

99. When does the President of India have a choice in the appointment of the Prime Minister
   (a) When no recognised party has a majority in the Lok Sabha
   (b) When no single party has an absolute majority in the Lok Sabha
   (c) When one party has an absolute majority in the Lok Sabha
   (d) In no case.

100. Power of administrator to Promulgare ordinaces during recess of legislative has been stated under Article
   (a) 130 (b) 123
   (c) 239 B (d) 239 A.

ANSWERS

1.	(d)	2.	(b)	3.	(b)	4.	(d)
5.	(c)	6.	(b)	7.	(b)	8.	(d)
9.	(c)	10.	(a)	11.	(c)	12.	(c)
13.	(b)	14.	(b)	15.	(b)	16.	(c)
17.	(c)	18.	(a)	19.	(b)	20.	(c)
21.	(c)	22.	(b)	23.	(d)	24.	(c)
25.	(d)	26.	(a)	27.	(c)	28.	(a)
29.	(b)	30.	(c)	31.	(a)	32.	(b)
33.	(a)	34.	(b)	35.	(c)	36.	(c)
37.	(b)	38.	(c)	39.	(a)	40.	(d)
41.	(b)	42.	(c)	43.	(c)	44.	(d)
45.	(d)	46.	(c)	47.	(a)	48.	(b)
49.	(d)	50.	(b)	51.	(a)	52.	(d)
53.	(c)	54.	(a)	55.	(c)	56.	(b)
57.	(c)	58.	(b)	59.	(c)	60.	(b)
61.	(c)	62.	(c)	63.	(a)	64.	(c)
65.	(c)	66.	(a)	67.	(d)	68.	(a)
69.	(b)	70.	(b)	71.	(a)	72.	(c)
73.	(b)	74.	(d)	75.	(b)	76.	(c)
77.	(c)	78.	(a)	79.	(c)	80.	(b)
81.	(a)	82.	(b)	83.	(a)	84.	(d)
85.	(c)	86.	(b)	87.	(a)	88.	(b)
89.	(b)	90.	(d)	91.	(a)	92.	(b)
93.	(c)	94.	(d)	95.	(c)	96.	(a)
97.	(d)	98.	(c)	99.	(b)	100.	(c)

The Vice-President of India

1. Who is ex-officio Chairman of the Rajya Sabha ?
   (a) Speaker, Lok Sabha
   (b) Prime Minister
   (c) Vice-President
   (d) Leader of the Oppostion.

2. The Vice-Presidnet of India is elected by an electoral college constituting of
   (a) The members of Rajya Sabha
   (b) Only elected member of Lok Sabha
   (c) Elected members of both the Houses of Parliament and the State Legislative Assemblies
   (d) The members of both the houses of Parliament at a joint sitting.

3. Under which article has the procedure of election of Vice-President been given
   (a) 66 (b) 68
   (c) 65 (d) 67.

4. The Vice-President is
   (a) A member of the Rajya Sabha
   (b) Not a member of Parliament
   (c) A wing of Parliament
   (d) A member of either Houses of Parliment.

5. The term of office of the Vice-President is
   (a) 5 years (b) 4 years
   (c) 6 years (d) 3 years.

6. The minimum age for election of the office of Vice President is
   (a) 30 years (b) 36 years
   (c) 35 years (d) 32 years.

7. Which one of the following Vice-Presidents of India was subseqently elected as President
   (a) Dr. S Radhakrishnan (b) Dr. Rajendra Prasad
   (c) B.D.Jatti (d) None of the above.

8. "The Vice-President of India shall be ex-officio Chairman of the Council of State". This has been mentioned under article
   (a) 89 (b) 92
   (c) 91 (d) 90.

9. The Vice-President may resign his office by writing under his hand addressed to the
   (a) Chief justice of India
   (b) Speaker of Lok Sabha
   (c) President of India
   (d) Prime Minister of India.

10. When the Vice-President discharges the duties of the President during his temporary absence, he is entitled to
   (a) An officiating allowances of Rs. 5000 in addition to his own salary
   (b) A fix salary of Rs. 20,000
   (c) The salary and allowances attached to the office of the president
   (d) The salary and allowances of both the office together.

11. During which one of the following situations does the Vice-President not discharge the functions of the President ?
   (a) When the President vacates office
   (b) When the President dies
   (c) When the President falls ill
   (d) When the President has been suspended.

12. After the death of the President, the Vice President holds that ofice upto a maximum period of
   (a) six months
   (b) one year
   (c) nine months
   (d) two years.

13. The Vice-President can be removed from office before expiry of his term by
   (a) The President
   (b) The members of the two Houses of Parliament
   (c) The Council of Ministers
   (d) The President on the recommendation of the Prime Minister.

14. Which one of the following is not a function of the Vice-President as ex-officio Chairman of the Rajya Sabha?
    (a) He protects the privileges of the members of Rajya Sabha
    (b) He acts as the spokesman of Rajya Sabha before the President and Lok Sabha
    (c) He dissolves the Rajya Sabha
    (d) He presides over the meetings of the Rajya Sabha and conducts its business.

15. The disputes regarding the election of the Vice-President are decided by
    (a) The Rajya Sabha
    (b) The Joint Session of Parliament
    (c) The President
    (d) The Supreme Court.

16. A Vice-President can
    (a) be elected only for two terms
    (b) be elected only for one term
    (c) be elected again and again for any number of times
    (d) be elected only for three terms.

17. If the Vice-President is not available to discharge the duties of the President if the latter dies or resigns, the responsibilities of the office fall on
    (a) The senior most Minister of Cabinet
    (b) The Chief Justice of India
    (c) The Speaker of Lok Sabha
    (d) None of the above.

18. When for the first time, the Vice-President dischared the functions of the President decrying the temporary absence of the President ?
    (a) June, 1960
    (b) January, 1965
    (c) May, 1958
    (d) None of the above.

19. "The Vice-President shall be ex-officio Chairman at the Council of States and shall not hold any other office of profit" This has been stated in article

(a) 61 (b) 63
(c) 62 (d) 64.

20. When the Vice-President acts as President?

(a) The Deputy Chairman presides over the meetings of Rajya Sabha
(b) The Speaker of Lok Sabha presides over Rajya Sabha sitting
(c) The post of Chairman of Rajya Sabha must remain vacant
(d) None of the above.

21. Who was the first Vice President of India

(a) Dr.S. RadhaKrishnan
(b) Dr. Zakir Hussain
(c) Sh. B.D.Jatti
(d) None of the above.

22. The oath of office to the Vice-President is administered by

(a) The Prime Minister
(b) The Speaker of the Lok Sabha
(c) The President of India
(d) None of the above

ANSWERS

1.	(c)	2.	(d)	3.	(a)	4.	(b)
5.	(a)	6.	(c)	7.	(d)	8.	(a)
9.	(c)	10.	(c)	11.	(d)	12.	(a)
13.	(b)	14.	(c)	15.	(d)	16.	(c)
17.	(b)	18.	(a)	19.	(d)	20.	(a)
21.	(a)	22.	(c)				

The Prime Minister and the Council of Ministers

1. The Council of Ministers in India is presided over by
   (a) The President
   (b) The Prime Minister
   (c) The Minister for Parliamentary Affairs
   (d) None of the above.

2. The Head of the government is
   (a) President (b) Prime Minister
   (c) Vice-President (d) Speaker, Lok Sabha.

3. The office of the Prime Minister of India is
   (a) A Constitutional post
   (b) A Non-Constitutional post
   (c) A Conventional post
   (d) Created by Parliamentary statute.

4. Under Article 75 (1) of the Constitution the Prime Minister is appointed by the
   (a) Speaker of Lok Sabha
   (b) Chief Justice of India
   (c) President
   (d) Vice-President.

5. The oath of office to the Prime Minister and other Ministers is administered by the
   (a) Vice-President of India
   (b) Speaker of Lok Sabha
   (c) Chief Justice of India
   (d) President of India.

6. Generally the Prime Minister is
   (a) The leader of the majority party in the Lok Sabha
   (b) A close friend of the President
   (c) The senior most member of the Parliament
   (d) Not a member of Parliament.

7. How long is the tenure of Prime Minister in India
   (a) It depends on the President's discretion
   (b) 5 years
   (c) So long as he enjoys the confidence of the Lok Sabha
   (d) So long as he is leader of the majority party in the Lok Sabha.

8. The President can dismiss a member of the Council of Ministers
   (a) on the recommendations of the Parliament
   (b) as recommended by the Prime Minister
   (c) as he is empowered
   (d) on the charges of negligence.

9. Which one of the following was not a member of Parliament at the time of appointment as Prime Minister?
   (a) P.V. Narasimha Rao (b) Chandra Sekhar
   (c) Indira Gandhi (d) Morarji Desai.

10. The Union Council of Ministers is collectively responsible to
    (a) The President (b) The Lok Sabha
    (c) The Parliament (d) The people.

11. Every decision of the cabinet is made in the name of
    (a) The Prime Minister
    (b) The Government of India
    (c) The Council of Ministers
    (d) The President.

12. The Prime Minister holds office
    (a) depends on the Parliament
    (b) for five years
    (c) till the new Lok Sabha is elected
    (d) as per the wish of the President.

13. Which one of the following Prime Ministers resigned after losing Vote of confidence in Lok Sabha ?
    (a) Indira Gandhi (b) V.P. Singh
    (c) Charan Singh (d) Chandra Shekhar.

14. In the Union Council of Ministers which of the following types of Ministers are second in ranking
    (a) Ministers of States
    (b) Deputy Ministers
    (c) Cabinet Ministers
    (d) None of these.

15. The Budget is prepared by the
    (a) Lok Sabha
    (b) Rajya Sabha
    (c) Cabinet
    (d) President.

16. In India generally the Prime Minister
    (a) Does not belong to any House of the Parliament
    (b) Belongs to the House of the People
    (c) Belongs to the Council of States
    (d) None of the above is correct.

17. In case, any minister is in disagreement with the decision of the cabinet, he
    (a) can complain to the Prime Minister
    (b) can register his protest in parliament
    (c) can compel the cabinet to change the decision
    (d) has to resign.

18. The base of the Indian Parliamentary system is
    (a) male franchise
    (b) universal adult franchise
    (c) adult franchise
    (d) proportional representation of the population.

19. Which of the following is not true about the Parliamentary secretary?
    (a) He is not a part of Council of Minister
    (b) He assists the minister with whom he is attached
    (c) He has no independent power or function
    (d) He directly reports to the Prime Minister.

20. Questions of disqualification of a member of Parliament have to be decided by
    (a) The President, according to the opinion of Election Commission
    (b) The Supreme Court
    (c) The Election Commission in consultation with the Speaker of Lok Sabha
    (d) None of the above.

21. A person can remain a Minister without being a member of either House of the Parliament upto a maximum period of
    (a) one year
    (b) six months
    (c) three months
    (d) nine months.

22. The Council of Ministers can remain in power only so long as it enjoys the confidence of the
    (a) Speaker
    (b) Prime Minister
    (c) Lok Sabha
    (d) Rajya Sabha.

23. · The President
    (a) is bound by the advice of the Cabinet
    (b) is not bound by the advice of the Cabinet
    (c) can act against the advice of the Cabinet
    (d) can ignore the advice given by the Cabinet.

24. The main characteristic of the Cabinet System is
    (a) Its decisions are binding on every minister
    (b) It includes the President
    (c) Leadership of the Prime Minister
    (d) Its decision are referred to the Parliament.

25. In case a "No-Confidence Motion" is passed against any minister
    (a) the Speaker, Lok Sabha asks him to resign
    (b) the entire Council of Ministers resign
    (c) he has to resign on his own
    (d) nothing happens.

26. The members of Union Council of Minister are
    (a) appointed by President
    (b) appointed by Prime Minister
    (c) appointed by Speaker, Lok Sabha
    (d) appointed by the President on the recommendation of the Prime Minister.

27. Which of the following articles has made it a duty of the Prime Minister to communicate to the President all decisions of the Union Council of Minister relating to the administration of the affairs of the Union and proposals for legislation
    (a) 78 (b) 80
    (c) 79 (d) 81.

28. Which one of the following officials is appointed by the President on the advice of the Prime Minister
    (a) Governor of the State
    (b) Chairman of UPSC
    (c) The Chief Justice of India
    (d) All of the above.

29. All the Ministers including Prime Minister hold their office during the pleasure of the
    (a) Parliament (b) Supreme court
    (c) President (d) Vice-President.

30. The Union Council of Ministers has to tender its resignation if a vote of confidence is passed against it
    (a) by the Lok Sabha
    (b) by the Rajya Sabha
    (c) by the two Houses at a joint sitting
    (d) by the Supreme Court.

31. Generally the Council of Ministers consists of
    (a) three different categories
    (b) two different categories
    (c) four different categories
    (d) none of the above.

32. The President can also appoint the Prime Minister from outside the Parliament. Such a person must get elected to the Parliament

(a) within four months (b) within one year
(c) within six months (d) none of the above.

33. Generally all important decisions are taken by

(a) The Prime Minister
(b) The Cabinet
(c) The Council of Ministers
(d) The Prime Minister and Parliamentary secretaries.

34. In India

(a) the proceedings of the cabinet meetings are not kept secret
(b) the proceedings of the cabinet meetings are made public
(c) the proceedings of the cabinet meetings are kept secret
(d) a cabinet minister is authorised to divulge the proceedings of the cabinet.

35. The portfolios of the Council of Minister are allocated by

(a) the Speaker of Lok Sabha
(b) the Prime Minister
(c) the Minister of parliamentary affairs
(d) the President on the recommendation of the Prime Minister.

36. The Prime Minister of India for the longest duration was

(a) Pt. Jawahar Lal Nehru
(b) Indira Gandhi
(c) Rajiv Gandhi
(d) Lal Bahadur Shastri.

37. Who presides over the meetings of the Union Council of Ministers ?

(a) the President
(b) the Prime Minister
(c) the Cabinet Secretary
(d) different ministers by rotation.

38. Under which of the following amendments has it been laid down that the President is bound to accept the advice of the cabinet
   (a) 42nd amendemnt
   (b) 34th amendment
   (c) 36th amendment
   (d) 43rd amendment.

39. When a minister loses the confidence of the Prime Minister the latter
   (a) can not dismiss him
   (b) can dismiss him
   (c) can get him dismissed by advising the President accordingly
   (d) must agree with him.

40. The Ministers in the Union cabinet are apointed by
   (a) the President
   (b) the Chairman, Rajya Sabha
   (c) the Speaker of the Lok Sabha
   (d) the Prime Minister.

41. Which one of the following is wrong?
   (a) The Prime Minister is the leader of the majority party in the Lok Sabha
   (b) The Prime Minister is the head of the government
   (c) The Prime Minister is the head of the state
   (d) The Prime Minister is the head of the cabinet.

42. The Union Ministry falls when
   (a) an advice on an important matter tendered by the Prime Minister to the President as rejected by the latter
   (b) the money bill presented on behalf of the government is defeated in the parliament
   (c) a vote of no-confidence is introduced against it in the parliament
   (d) in case of (a) and (b).

43. Which one of the following things the President can do ?
    (a) He can tell the Prime Minister to submit a particular problem for consideration to the cabinet and inform him regarding the decision of the same
    (b) He has the power to make the rules for the convenient transaction of the business of the government and the administration
    (c) He can ask any information regarding the administration or the government from the Prime Minister
    (d) All the above.

44. Which one of the following is not a function of the Prime Minister of India?
    (a) The Prime Minister presides over the meetings of the cabinet
    (b) It is the duty of the Prime Minister to communicate to the President all the decisions of the cabinet meetings
    (c) The Prime Minister advises the President on the allocation of portfolios to the members of his cabinet
    (d) The Prime Minister promulgates its ordinances when parliament is not in session.

45. Who appoints the Prime Minister
    (a) the Speaker, Lok Sabha
    (b) the President
    (c) the Chairman, Rajya Sabha
    (d) the President on the advice of the Vice-President.

46. The other ministers are
    (a) appointed by the Prime Minister
    (b) also chosen and appointed by the President
    (c) appointed by the President on the advice of the prime Minister
    (d) appointed by the Vice-President.

47. The powers of the Union Council of Ministers with regard to the foreign relations include
    (a) determining the foreign policy of the country
    (b) receiving the ambassadors and diplomates from foreign countries
    (c) Concluding treaties and agreements with foreign countries
    (d) helping in the recuirtment of members of the Indian Foreign Service.

48. Which one of the following hold office of the Prime Minister for the shortest period of time
    (a) Chandra Shekhar
    (b) Moraji Desai
    (c) Charan Singh
    (d) V.P. Singh.

49. The Prime Minister of India recieves monthly
    (a) a fixed salary of Rs. 25,000/-
    (b) a fixed salary of Rs. 20,000/-
    (c) a fixed salay of Rs. 15,000/-
    (d) the same salary and allowances which are paid to MPs and certain other allowances.

50. The legislatative functions of the Union Council of Ministers include the right to
    (a) nominate some members to Rajya Sabha
    (b) summon and prorogue the two Houses of parliament
    (c) introduce important bills and resolutions in the parliament
    (d) nominate two Anglo-Indian members of Lok Sabha.

ANSWERS

1.	(b)	2.	(b)	3.	(a)	4.	(c)
5.	(d)	6.	(a)	7.	(c)	8.	(b)
9.	(a)	10.	(c)	11.	(d)	12.	(c)

13.	(b)	14.	(a)	15.	(c)	16.	(b)
17.	(d)	18.	(b)	19.	(d)	20.	(a)
21.	(b)	22.	(c)	23.	(a)	24.	(c)
25.	(b)	26.	(d)	27.	(a)	28.	(d)
29.	(c)	30.	(a)	31.	(a)	32.	(c)
33.	(b)	34.	(c)	35.	(d)	36.	(b)
37.	(b)	38.	(a)	39.	(c)	40.	(d)
41.	(c)	42.	(b)	43.	(d)	44.	(d)
45.	(b)	46.	(c)	47.	(a)	48.	(c)
49.	(d)	50.	(c)				

VI
THE PARLIAMENT

1. Parliament is a
   (a) unicameral legislature
   (b) tricameral legislature
   (c) bicameral legislature
   (d) none of the above.

2. The name of Union Legislature is the
   (a) Lok Sabha (b) Rajya Sabha
   (c Parliament (d) Vidhan Sabha.

3. A person can not be elected a member of the Lok Sabha unless he attains the age of
   (a) 21 years (b) 30 years
   (c) 32 years (d) 25 years.

4. How many times at least has the parliament to meet in a year?
   (a) once
   (b) thrice
   (c) twice
   (d) there is no specifaction.

5. The member of the Lok Sabha are
   (a) appointed by the Speaker, Lok Sabha
   (b) directly elected the people
   (c) nominated by the President
   (d) none of the above.

6. Who is known as the ex-officio man of the Rajya Sabha?
   (a) The Vice-President (b) The Speaker
   (c) The President (d) The Home Minister.

7. How many members of the Lok Sabha are elected by the states?
   (a) nearly 535 (b) nearly 530
   (c) nearly 540 (d) nearly 528.

8. What is the maximum strength of Lok Sabha?
   (a) 525 (b) 500
   (c) 545 (d) 552.

9. The maximum strength of Rajya Sabha
   (a) 270 (b) 240
   (c) 250 (d) 245.

10. How many members of the Lok Sabha are elected by the Union Territories ?
    (a) 20 (b) 19
    (c) 18 (d) 17.

11. The Deputy Chairman of the Rajya Sabha is
    (a) the senior-most member of the House
    (b) the leader of the largest party in the House
    (c) elected from amonst the members of the Rajya Sabha
    (d) appointed by the chairman.

12. According to Article 79, parliament does not consist of the
    (a) Rajya Sabha
    (b) President
    (c) Lok Sabha
    (d) Attorney General of India.

13. Salaries and allowances of the members of both Houses of Parliament have been provided under article
    (a) 105 (b) 106
    (c) 108 (d) 104.

14. The minimum age for a person to be elected as a member of Rajya Sabha is

(a) 30 years (b) 21 years
(c) 35 years (d) 25 years.

15. Each member of the Rajya Sabha enjoys the term of

(a) 5 years (b) 2 years
(c) 6 years (d) 4 years.

16. The minimum age for casting vote in India

(a) 20 years (b) 18 years
(c) 21 years (d) 25 years.

17. In Rajya Sabha, the states are represented

(a) equal representation
(b) on the basis of size
(c) on the basis of language
(d) on the basis of population.

18. Can the Lok Sabha be dissolved before the expiry of its term?

(a) No (b) Yes
(c) Sometimes (d) Not always.

19. The sole power to control the expenditure of the government rests with

(a) the Prime Minister
(b) the Parliament
(c) the Lok Sabha
(d) the Finance Minister.

20. The tenure of the Union Council of Minister is

(a) uncertain
(b) 5 years
(c) fixed and co-terminus with the President
(d) co-terminus with the Lok Sabha.

21. The Rajya Sabha can be dissolved before expiry of its term by
    (a) the Vice-President
    (b) the President
    (c) the President on the recommendation of the Council of Ministers
    (d) none of the above.

22. A member of the Union Council of Ministers can be dismissed by the President
    (a) on the recommendation of the Lok Sabha
    (b) on his own
    (c) on the recommendation of the parliament
    (d) on the recommendation of the Prime Minister.

23. The Lok Sabha secretariat comes under the direct supervision of the
    (a) Minister of Parliamentary affairs
    (b) Ministry of Home Affairs
    (c) Speaker of Lok Sabha
    (d) President.

24. The estimate committee of the Lok Sabha consists of
    (a) 40 members (b) 30 members
    (c) 50 members (d) 20 members.

25. The power to establish new states or change the boundaries of any state is vested in
    (a) the Union Cabinet (b) the Parliament
    (c) the President (d) none of the above.

26. The lower chamber or the first chamber of the parliament in India is known as
    (a) House of People
    (b) Legislative Council
    (c) Council of States
    (d) Legislative Assembly.

27. The Lok Sabha can be dissolved before the expiry of its normal term of 5 years by
    (a) the President
    (b) the Prime Minister
    (c) the Speaker of Lok Sabha
    (d) the President on the recommendation of Prime Minister.

28. The Lok Sabha and Rajya Sabha sit jointly when
    (a) both the Houses have to discuss some matter jointly
    (b) it is necessary
    (c) there is a disagreement between the two Houses
    (d) none of the above.

29. How many members are nominated to the Rajya Sabha by the President of India
    (a) 10 (b) 12
    (c) 13 (d) 30.

30. The Speaker of Lok Sabha is
    (a) nominated by the Prime Minister
    (b) nominated by the President
    (c) elected by the members of the Lok Sabha
    (d) nominated by the Vice-President.

31. Out of the maximum strength of 250 members in Rajya Sabha, how many of them represent the state and the union territories
    (a) 240 (b) 238
    (c) 235 (d) 241.

32. The proceedings regarding impeachment against the President can be started in
    (a) the Lok Sabha
    (b) the Rajya Sabha
    (c) either of the House
    (d) neither of the House.

33. Who takes a final decision upon the disqualification of a member of Parliament
    (a) the Prime Minister
    (b) the Vice-president
    (c) the President
    (d) the Speaker of Lok Sabha.

34. What is the maximum period during which the parliament may not meet ?
    (a) not more than five months
    (b) not more than one year
    (c) not more than six months
    (d) none of the above.

35. A motion for no confidence can be moved in the Lok Sabha if it is supported by at least
    (a) 50 members (b) 60 members
    (c) 100 members (d) 55 members.

36. Who was the first Speaker of Lok Sabha?
    (a) Hukum Singh
    (b) G.V. Mavalankar
    (c) G.S. Dhillon
    (d) A.S. Ayyangar.

37. The Chairman of the Estimates Committee of the Lok Sabha is appointed from amongst the members themselves by the
    (a) Minister for Parliamentary Affairs
    (b) Deputy Speaker of the Lok Sabha
    (c) Prime Minister
    (d) Speaker of the Lok Sabha.

38. Which one of the following committees contains members of the Lok Sabha as well as Rajya Sabha?
    (a) Committee on Public Undertakings
    (b) Privileges Committee
    (c) Business Advisory Committee
    (d) All of the above.

39. The members of Public Accounts Committee are elected by the Parliament on the basis of
    (a) their financial and business background
    (b) proportional representation
    (c) both of the above
    (d) none of the above.

40. The quorum of the parliament is fixed at
    (a) one half of the membership of the House
    (b) one third of the membership of the House
    (c) one fourth of the membership of the House
    (d) one tenth of the membership of the House.

41. Which legislative body is presided over by a non-member?
    (a) Lok Sabha
    (b) Rajya Sabha
    (c) State Legislative Council
    (d) State Legislative Assembly.

42. The Union list of legislation consists of
    (a) 27 subjects
    (b) 12 subjects
    (c) 30 subjects
    (d) 32 subjects.

43. In both the Houses of Parliament, the first item of business is
    (a) the question hour
    (b) the private members bill
    (c) the zero hour
    (d) the debate on national issues.

44. The relation between parliament and President is that the
    (a) President is a wing of parliament
    (b) President is superior to parliament
    (c) President has nothing to do with parliament
    (d) none of the above.

45. Why is the Government of India called "Parliamentary" because
    (a) the parliament is a sovereign body
    (b) the executive is accountable to the legislature
    (c) the people elect the democratice government
    (d) none of the above.

46. The upper chamber or the second chamber of the Indian Parliament is known as
    (a) Legislative Council
    (b) Council of States
    (c) House of the People
    (d) Legislative Assembly.

47. Special procedure relating to money bills has been laid down under article
    (a) 108 (b) 110
    (c) 111 (d) 109.

48. The residuary powers have been given to the
    (a) State legislature
    (b) Union Parliament
    (c) Both to the State legislature and the Union Parliament
    (d) None of the above.

49. If a no-confidence motion is adopted by the Lok Sabha, the
    (a) the council of ministers resigns
    (b) the Prime Minister resigns from office
    (c) the parliament is dissolved
    (d) all of the above happens.

50. After being elected as Speaker of the Lok Sabha a person
    (a) is not a member of Parliament
    (b) remains a member of his party
    (c) becomes a non-party man
    (d) may or may not remain a party man.

51. In a parliamentary system the executive is responsible
    (a) directly to the people (b) to the judiciary
    (c) to the legislature (d) none of the above.

52. Either House of the Parliament is authoriesed to declare the seat of a member vacant who remains absent without permission from all the meetings of that House for a period of

(a) 60 days (b) 90 days
(c) 70 days (d) 80 days.

53. Members of the Parliament/state legislature can focus the attention of government on matters of public importance through

(a) no-confidence motion
(b) adjournment motion
(c) cut motion
(d) censure motion.

54. Vacation and resignation of, and removal from the offices of speaker and deputy speaker has been stated under article

(a) 95 (b) 96
(c) 97 (d) 94.

55. Which one of the following Lok Sabha enjoyed a term of more than five years ?

(a) 6th Lok Sabha (b) 4th Lok Sabha
(c) 5th Lok Sabha (d) 8th Lok Sabha.

56. When a member of Parliament casts his vote without regard to party affiliation it is called

(a) crossing the floor (b) defection
(c) cross-voting (d) free voting.

57. The life of the Estimates Committee of the Lok Sabha is

(a) 2 years (b) 6 months
(c) 1 year (d) 1 year.

58. The number of seats reserved for the members of scheduled tribes in Lok Sabha is

(a) 24 (b) 42
(c) 30 (d) 45.

59. The Lok Sabha is superior to Rajya Sabha because
    (a) it controls the finance matters
    (b) it is the House of directly elected members
    (c) through a no-confidence motion, it can oust the government
    (d) all the above.

60. During a national emergency, the President can extend the life of the Lok Sabha in the first instance for a period of
    (a) 6 months (b) 1 year
    (c) 9 months (d) 1 month.

61. The President of India nominates to the Rajya Sabha members out of these who
    (a) have distinguished themselves in the field of literature, science, art and social services
    (b) belong to the armed forces
    (c) belong to the backward class
    (d) belong to the royal familes.

62. The term of Lok Sabha is
    (a) 4 years (b) 5 years
    (c) 6 years (d) 3 years.

63. Who presides over the meetings of the Rajya Sabha in the absence of the Chairman?
    (a) Speaker
    (b) Deputy Speaker
    (c) Deputy Chairman
    (d) Deputy Minister for Parliamentary Affairs.

64. The members of the Rajya Sabha are elected by the elected members of the
    (a) Legislative Assemblies of the States
    (b) Lok Sabha
    (c) Legislative Council of the States
    (d) none of the above is correct.

65. Any new all India service can be created if a resolution by a 2/3rd majority is passed by
    (a) the Lok Sabha
    (b) the Rajya Sabha
    (c) both the Houses of the Parliament
    (d) none of the above.

66. Regarding a bill being a Money bill the certificate of the
    (a) President is final
    (b) Vice-President is final
    (c) Finance Minister is final
    (d) Speaker is final.

67. Various definitions of "Money Bills" have been provided under article
    (a) 109 (b) 108
    (c) 110 (d) 107.

68. In case there is a dead lock regarding a bill between Lok Sabha and Rajya Sabha, it would be solved by
    (a) the Speaker
    (b) the Prime Minister
    (c) the joint session of both Houses
    (d) the President.

69. The term of the Public Accounts Committee of the Parliament is
    (a) one year (b) two years
    (c) three years (d) six months.

70. The quorum for the meetings of the public accounts committee is
    (a) six members (b) four members
    (c) five members (d) ten members.

71. Which of the following report is not placed before the Parliament ?
    (a) Annual reports of the Ministers
    (b) Election Commission's report
    (c) Auditor General's report
    (d) Union Public Service Commission's report.

72. The main function of the Speaker of Lok Sabha is
    (a) to decide wheter a bill is money bill or not
    (b) to run the house effectively
    (c) to give proper direction to the government
    (d) to give rulings on the points of order raised in parliament.

73. In a voting, the absolute majority means
    (a) two third of the votes
    (b) half of the votes
    (c) three fourth of the votes
    (d) cent per cent votes.

74. The Parliament has been given supremacy through the Constitution
    (a) 24th amendment (b) 42nd amendment
    (c) 43rd amendment (d) 54th amendment.

75. The maximum number of nominated members in both the Houses of Parliament can be
    (a) 22 (b) 12
    (c) 14 (d) 20.

76. The Public Accounts Committee comprises
    (a) 12 members (b) 24 members
    (c) 25 members (d) 22 members.

77. A select or joint committee can be appointed by
    (a) the Speaker, Lok Sabha
    (b) the Prime Minister
    (c) the Union Minister for parliamentary affairs
    (d) the President.

78. If any government is defeated on the Floor of the Rajya Sabha
    (a) the Prime Minister submits his resignations
    (b) nothing happens
    (c) Parliament is dissolved
    (d) President's rule imposed.

79. A money bill cannot be introduced in
   (a) Lok Sabha
   (b) the joint sitting of both the houses
   (c) Rajya Sabha
   (d) none of the above.

80. The members of Parliament enjoy the freedom from arrest, but this privilege is not available to members in
   (a) cases of legal nature
   (b) FERA violation cases
   (c) criminal cases
   (d) economic offences.

81. The maximum number of days, within which the Rajya Sabha has to return back a bill to the Lok Sabha after rejection or acceptance is
   (a) 10 days (b) 2 days
   (c) 1 month (d) 2 months.

82. What is the duration of the Rajya Sabha?
   (a) 4 years
   (b) 5 years
   (c) its duration is of permanent nature as after individual terms of six years each, one third members retire after two years
   (d) none of the above.

83. The Chief Spokesman of the government in Parliament is
   (a) the Speaker of Lok Sabha
   (b) the Prime Minister
   (c) the Vice-President
   (d) the Minister for Parlimentary affairs.

84. Which of the following articles has provided the right to President to address and send messages to either House of Parliament ?
   (a) 84 (b) 85
   (c) 87 (d) 86.

85. The Union Council of Ministers can remain in power only so long as it enjoys the confidence of the

(a) Prime minister

(b) Rajya Sabha

(c) Lok Sabha

(d) Speaker of the Lok Sabha.

86. Which of the following can form new states and alter the areas boundaries or names of existing states

(a) Parliament
(b) Union Cabinet
(c) Supreme Court
(d) State Legislatures.

87. When a money bill passed by the Lok Sabha is sent to the Rajya Sabha, it must be returned to the Lok Sabha by the Rajya Sabha within

(a) 7 days
(b) 1 month
(c) 14 days
(d) 15 days.

88. No money bill can be introduced in the Lok Sabha without the prior approval of the

(a) Finance Minister
(b) President
(c) Prime Minister
(d) Vice President.

89. The certificate of the Speaker regarding a money bills is

(a) subject to the approval of the President

(b) final, but can only be challenged in the Supreme Court

(c) final and it can not be callenged in any court of law

(d) not final.

90. No taxes can be levied or expenditure incurred without the approval of

(a) the Parliament

(b) the President

(c) the Council of Ministers

(d) all of the above.

91. Proclamation of emergency must be submitted to the Parliament for approval within

(a) two months
(b) six months
(c) one year
(d) one month.

92. The Speaker
   (a) votes on every bill
   (b) votes only to help the party in power
   (c) vote on money bills only
   (d) has a casting vote in case of a tie.

93. Power of Parliament to vary or revoke conditions of service of officers of certain services has been granted under article
   (a) 312 (b) 312 A
   (c) 308 (d) 309.

94. A select or joint committee can be appointed by
   (a) Chairman of Rajya Sabha
   (b) The Speaker of Lok Sabha
   (c) The Prime Minister
   (d) None of the above.

95. What does Business Advisory Committee do?
   (a) It plans and regulates the business of the House
   (b) it determines the dates on which the session of Parliament should be called
   (c) it allocates time for discussion of different matters
   (d) it does all the above duties.

96. The privsions regarding the Speaker and Deputy Speaker of the House of the People has been included under article
   (a) 93 (b) 96
   (c) 94 (d) 95.

97. Which of the following articles says that the Council of States shall not subject to dissolution
   (a) 84 (b) 90
   (c) 83 (d) 91.

98. Which one of the following is not a qualification for a member of the Lok Sabha
   (a) he should not hold any office of profit under the government
   (b) he should not be less than 30 years of age

(c) he must be a citizen of India

(d) He should possess such other qualifications as may be prescribed by the parliament from time to time.

99. All speeches and the remarks made in the House of the People are addressed to the

(a) Prime Minister

(b) Minister concerned

(c) Speaker

(d) President of India.

100. Power of Parliament to legislate with respect to any matter in the state list if a proclamation of emergency is in operation has been stated under article

(a) 250 (b) 150

(c) 350 (d) 50.

101. The members of Rajya Sabha are

(a) directly elected

(b) indirectly elected

(c) nominated

(d) indirectly elected and some are nominated.

102. The Parliament exercises control over Union Council of Ministers

(a) through debates on issues

(b) by putting questions in the Parliament

(c) by moving adjournment or censure motion

(d) by all of the above means.

103. In which of the following articles has power of Parliament to amend the Constitution and procedure—therefore been laid down?

(a) 368 (b) . 367

(c) 267 (d) 268.

104. Which one of the following authorities is authorised by the Constitution to impose reasonable restrictions on Fundamental Rights?

(a) The Supreme Court (b) The Parliament

(c) The President (d) None of the above.

105. Which of the following are Financial Committees of Parliament in India?
(1) Estimates Committee
(2) Public Accounts Committee
(3) Committee on Public Undertakings
(4) select the correct answer using the codes given below
(a) 1 only (b) 1 and 3
(c) 1 and 2 (d) 1,2 and 3.

106. The Council of Ministers is jointly responsible to
(a) the President
(b) the Prime Minister
(c) the Parliament
(d) the Sepaker, Lok Sabha.

107. With the approval of Parliament, the national emergency can remain in operation
(a) indefinitely
(b) for a period of one year
(c) for a maximum period of six months
(d) for a maximum period of four months.

108. Atleast how many times the parliament meets in a year
(a) once (b) thrice
(c) twice (d) not necessary to meet.

109. Who has the sole power to control the expenditure of the government?
(a) the President
(b) the Parliament
(c) the Prime Minister
(d) the Comptroller and Auditor General.

110. The Council of States, i.e. Rajya Sabha is a permanent House, but
(a) one third of its members retire every year
(b) one half of its members retire every year
(c) one third of its members retire every two years
(d) one third of its members retire every four years.

111. A bill is send to the select committees after
   (a) the first reading
   (b) the second reading
   (c) the formal introduction
   (d) none of the above.

112. A joint session of both the Hosues of Parliament can be called by the President
   (a) if any of the House does not take any action for six months on a bill remitted by the other
   (b) if a bill passed by one House is rejected by the other House
   (c) if the amendment to a bill proposed by one House is not acceptable to the other House
   (d) all the above conditions.

113. If the President thinks that the Anglo-Indian Community has not been adequately represented in the Lok Sabha he may nominate
   (a) not more than five members from this commnity
   (b) not more than two members from this community
   (c) one member only
   (d) none of the above.

114. Under the 65th Constitution Amendment to the Constitution the reservation of seats in the Lok Sabha for SCs and STs would continue
   (a) upto 1999 (b) upto 2010
   (c) upto 2001 (d) none of the above.

115. The Union List of legislation consists of
   (a) 30 subjects (b) 12 subjects
   (c) 32 subjects (d) 97 subjects.

116. The Committees of Parliament are created
   (a) to ensure speedy enactment of the laws
   (b) to provide expertise for the consideration of laws which are highly technical and complex
   (c) to ensure detailed examination of laws before they are considered by the Parliament
   (d) for all the above.

117. The term of office, salaries, allowances and other conditions of the Chairman and other members of Finance Commission

(a) are determined by the President
(b) have been specified in the Constitution
(c) are specified by the Finance Ministry
(d) are determined by the Parliament from time to time.

118. The right to pass a vote of no-confidence is exclusively vested in

(a) the Rajya Sabha
(b) the Lok Sabha
(c) the joint sitting of both the Houses
(d) none of the above.

119. Which article of the Constitution empowers Parliament to provide for establishment of additional courts for better administration of union laws ?

(a) Art. 246 (b) Art. 245
(c) Art. 247 (d) Art. 248.

120. The convention that once a speaker is alway a speaker is followed in

(a) U.K (b) U.S.S.R.
(c) U.S.A (d) India.

121. The various subjects of legislation are enumerated in the seventh schedule of the Constitution in

(a) four lists
(b) two lists
(c) one list
(d) three lists.

122. The Lok Sabha enjoys co-equal powers with Rajya Sabha regarding the

(a) election of the Vice-President
(b) Impeachment of President
(c) Amendment of the Constitution
(d) all the above.

123. A money bill can originate
   (a) in either of the house
   (b) only in the Rajya Sabha
   (c) only in the Lok Sabha
   (d) only in joint sitting of both the Houses of Parliament.

124. Through the calling attention notice the members of Parliament
   (a) can elicit information on important matters of urgent public importance
   (b) can call the attention of the Speaker
   (c) can call the attention of the President on national issues
   (d) none of the above.

125. How many members are nominated to the Lok Sabha by the President of India
   (a) three (b) ten
   (c) two (d) twelve.

126. Powers, privileges etc. of the Houses of Parliament and of the members and committees has been stated under article
   (a) 106 (b) 107
   (c) 105 (d) 108.

127. Who presides over the meetings of Lok Sabha in the absence of the Speaker ?
   (a) The Minister for Parliamentary Affairs
   (b) Deputy Speaker
   (c) The Vice President
   (d) None of the above.

128. Which of the following is not correct?
   (a) The presiding officer of the Lok Sabha is called Chairman
   (b) The speaker is elected by the members of the House from among themselves
   (c) We have borrowed the office of speaker from the British Constitution
   (d) The Speaker should be a member of the House of the People.

129. The Parliament can make laws in respect of Jammu and Kashmir

(a) only on subjects in the concurrent list
(b) only on subjects in the union list
(c) on those matters in the union list as well as concurrent list in consultation with the government of the state
(d) on subjects included in all the three lists.

130. The Budget is first passed by the

(a) Rajya Sabha
(b) Lok Sabha
(c) Either of the above
(d) Neither of the above.

131. A bill becomes a law only when it

(a) gets the President's consent
(b) is approved by Parliament
(c) is passed by Rajya Sabha
(d) is passed by Lok Sabha.

132. To maintain order in the Lok Sabha the Speaker can take the help of the

(a) Border Security Force
(b) Military Police
(c) Central Reserve Police
(d) Sergeant-at arms.

133. Powers of Parliament to make provisions with respect to elections to legislatures has been granted under article

(a) 327 (b) 325
(c) 324 (d) 326.

134. Which one of the following committee comprises members of the Lok Sabha as well as Rajya Sabha

(a) The Public Accounts Committee
(b) Committee on Public undertakings
(c) The Estimate Committee
(d) (a) and (b).

135. Vote on account is made by the Lok sabha

(a) to meet expenditure on secret service

(b) to meet the additional expenditure incurred by the government on any approved item of expenditure during the supplementary budget

(c) to meet expenditure for a period before the passing of the annual budget

(d) to meet expenditure on unexpected demand.

136. Who acts as the Friend, Philosopher and Guide of the Public Accounts Committee?

(a) Chairman, Finance Commission

(b) Comptroller and Auditor General

(c) Union Finance Minister

(d) none of the above.

137. The Freedom of Speech of a member of Parliament is

(a) almost absolute

(b) subject to normal restrictions

(c) similar to that of a citizen

(d) none of the above.

138. After the inclusion of three new regional languages in the VIIIth Schedule, the total number of regional languages has risen to

(a) 15 (b) 18

(c) 9 (d) 12.

139. Who presents the Union Budget in Lok Sabha?

(a) The Union Finance Minister

(b) The Prime Minister

(c) The Chairman, Finance Commission

(d) The Dy. Chairman, Planning Commission.

140. A bill introduced by a member or a minister, goes through

(a) one reading

(b) two readings

(c) three readings

(d) unlimited readings.

141. During question hour, the starred questions are
  - (a) The questions which are answered by the minister orally
  - (b) The questions with star mark
  - (c) The question which need greater attention
  - (d) None of the above.

142. The President can return a bill to the Houses of Parliament
  - (a) any number of times
  - (b) twice
  - (c) thrice
  - (d) only once.

143. The power to promulgate ordinance during recess of Parliament has been given to
  - (a) The Chairman, Rajya Sabha
  - (b) The Speaker, Lok Sabha
  - (c) The Union Law Minister
  - (d) The President.

144. Which one of the following is not the legislative power of the Parliament?
  - (a) Law-making or legislation
  - (b) appointment of the Prime Minister
  - (c) approval of ordinances
  - (d) none of the above.

145. The Parliament works through numerous committees, whose members are
  - (a) appointed by the speaker
  - (b) appointed by the Council of Ministers
  - (c) either appointed by the Speaker or elected by the House
  - (d) appointed by the Minister for Parliamentary Affairs.

146. A bill shall be deemed to be a money bill if it contains provisions dealing with
  - (a) the appropriation of money out of the consolidated fund of India
  - (b) imposition, abolition, remission, alteration or regulation of any tax

(c) the declaring of any expenditure to be expenditure charged on the consolidated fund of India
(d) all the above.

147. Under which article has this been mentioned that "The validity of any proceeding in Parliament shall not be called in question on the ground of any alleged irregularity of procedure"?

(a) 122 (b) 120
(c) 121 (d) 123.

148. Which one of the following is a disqualification for a member of the Lok Sabha?

(a) An alien
(b) Unsound mind
(c) Undischarged insolvent
(d) All the above.

149. The impeachment proceedings against the Vice-President can be initiated

(a) only by the Rajya Sabha
(b) only by the Lok Sabha
(c) by neither of the House of Parliament
(d) by either of the House of Parliament.

150. The Parliament has also the power to make a law for the whole or any part of the territory of India for implementing

(a) the five year plans
(b) its financial policies
(c) any treaty, agreement or convention with any other country or countries
(d) its industrial policy.

151. The list which contains the subjects over which the Centre and the states both have jurisdiction is called the

(a) Union list (b) Concurrent list
(c) Joint list (d) none of the above.

152. The power of Central Government are enumerated in the

(a) Federal list (b) Union list
(c) Concurrent list (d) State list.

153. If there is any disagreement between the Rajya Sabha and the Lok Sabha over a bill the President will convene a joint sitting of both Houses of Parliament within a period of

(a) one year (b) five years
(c) six months (d) two years.

154. Who presides over the meetings of the Rajya Sabha?

(a) The President
(b) The Vice-President
(c) Deputy Speaker
(d) None of the above.

155. When a member of either of the House of Parliament is absent without permission of the House from all the meetings for a period of sixty days, the house may declare his seat vacant. In which of the following article has this been stated ?

(a) 101 (b) 103
(c) 102 (d) 104.

156. "The Speaker or the Deputy Speaker shall not preside while a resolution for his removal from office is under consideration". This has been mentioned under article

(a) 95 (b) 96
(c) 97 (d) 94.

157. The term of Lok Sabha may be extended by

(a) two years (b) one year
(c) three years (d) none of the above.

158. Which of the following powers is enjoyed by the Parliament of India?

(a) It can elect the Vice President
(b) It can initiate impeachment proceedings against the President of India
(c) It can recommend removal of judges of Supreme Court and high courts to the President
(d) It enjoys all the above powers.

159. In addition to the Speaker, the Lok Sabha has a Deputy

Speaker who is

(a) appointed by the President
(b) appointed by the Speaker
(c) appointed by the Prime Minister
(d) elected by the members of the Lok Sabha.

160. The Lok Sabha and the Rajya Sabha participate in the election of

(a) Chairman of UPSC and other members of the UPSC
(b) The President and the Vice-President
(c) Prime Minister and other Minister
(d) Chief Election Commissioner and the Election Commissioners.

161. The President shall cause a copy of the report together with a memorandum explaining the cases, if any, where the advice of the commission was not accepted and the reasons for such non-acceptance are to be laid before

(a) The Council of Ministers
(b) The Lok Sabha
(c) The Rajya Sabha
(d) Each House of the Parliament.

162. Which of the following is not correct about the function of the Indian Parliament?

(a) It is final the law making body of the country
(b) It can make laws mentioned in the concurrent and union list
(c) It can appoint judges of the Supreme Court and High Court
(d) It has powers to amend the Constitution through a specific procedure.

163. The Parliament of India cannot be regarded as a sovereign body because

(a) of the presence of certain Fundamental Rights of citizens
(b) law passed by Parliament can be declared unconstitutional by the Supreme Court

(c) its authority is confined to jurisdiction earmarked by the Constitution
(d) of all these factors.

164. The term of office of the members of the estimate committee is

(a) six months (b) one year
(c) two years (d) three years.

165. Which of the following articles deals with the salaries and allowances of Chairman, Deputy Chairman of Rajya Sabha, Speaker of the Lok Sabha

(a) 97 (b) 98
(c) 99 (d) 100.

166. Can the Rajya Sabha be dissolved by the President?

(a) sometimes (b) yes
(c) no (d) at any time he likes.

167. Mark the correct statement

(a) The Parliament can create a new state
(b) The Parliament can create an Union Territory
(c) The Parliament can convert the Union Territory into a full state
(d) All of the above.

168. The power to remove which one of the following is not vested with Parliament?

(a) Attorney General
(b) Judges of the Supreme Court and High Courts
(c) Chief Election Commissioner
(d) Comptroller and Auditor General.

169. The legislature also influences the public opinion by

(a) passing a vote of no-confidence against the Council of Ministers
(b) discussing the various burning problems faced by the people and the country
(c) passing laws to please the public

(d) giving concessions to certain sections of the society.

170. When a joint sitting of both Houses of the Parliament is convened?

(a) If more than six months is elapsed from the date of the reception of the bill

(b) If after a bill has been passed by one House and transmitted to the other House, the bill is rejected by the other House

(c) If the Houses have finally disagreed as to the amendments to be made in the bill

(d) In all the above cases.

ANSWERS

1.	(c)	2.	(c)	3.	(d)	4.	(c)
5.	(b)	6.	(a)	7.	(b)	8.	(d)
9.	(c)	10.	(a)	11.	(c)	12.	(d)
13.	(b)	14.	(a)	15.	(c)	16.	(b)
17.	(d)	18.	(b)	19.	(c)	20.	(a)
21.	(d)	22.	(d)	23.	(d)	24.	(b)
25.	(b)	26.	(a)	27.	(d)	28.	(c)
29.	(b)	30.	(c)	31.	(b)	32.	(c)
33.	(c)	34.	(c)	35.	(a)	36.	(b)
37.	(d)	38.	(a)	39.	(b)	40.	(d)
41.	(b)	42.	(a)	43.	(c)	44.	(a)
45.	(b)	46.	(b)	47.	(d)	48.	(b)
49.	(a)	50.	(c)	51.	(c)	52.	(a)
53.	(b)	54.	(d)	55.	(c)	56.	(d)
57.	(c)	58.	(c)	59.	(d)	60.	(d)
61.	(a)	62.	(b)	63.	(c)	64.	(a)
65.	(b)	66.	(d)	67.	(c)	68.	(c)
69.	(a)	70.	(b)	71.	(c)	72.	(d)
73.	(a)	74.	(b)	75.	(c)	76.	(d)
77.	(a)	78.	(b)	79.	(c)	80.	(c)
81.	(a)	82.	(c)	83.	(b)	84.	(d)
85.	(c)	86.	(a)	87.	(c)	88.	(b)
89.	(c)	90.	(a)	91.	(d)	92.	(d)
93.	(b)	94.	(b)	95.	(d)	96.	(a)
97.	(c)	98.	(b)	99.	(c)	100.	(a)

101. (d)	102. (d)	103. (a)	104. (b)
105. (d)	106. (c)	107. (a)	108. (d)
109. (b)	110. (c)	111. (a)	112. (d)
113. (b)	114. (c)	115. (d)	116. (d)
117. (d)	118. (b)	119. (c)	120. (a)
121. (d)	122. (d)	123. (c)	124. (a)
125. (b)	126. (c)	127. (b)	128. (a)
129. (c)	130. (b)	131. (a)	132. (d)
133. (a)	134. (d)	135. (c)	136. (b)
137. (a)	138. (b)	139. (a)	140. (a)
141. (a)	142. (d)	143. (d)	144. (b)
145. (c)	146. (d)	147. (a)	148. (d)
149. (a)	150. (c)	151. (c)	152. (b)
153. (c)	154. (b)	155. (a)	156. (b)
157. (d)	158. (d)	159. (d)	160. (b)
161. (d)	162. (c)	163. (d)	164. (b)
165. (a)	166. (c)	167. (d)	168. (a)
169. (b)	170. (d)		

7
UNION JUDICIARY

1. The Supreme Court of India was
   (a) created by the Constitution
   (b) created by an Act of Parliament in 1950
   (c) created by the Indian Independence Act, 1951
   (d) created by the Indian Independence Act, 1947.

2. The Supreme Court originally consisted of a Chief Justice of India and not more than
   (a) 7 other judges
   (b) 14 other judges
   (c) 18 other judges
   (d) 17 other judges.

3. Which one of the following is a power of the Supreme Court?
   (a) The Supreme Court is a court of record
   (b) Under article 32 of the Constitution the Supreme Court has the power to issue writs for enforcement of the fundamental rights of the citizens
   (c) The law declared by the Supreme Court is binding on all courts within the Territory of India
   (d) All of above.

4. Can a retired judge be asked to sit in the Supreme Court?
   (a) Yes (b) No
   (c) Never (d) None of these.

5. When can the salaries of the judges of the Supreme Court be reduced?
   (a) During a National Emergency due to external aggression
   (b) During a National Emergency due to internal disturbance
   (c) During financial emergency
   (d) None of these.

6. What is reflected by the separation of the judiciary from executive?
   (a) Gandhian Philosophy
   (b) Socialism
   (c) Secularism
   (d) Liberal and intellectual philosophy.

7. Which one of the following cases is not included within the original jurisdiction of the Supreme Court of India?
   (a) Any dispute between the Government of India and one or more states
   (b) Any dispute between the Government of India and any state or states on the one side and one or more other states on the other
   (c) Any dispute between two or more states
   (d) Any dispute between a citizen of India and a state.

8. When a High Court certifies that a case involves a substantial question of law as to the interpretation of the Constitution under its
   (a) original jurisdiction
   (b) appellate jurisdiction
   (c) advisory jurisdiction
   (d) none of the above.

9. In 1980, in the case of Minerva Mills Vs. Union of India, the Supreme Court struck down articles
   (a) 361 (b) 368
   (c) 31 (c) (d) both (b) and (c).

10. Appellate jurisdiction of Supreme Court in appeals from High Courts in regard to civil matters has been provided under articles?
    (a) 133 (b) 135
    (c) 137 (d) 139.

11. When can a President refer a matter to the Supreme Court for its opinion?
    (a) When the cabinet is not functioning properly
    (b) When emergency has to be promulgated
    (c) When a matter is of public importance
    (d) Whenever the President feels like it.

12. A case of dispute in the presidential election is referred to the
    (a) Chief Election Commissioner
    (b) Supreme Court
    (c) Parliament
    (d) None of the above.

13. In which of the following articles has Appellate jurisdiction of Supreme Court in regard to criminal matters mentioned?
    (a) 130 (b) 132
    (c) 134 (d) 136.

14. In a case where a certificate that the case is fit to be heard by the Supreme Court is not granted by a High Court the Supreme Court
    (a) will not hear any appeal against this case
    (b) cannot hear any appeal against this case
    (c) may grant special leave to appeal and hear the case
    (d) none of the above.

15. An appeal shall lie to the Supreme Court from any judgment, final order or sentence in a criminal proceeding of High Court if the High Court
    (a) has an appeal reversed on order of acquittal of an accused person and sentenced him to death
    (b) his withdrawal for trial before itself any case from any

court subordinate to its authority and has such trial convicted the accused person and sentenced him to death

(c) certifies that the case is fit for appeal to the Supreme Court

(d) In all the above cases.

16. The President of India may seek the advice of the Supreme Court on any question of law or fact of public importance under the Supreme Court's

(a) Original Jurisdiction

(b) Advisory Jurisdiction

(c) Appellate Jurisdiction

(d) None of the above.

17. Which one of the following is a limitation on the powers of the Supreme Court?

(a) The Supreme Court cannot question the decision of the President regarding the proclamation of emergency

(b) The Supreme Court cannot question the decision of the Speaker as to whether a Bill is a money bill or not

(c) The Supreme Court cannot interfere with the delimitation of constituencies

(d) All the above.

18. Under which one of the following Articles the Supreme Court has been given the power to review any judgement pronounced or ordered made by it previously?

(a) Art. 130 (b) Art.139

(c) Art. 138 (d) Art.137.

19. In India the power of Judicial review is

(a) Extra constitutional (b) Unconstitutional

(c) Constitutional (d) None of the above.

20. What is meant by the Independence of Judiciary?

(a) An organisation of Judges acting in an independent manner

(b) An organisation of Judges not influenced by the party in power

(c) An organisation of Judges who are political
(d) An organisation of Judges who enjoy security of tenure and cannot be removed except by a special procedure.

21. In India the Judiciary is
(a) Independent
(b) Under the Parliament
(c) Under the President
(d) Under the Prime Minister.

22. The concept of judical review has been borrowed from the Constitution of
(a) Former U.S.S.R (b) U.K
(c) U.S.A (d) Switzerland.

23. The Power of Judicial Review
(a) has been specifically given to the higher court
(b) is not the inherent power of the higher court
(c) is the inherent power of the higher court
(d) none of the above.

24. Under which one of the following Amendments of the Constitution the power of judical review of the Supreme Court and the High Courts was curtailed to a great extent
(a) 24th Amendment
(b) 26th Amendment
(c) 38th Amendment
(d) 42nd Amendment.

25. Which one of the following is not correct?
(a) The Supreme Court of India is the guardian of the Constitution
(b) The Supreme Court cannot declare the laws passed by the Parliament as null and void
(c) The Power of Judicial Review of the Supreme Court of India is not so wide as that of the Supreme Court of U.S.A
(d) None of the these.

26. Which one of the following is not correct?
    (a) The phrase 'procedure established by the law' has placed much authority in the hands of the legislature
    (b) The phrase 'procedure established by the law' limits the authority of the court in the matter of Judicial Review
    (c) The phrase 'procedure established by the law' increase the authority of the Indian Courts even more than the American Supreme Court in the matter of Judicial Review
    (d) None of these.

27. Supreme Court has been granted power to issue certain writs for any purpose other than those mentioned in clause (2) of article 32 under article
    (a) 137 (b) 138
    (c) 139 (d) 140.

28. Who decides disputes regarding the election of Vice-President?
    (a) The Speaker
    (b) The President
    (c) The Parliament
    (d) The Supreme Court.

29. If the Union Government sues a private individual the suit will be instituted in
    (a) a High Court
    (b) Supreme Court
    (c) a court of the lowest jurisdiction
    (d) any one of the above.

30. In a case where a certificate that the case is fit to be heard by the Supreme Court is not granted by a High Court the Supreme Court
    (a) will not hear any appeal against this case
    (b) cannot hear any appeal against this case
    (c) may grant special leave to appeal and hear this case
    (d) none of the above.

31. The law declared by the Supreme Court shall be binding on all courts by virtue of
   (a) Art. 134 (b) Art. 136
   (c) Art. 140 (d) Art. 141.

32. All authorities in India, both civil and judicial are duty bound to act in and of Supreme Court by virtue of
   (a) Art. 144 (b) Art. 145
   (c) Art. 146 (d) Art. 147.

33. Which of the following is not a function of Judiciary?
   (a) Acting as the guardian of citizen's right
   (b) Settling the conflict between State and Centre
   (c) Catching criminals and punishing them
   (d) Issuing writs

34. Which of the following is not a writ issued only by a superior court to an inferior court?
   (a) Prohibition (b) Mandamus
   (c) Certiorari (d) None of the above.

35. The writ of prohibition issued by the Supreme Court or a High Court is issued against
   (a) judicial or quasi-judicial authorties
   (b) administrative and judicial authorties
   (c) administrative authorities only
   (d) administrative authorities and government.

36. The Appellate Jurisdiction of the Supreme Court does not involve
   (a) Civil cases
   (b) Criminal cases
   (c) Cases involving interpretation of the Constitution
   (d) Disputes arising out of pre-constitution treaties and agreements.

37. In India, mandamus will lie against
   (a) officers bound to do a public duty
   (b) government

(c) both officers and the government

(d) none of the above.

38. Consider the following statement with regard to the Supreme Court of India

(a) The Supreme Court of India has been created under the Constitution of India

(b) The Supreme Court at present comprises a Chief Justice and 25 ordinary judges

(c) The Supreme Court has its permanent seat at New Delhi, but it can met elsewhere if the Chief Justice of India so decides, in consultation with the President of India

(d) The original jurisdiction of Supreme Court extend over disputes between India and foreign countries.

39. Which of the following cases was connected with the Supreme Court's Judgement in 1980 that the amendment made to Article 31 (C) and article 368 are invalid

(a) Golaknath case

(b) Sajjan Singh case

(c) Keshvanand Bharati case

(d) Minerva Mills.

40. In which one of the following cases did the Supreme Court declare that the Parliament had no right to amend the basic structure of the Indian Constitution?

(a) Gopalan's case

(b) Bank Nationalisation case

(c) Golaknath vs: the State of Punjab case

(d) Keshavanand Bharti's case.

41. In which of the following cases was the Power of the Parliament to amend the Constitution curbed by the Supreme Court Judgement?

(a) Keshavanand Bharti case

(b) Minerva Mills case

(c) Habeas Corpus case

(d) Golaknath case.

42. In which one of the following cases did the Supreme Court declare that a constituent assembly should be convened to amend the fundamental rights?
   (a) Golaknath vs. the State of Punjab
   (b) Gopalan's case
   (c) Keshavanand Bharti case
   (d) None of the above.

43. Article Subject matter

130 (A) Appellate Jurisdiction of Supreme Court's in appeals from High Court in certain cases

131 (B) Appellate Jurisdiction of Supreme Court in appeals from High Courts in regard to civil matters

132 (C) Seat of Supreme Court

133 (D) Original Jurisdiction of the Supreme Court

Select the correct answer using the codes given below

	(130)	(131)	(132)	(133)
(a)	D	B	C	A
(b)	C	D	A	B
(c)	A	B	C	D
(d)	B	C	D	A

44. Article Subject matter

138 (A) confirmation of the Supreme Court of power to issue certain writs

139 (B) Enlargement of the Jurisdiction of the Supreme Court

140 (C) Ancillary Powers of Supreme Court

141 (D) Law declared by Supreme Court to be binding on all courts

	138	139	140	141
(a)	B	A	C	D
(b)	A	B	C	D
(c)	C	D	A	B
(d)	D	C	A	B

45. The Supreme Court holds its meetings at New Delhi but it can meet elsewhere
    (a) if a majority of judges of the Supreme Court so decides
    (b) with the approval of Parliament
    (c) with the approval of the President
    (d) on the request of the state legislature.

46. The Supreme Court call be a court of record and shall have all the powers of such a court including the power to punish for contempt of itself" This has been mentioned under the article
    (a) 102 (b) 129
    (c) 128 (d) 125.

47. The seat of the Supreme Court of India is
    (a) Bombay (b) Calcutta
    (c) Madras (d) New Delhi.

48. Which article of the Constitution provides for appointment of ad hoc judges?
    (a) Art. 124 (b) Art. 126
    (c) Art. 127 (d) Art. 128.

49. Can the Parliament vote on the salaries of the judges of the Supreme Court?
    (a) No (b) Sometimes
    (c) Always (d) None of these.

50. The oath offers to the Judges of the Supreme Court is administered by
    (a) The President
    (b) The Vice-President
    (c) The Speaker of Lok Sabha
    (d) The Law Minister.

51. Which of the following jurisdiction is enjoyed by the Supreme Court?
    (a) Appellate Jurisdiction
    (b) Original Jurisdiction

(c) Advisory Jurisdiction
(d) All the above.

52. The Supreme Court hears cases involving a substantial question of law as to the interpretation of the Constitution under its
(a) Original Jurisdiction
(b) Appellate Jursdiction
(c) Advisory Jurisdiction
(d) None of the above.

53. Which of the following articles deal with original jurisdiction of the Supreme Court?
(a) 128 (b) 129
(c) 130 (d) 131.

54. Who can be appointed as an ad-hoc judge of the Supreme Court?
(a) A retired judge of the Supreme Court
(b) A sitting judge of a High Court duly qualified for appointment as a Supreme Court judge
(c) An acting judge of the Supreme Court
(d) A person fully qualified for appointment as a judge to the Supreme Court.

55. All cases involving an interpretation of the Constitution fall within the
(a) Original Jurisdiction of the Supreme Court
(b) Advisory Jurisdiction of Supreme Court
(c) Appellate Jurisdiction of the Supreme Court
(d) None of the above.

56. The Supreme Court tenders advice to the President on a matter of law or fact
(a) On its own
(b) Only if he seeks such an advice
(c) Only if the matter relates to the Fundamental Rights of citizens
(d) Only if the issue poses a threat to the unity and integrity of the country.

57. The judges of the Supreme Court, after retirement, are not permitted to carry on practice before
    (a) The Supreme Court of India
    (b) The High Courts
    (c) The District and Session Courts
    (d) Any of the above.

58. The condition that in civil matters a case can only be taken to the Supreme Court if it involved an amount of Rs. 20,000 has been waived under
    (a) 40th amendment
    (b) 30th amendment
    (c) 42nd amendment
    (d) None of these.

59. Which one of the following is not correct?
    (a) All the authorities, civil and judicial in the territory of India are bound to act in aid of the Supreme Court
    (b) The Supreme Court may from time to time with the approval of the President make rules for regulating the practice and procedure of the Supreme Court
    (c) The judgements of the Supreme Court are not delivered in the open court
    (d) The judgements of the Supreme Court are delivered with the concurrence of majority of the Judges present and hearing the case.

60. The advice given by the Supreme Court to the President under its Advisory Jurisdiction is
    (a) Binding on the President of India
    (b) Not binding on the President of India
    (c) Always binding on the President of India
    (d) None of the above.

61. The Supreme Court of India
    (a) does not enjoy the power of judicial review
    (b) cannot enjoy the power of judicial review
    (c) enjoys the power of judicial review
    (d) none of the above is correct.

62. While interpreting the Constitution the courts are expected to

    (a) Resolve the conflict between the Directive Principles and Fundamental Rights

    (b) Ignore the Directive Principles, while interpreting Fundamental Rights

    (c) Give precedence to the Fundamental Rights over Directive Principles

    (d) Interpret the provisions of Fundamental Rights and Directive Principles as harmoniously as possible.

63. Which of the following is not one of the provisions made in the Constitution to secure independence of the Supreme Court judges ?

    (a) The judges of the Supreme Court hold office not during President's pleasure but on 'good behaviour'

    (b) They can be removed by the President only after a joint address by both Houses of Parliament passed by two thirds majority of members, President and voting in each House

    (c) The allowances, leave and pension etc. of the judges cannot be changed to the disadvantage of the judge during his term of office

    (d) A judge of the Supreme Court can practise only after ten years of his retirement.

64. The judges of the Supreme Court can be removed from their office during their tenure

    I by the President on the recommendation of the parliament

    II by the President on the recommendation of the Prime Minister

    III by the President of his discretion.

    Select the correct answer using the codes given below

    (a) I only

    (b) I and II

    (c) III only

    (d) In no case

65 The Supreme Court propounded the theory of basic structure of the Constitution in the

(a) Gopalan Vs. State of Madras case

(b) Golaknath case

(c) Keshavanand Bharti case

(d) Minerva Mills case.

66. Judicial Review means

(a) The power of the courts to make laws

(b) The power of the courts to define laws

(c) The power of the courts to define constitution

(d) The power of the courts to amend any legislative or executive act which is against the provisions of the Constitution.

67. In India the Power of Judicial Review is enjoyed by the

(a) High Court only

(b) Supreme Court only

(c) Lower Courts only

(d) Supreme Court and High Court

68. Under which one of the following amendments of the Constitution the power of judicial review of the Supreme Court and High Courts has been restored to them ?

(a) 42nd amendment

(b) 43rd amendment

(c) 44th amendment

(d) 45th amendment.

69. While exercising the power of judicial review, the Supreme Court of India

(a) has to see as to whether a law has been passed according to the procedure established by the law or not

(b) Has to see whether the law has been passed according to the due process of law or not

(c) Has not to see whether a law has been passed according to the procedure established by the law

(d) None of the above.

70. The Constitution has tried to ensure the independence of judges of the Supreme Court by
   (a) charging their salaries and allowances on the consolidated fund of India
   (b) by making the removal of judges quite difficult
   (c) by debarring judges from carrying on practice before any court in India after retirement
   (d) all of the above

71. The privileges of the judges of Supreme Court
   (a) cannot be modified to their disadvantage during their tenure of office
   (b) can be modified to their advantage or disadvantage during their term of office
   (c) can be modified by the Parliament only by two-third majority
   (d) can be modified only with the approval of the Chief Justice of India.

72. A case can come up for hearing before the Supreme Court against the judgement of lower courts
   (a) If high court certifies that the case involves a substantial question of law regarding interpretation of Constitution
   (b) On the Supreme Court granting special leave
   (c) If the Supreme Court has in an appeal reversed the order of acquittal of an accused person and sentenced him to death
   (d) In all the above cases.

73. Ancillary powers of Supreme Court has been stated under article
   (a) 140
   (b) 141
   (c) 142
   (d) 143.

ANSWERS

1.	(a)	2.	(a)	3.	(d)	4.	(a)
5.	(c)	6.	(d)	7.	(d)	8.	(b)
9.	(d)	10.	(a)	11.	(c)	12.	(b)
13.	(d)	14.	(d)	15.	(b)	16.	(d)
17.	(d)	18.	(c)	19.	(d)	20.	(a)
21.	(c)	22.	(d)	23.	(d)	24.	(b)
25.	(a)	26.	(c)	27.	(a)	28.	(d)
29.	(c)	30.	(c)	31.	(d)	32.	(a)
33.	(c)	34.	(b)	35.	(a)	36.	(d)
37.	(c)	38.	(b)	39.	(c)	40.	(d)
41.	(d)	42.	(a)	43.	(b)	44.	(a)
45.	(c)	46.	(b)	47.	(d)	48.	(c)
49.	(a)	50.	(a)	51.	(d)	52.	(b)
53.	(d)	54.	(b)	55.	(a)	56.	(b)
57.	(d)	58.	(b)	59.	(c)	60.	(b)
61.	(c)	62.	(d)	63.	(d)	64.	(a)
65.	(c)	66.	(d)	67.	(d)	68.	(b)
69.	(a)	70.	(d)	71.	(a)	72.	(d)
73.	(a)						

8
THE STATE EXECUTIVE

THE GOVERNOR

1. The Governor of the state nominates to the legislative council
   - (a) one-sixth of its members
   - (b) one-third of its members
   - (c) one-twelfth of its members
   - (d) one fourth of its members.

2. The Governor nominates those person in legislative council who
   - (a) are recommended by his friends
   - (b) are recommended by the ministers
   - (c) are famous politicians
   - (d) cooperate movement and social service.

3. How is a Governor paid if he acts as the Governor of more than one state?
   - (a) His salary is paid by the Central Government
   - (b) His salary is paid by the state where his headquarter is located
   - (c) His salary is shared by the concerned states in equal proportion
   - (d) He cannot be governor for more than one state.

4. Is there any constitutional provision for the impeachment of the Governor?
   (a) Yes, by the parliament
   (b) Yes
   (c) No
   (d) No by the state government.

5. The Governor of the State is
   (a) Real head of the government of the state
   (b) Constitutional head of a state
   (c) Head of the government of a state
   (d) None of these.

6. Every state has a legislature consisting of one or two houses with _______ as the executive head
   (a) The President
   (b) The Governor
   (c) The Chief Minister
   (d) The State Council of Ministers.

7. The Governor is the agent of the
   (a) Prime Minister in the state
   (b) President in the state
   (c) Home Minister in the state
   (d) None of these.

8. The Governor may exercise his discretion in the selection of the Chief Minister when
   (a) no single party
   (b) he does not like the leader of the majority party in the legislative assembly
   (c) one single party has achieved absolute majority in the legislative assembly
   (d) none of the above.

9. Can a person be appointed Governor of more than one state?
   (a) Yes (b) No
   (c) Only temporarily (d) Never.

10. The usual term of office of the Governor of a state is

(a) six years (b) five years
(c) four years (d) ten years.

11. Article Subject matter

157 (A) Qualification for appointments as Governor of a state
158 (B) Oath or affirmation by the Governor
159 (C) Discharge of the functions of the Governor in certain contingencies
160 (D) Conditions of Governor's office

Select the correct answer using the codes given below :

	157	158	159	160
(a)	A	D	B	C
(b)	B	C	D	A
(c)	C	D	A	B
(d)	D	C	A	B

12. Article Subject matter

153 (A) Governors of states
154 (B) Term of office of Governor
155 (C) Executive power of state
156 (D) Appointment of Governor of a state

Select the correct answer using the codes given below :

	153	154	155	156
(a)	A	C	D	B
(b)	B	C	D	A
(c)	C	D	A	B
(d)	D	C	A	B

13. Consider the following statements regarding the Governor of a state

(1) the Governor is the Constitutional head of the state
(2) the Governor always acts as an agent of the Centre
(3) the Governor is an integral part of the state legislature
(4) the Governor appoints the judges of the High Court.

Out of these statements
(a) 1 and 3 are correct
(b) 1, 3 and 4 are correct
(c) 1 and 2 are correct
(d) 2, 3 and 4 are correct.

14. The holding of elections for the Panchayats is decided by
(a) the District Magistrate
(b) constitutional mandate
(c) the state government
(d) the Election Commission.

15. Which one of the following is not correct?
(a) In the discharge of his official functions and duties the Governor will be only answerable before the Supreme Court of India
(b) The Governor cannot be arrested nor any proceedings to that effect be undertaken
(c) No criminal suit can be filed against the Governor
(d) In civil matters also no proceeding can be undertaken against the Governor.

16. Which one of the following is correct?
(a) No money bill can be introduced in the state legislature without the prior permission of the Governor
(b) The Governor has the power of issuing ordinances when the legislature is not in session
(c) The Governor can recommend to the president to impose President's rule on the state
(d) All of the above.

17. Which one of the following qualifications for the office of the governor has been wrongly listed?
(a) He must be a citizen of India
(b) He must not be less than thirty years of age
(c) He must not be a member of either House of Parliament or state legislature
(d) He must not hold any other office of profit.

18. Which one of the following alternatives is not available to the Governor of a state with regard to a bill passed by both the houses of the state legislature?
    (a) He can return the bill for reconsideration
    (b) He can reserve the bill for the approval of the President
    (c) He can kill the bill by not returning the same to the House where it originated
    (d) He can record his assent.

19. Which one of the following is not correct?
    (a) The Governor is a part and parcel of the state legislature
    (b) The Governor nominates one seventh members to the legislative council
    (c) The Governor has the power to summon the state legislature, address it and send messages to it
    (d) The Governor can prorogue the legislature and dissolve the state legislative assembly.

20. The formalities for contracts made in the exercise of the executive power of a state that the contract must be executed by a person duly authorised by the
    (a) Governor
    (b) Chief Minister
    (c) Prime Minister
    (d) Chief Secretary.

21. Under which article has power of Governor to promulgate ordinances during recess of legislature been mentioned?
    (a) 213 (b) 212
    (c) 112 (d) 113.

22. "The Governor shall in respect of every financial year cause to be laid before the House of the legislature of the state a statement of the estimated receipts and expenditure of the state for that year". This has been stated under article
    (a) 202 (b) 302
    (c) 102 (d) 42.

23. If the Governor wishes to relinquish office before the expiry of his term he has to address his resignation to
    (a) The Chief Minister of the State
    (b) The Speaker of the State Legislative Assembly
    (c) The President
    (d) The Prime Minister.

24. The Lt. Governor of Daman and Diu is concurrently the administrator of
    (a) Lakshadweep
    (b) Pondicherry
    (c) Chandigarh
    (d) Dadra and Nagar Haveli.

25. The Lt. Governor of a Union Territory
    (a) can issue an ordinance only after obtaining instructions from the President.
    (b) can issue ordinance on the recommendation of legislative assembly, if any
    (c) can issue ordinances of his own discretion
    (d) cannot issue any ordinance.

26. "All executive action of the Government shall be expressed to be taken in the name of the Governor". This has been mentioned under article
    (a) 166 (b) 176
    (c) 186 (d) 196.

27. The judicial powers of the Governor do not include the right to
    (a) be consulted by the president about appointment of judges of state High Court
    (b) grant pardon
    (c) remit punishment
    (d) pardon death sentence.

28. Article 161 of the Constitution does not empower the Governor of a state to grant pardon, reprieve respites of punishment convicted of an offence against

(a) panchayat laws (b) municipal laws
(c) state laws (d) central laws.

29. The ordinance issued by the Governor is valid for a maximum period of
(a) one year
(b) two years
(c) three years
(d) six months and six weeks.

30. The Governor recommends the imposition of the President's rule in a state
(a) when he is satisfied that the Government of the state cannot be carried on in accordance with the provisions of the Constitution
(b) when the Chief Minister of the state does not obey him
(c) when the Chief Minister of the state does not agree with him.
(d) None of the above.

31. Who is decide whether any matter is or is not a matter where the Governor has to act in his discretion?
(a) The Chief Minister (b) The Governor
(c) The President (d) The Prime Minister.

32. The Governor can issue ordinances
(a) only in case of between breakdown of constitutional machinery in the state
(b) only when the Chief Minister asks him to do so
(c) only during the recess of the state legislature
(d) only after taking format approval of the President.

33. The power of the Governor of issue ordinances covers all the matter
(a) included in the concurent list
(b) included in the union list
(c) on which the state legislature has the power to make the laws
(d) included in the union list as well as the concurrent list.

34. The Governor of a state exercises his discretionary powers
    (a) on the advice of the Prime Minister
    (b) on the advice of the chief secrotary of the state
    (c) on the advice of the state council of ministers
    (d) on his own.

35. A money bill can originate in the state legislature only with the prior consent of the
    I Chief Minister
    II President
    III Governor.

    Select the correct answer using the codes given below
    (a) I (b) II
    (c) III (d) I & III.

36. The Governor can reserve
    (a) all bill passed by state legislature for the assent of the President
    (b) certain types of bills passed by state legislature for the approval of the President
    (c) no
    (d) only financial bills for the approval of the President.

37. When can the Governor exercise his discretionary powers?
    (a) In appointment of Chief Minister if not a single party has clearcut majority in the House or there is no recognised leader of the majority party
    (b) In reservation of a bill passed by state legislature for the assent of the President
    (c) Dismissing a ministry if he is convinced that it has lost majority support in the assembly
    (d) all of the above.

38. "The Governor of a state shall have the power to grant pardons reprieves, respites on remissions of punishment or to suspend, remit or commute the sentence of any person convicted of any offence against any law relating to a matter to which the excutive power of the state extends." In which of the following article has this been stated?

(a) 161 (b) 171
(c) 181 (d) None of the above.

39. Who is the head of a state of the Indian Union?
(a) Government (b) Chief Minister
(c) President (d) Prime Minister.

40. In whom is the executive power of a state of the Indian Union vested?
(a) Prime Minister (b) Chief Minister
(c) Governor (d) President.

41. Under which article, it is possible to appoint the same person as the Governor for two or more states?
(a) Art. 53. (b) Art. 253
(c) Art. 353 (d) Art. 153.

42. Under which of the following article has this been mentioned that the executive power of the state shall be vested in the Governor and shall be exercised by him either directly or through officers subordinate to him in accordance with this Constitution?
(a) 154 (b) 155
(c) 156 (d) 157.

43. Under Article 155 of the Governor of a state is appointed by the
(a) Chief Justice of Inida
(b) Chief Justice of the High court
(c) Prime Minister
(d) President.

44. Qualifications for appointment as Governor have been stated under article
(a) 156 (b) 157
(c) 160 (d) 165.

45. Conditions of Governor's office has been stated under article
(a) 156 (b) 157
(c) 158 (d) 159.

46. The Governor may, resign his office by willing under his hand addressed to the

(a) Chief Minister (b) Prime Minister
(c) Vice President (d) President.

47. The Governor holds office during the pleasure of the

(a) President (b) Prime Minister
(c) Vice-President (d) President.

48. The Governor of a State can be dismissed by the

(a) Prime Minister (b) President
(c) Vice President (d) None of the above.

49. The President

(a) can transfer the Governor of a state
(b) cannot transfer the Governor of a state
(c) cannot always transfer the Governor of a state
(d) none of the above.

50. Which one of the following is not a qualification for the Governor of a state?

(a) He should be a citizen of India
(b) He should have completed the age of forteen years
(c) He should not hold any other office of profit under the Government
(d) None of the above.

51. What is the minimum age below which a person cannot be appointed a Governor of a state?

(a) 25 years (b) 30 years
(c) 35 years (d) 40 years.

52. At what age does a Governor of a state retire?

(a) 60 years (b) 62 years
(c) 65 years (d) There is no age limit.

53. The salary of the Governor of a state is

(a) Rs. 9000 per month
(b) Rs. 10,000 per month

(c) Rs. 11,000 per month
(d) Rs. 12,500 per month.

54. Which one of the following is not correct?
(a) The salary of the Governor of a state is charged on consolidated fund of the state
(b) The salary of the Governor cannot be reduced during his term of office
(c) The salary of the Governor of a state is charged on the consolidated fund of Inida
(d) The salary of the Governor of a state can only be reduced by the President during the promulgation of financial emergency in the country.

55. Every Governor before entering upon his office has to take an oath of his office in the presence of the
(a) Chief Justice of India
(b) Chief Justice of the High court
(c) President of India
(d) Chief Minister of the state.

ANSWERS

1.	(a)	2.	(d)	3.	(c)	4.	(c)
5.	(b)	6.	(d)	7.	(b)	8.	(b)
9.	(a)	10.	(a)	11.	(a)	12.	(a)
13.	(a)	14.	(a)	15.	(a)	16.	(d)
17.	(b)	18.	(c)	19.	(b)	20.	(a)
21.	(a)	22.	(a)	23.	(c)	24.	(d)
25.	(a)	26.	(a)	27.	(d)	28.	(d)
29.	(d)	30.	(a)	31.	(a)	32.	(b)
33.	(c)	34.	(a)	35.	(c)	36.	(d)
37.	(a)	38.	(a)	39.	(a)	40.	(c)
41.	(a)	42.	(a)	43.	(d)	44.	(b)
45.	(c)	46.	(d)	47.	(a)	48.	(b)
49.	(a)	50.	(b)	51.	(c)	52.	(c)
53.	(d)	54.	(c)	55.	(b)		

Chief Minister and State Council of Ministers

1. Who is the head of the State Council of Ministers?
   (a) Governor (b) Prime Minister
   (c) Chief Minister (d) None of the above.

2. The Chief link between the Governor and the Council of Ministers in a state is
   (a) Speaker
   (b) Cabinet Minister
   (c) Chief Justice of the High Court
   (d) None of the above.

3. Can the courts inquire as to what advice was tendered by the Ministers to the Governor?
   (a) No (b) Yes
   (c) Always (d) Sometimes.

4. The Chief Minister is appointed by the
   (a) President (b) Vice President
   (c) Governor (d) Prime Minister.

5. The other Ministers of the State Council of Minister
   (a) are appointed by the Governor at his sweet will
   (b) are appointed by the Governor on the advice of the Chief Minister
   (c) are appointed by the Chief Minister
   (d) none of the above.

6. The Chief Minister and the other Ministers hold office during the pleasure of
   (a) The Prime Minister (b) Governor
   (c) Legislaure (d) Legislative Council.

7. The State Council of Minister is collectively responsible to the
   (a) Legislative council of the State
   (b) Governor

(c) Chief Minister
(d) Legislative Assembly of the state.

8. The oath of office and secrecy is administered to the ministers by the
(a) Chief Secretary of the state
(b) Chief justice of the High Court
(c) Governor
(d) Chief Minister.

9. How long can a person remain as a minister without becoming a member of either house of the state legislature?
(a) one year (b) six months
(c) three months (d) four months.

10. The Chief Minister generally
(a) belongs to the legilative assembly
(b) belongs to the legislative council
(c) belongs to the Lok Sabha
(d) belongs to the Rajya Sabha.

11. The head of the Government in a state is
(a) the Chief Minister (b) the Governor
(c) the Lt. Governor (d) none of the above.

12. Can a member of the legislative council be appoint a Chief Minister of the state?
(a) Yes, but he should got himself elected to the legislative assembly at the earliest in conformity with the spirit of the Constitution
(b) No, it is against the constitutional provisions
(c) Never
(d) The constitution has specifically forbidden it.

13. For all practical purposes, the Chief Minister of a state is the
(a) Constitutional executive of the state
(b) Real executive of the state
(c) Nominal head of the state
(d) None of the above.

14. The position of the Chief Minister is
    (a) similar to that of the Prime Minister
    (b) identical to that of the President
    (c) a combination of the position of the Prime Minister and President
    (d) not constitutional.

15. Which one of the following factors does not play any role in determining the position of the Chief Minister ?
    (a) His personality
    (b) His position in the party
    (c) His financial status
    (d) The position of his party in the state legislature.

16. If a Chief Minister dies
    (a) the senior-most member of the Council of Minister automatically becomes the chief minister
    (b) the Council of Minister automatically stands dissolved
    (c) the Chief Justice of the High Court succeeds him as the Chief Minister
    (d) the Governor immediately appoints a new Chief Minister.

17. The Chief Minister is the principal advisor to the Governor and acts as a link between
    (a) Governor and the President
    (b) Legislative Council and the government
    (c) Governor and the Council of Ministers
    (d) Governor and other bodies reffered in (a) and (c) above.

18. The Council of Ministers stays in office
    (a) for a period of 5 years
    (b) as long as it enjoys the confidence of the majority party in the legislative assembly
    (c) as long as the Governor of the state wants it
    (d) as long as it enjoys the confidence of the opposition.

19. The portfolio are allocated to the ministers by
    (a) the Governor according to his sweet will
    (b) the Governor according to the abilities of the minister
    (c) the Governor according to the recommendations of the Chief Minister
    (d) The Chief Minister according to the advice of the Governor.

20. The Governor of a state can dismiss a Minister
    (a) on the advice of the leader of the Opposition party
    (b) on the advice of the Speaker of the legislative assembly
    (c) as his own sweet will
    (d) on the advice of the Chief Minister.

21. The state budget is formulated and presented to the state legislature by
    (a) Chief Minister
    (b) Governor
    (c) Council of Minster
    (d) Speaker.

22. A ministe can be asked to submit his resignation if he loses the confidence of the
    (a) Governor
    (b) Speaker of the Legislative Assembly
    (c) Chairman of the Legislative Council
    (d) Chief Minister.

23. Which of the following is a function of the Chief Minister?
    (a) He recommends the names of ministers for his Council of Ministers
    (b) He has to aid and advise the Governor in the exercise of his powers
    (c) He has to communicate to the Governor of the state all decisions of the Council of Ministers relating to the administration of the affairs of the state and proposal for legislation
    (d) All of the above.

24. Which one of the following is not a function of the Chief Minister
    (a) He allots business among his colleagues
    (b) He can ask any Minister to resign and in case of his refusal advise the Governor to dismiss him
    (c) He can dissolve the legislative assembly
    (d) He presides over the meetings of the Cabinet and controls the agenda thereof.

25. The Chief Minister is not responsible for
    (a) running the entire administration of the state
    (b) the maintenance of the law and order in the state
    (c) the defence of the state
    (d) none of the above.

26. The position of a Chief Minister depends upon
    (a) the position of his party in the state legislative assembly
    (b) his position in his pary
    (c) his personality and his popularily
    (d) all the above factors.

27. Which one of the followin is wrong?
    (a) It is the duty of the Chief Minister to keep the Governor informed of all the decisions of the cabinet
    (b) The Governor has the power to ask for any information from the Chief Minister regarding the administration of the state
    (c) The Governor is the real head of the state administration
    (d) As an agent of the Central Government the Governor may have to act sometimes independently on the advice of the Council of Ministers.

28. Which article of the Constitution defines the duties of the Chief Minister?
    (a) Art. 163 (b) Art. 164
    (c) Art. 166 (d) Art. 167.

29. The Chief Minister of a state asks the Governor to dissolve the legislature when

(a) the President issues a proclamation of state emergency
(b) he fears large scale defections for his ruling party
(c) he has no confidence in the cabinet
(d) his ministry loses absolute majority in the legislature.

30. Of the following methods which can be adopted by the Chief Minister to get rid of a Minister who has lost his confidence?

(a) Ask him to give his resignation
(b) Ask him from the council while reshuffling it
(c) Ask the Governor to dismiss him
(d) All the above.

31. The strength of the State Council of Ministers

(a) is fixed by the constitution
(b) is determined by the government
(c) is determined by the state legislature of every state
(d) is determined by the Chief Minister.

32. Which one of the following was not a member of the state legilsature at the time of appointments as Chief Minister of the state?

(a) Bansi Lal in Haryana
(b) N.D.Tewari in Uttar Pradesh
(c) S.B. Chavan in Mahrashtra
(d) All of the above.

33. The meetings of the state cabinet are presided over by the

(a) Governor
(b) Chief Minister
(c) Chief Secretary of the State
(d) Vice-President.

34. Which one of the following is not an executivr function of the Council of Ministers of a state?

(a) To run the administration of the state in accordance with the provisions of a Consitituion

(b) To bring about necessary cohesion in the policies of the various ministries

(c) To formulate the policy of the state government and give it practical shape

(d) To assist the President in the administration of the state during the President's rule in the state.

ANSWERS

1.	(c)	2.	(d)	3.	(a)	4.	(c)
5.	(b)	6.	(b)	7.	(d)	8.	(c)
9.	(b)	10.	(a)	11.	(a)	12.	(a)
13.	(b)	14.	(a)	15.	(c)	16.	(b)
17.	(c)	18.	(b)	19.	(c)	20.	(d)
21.	(c)	22.	(d)	23.	(d)	24.	(c)
25.	(c)	26.	(d)	27.	(c)	28.	(d)
29.	(d)	30.	(d)	31.	(d)	32.	(d)
33.	(b)	34.	(d)				

9
STATE LEGISLATURE

1. Which of the following functionaries has the right to participate in the proceedings of state legislatures?
   (a) Chairman, State Public Service Commission
   (b) Chief Justice of High court
   (c) Advocate General
   (d) Chief of the police force in the state.

2. Which of the following is a limitation on the powers of a state legislature?
   (a) Parliament can make laws on state subjects during the proclamation of emergency
   (b) During the presidential rule in a state the President can authorise the Parliament to make laws on the subjects included in the state list
   (c) Certain types of bills cannot be introduced in the state legislature without the prior sanction of the president
   (d) All of above.

3. If a money bill is not returned by the legislative council within a period of fourteen days of its receipt the bill is
   (a) considered to be rejected by both the houses
   (b) considered to be rejected by the legislative council
   (c) considered to have been passed by both the houses at the end of this period
   (d) None of the above.

4. After a money bill is passed by the legislative assembly the legislative council is required to return the bill to the legislative assembly with its recommendations within a period of
   (a) 14 days of the receipt of the bill
   (b) 20 days of the receipt of the bill
   (c) 21 days of the receipt of the bill
   (d) 22 days of the receipt of the bill.

5. Which one of the following is not a power of the legislative council?
   (a) The legislative council can remove a council of ministers by passing a vote of no-confidence against it
   (b) A non-money bill may be initiated in the legislative council
   (c) The legislative council can control the council of ministers by asking questions by discussing the bills, by introducing adjournment motions etc.
   (d) None of these.

6. Which of the following is not a power of the legislative assembly?
   (a) It can dismiss the Council of Ministers by passing a vote of no-confidence against them
   (b) All money bill must originate in the legislative assembly
   (c) It can initiate amendment of the constitution
   (d) The elected members of the legislative assembly participate in the election of the President of India along with the elected members of the Parliament.

7. The presiding officer of the legislative assembly is speaker who
   (a) is elected by the members of the legislative assembly from amongst themselves
   (b) is elected by the members of the legislative assembly from amongst persons who is not members of legislative assembly
   (c) is appointed by government of the state on the recommendation of the Chief Minister
   (d) is appointed by the Chief Minister of the state

8. Who of the following persons has the right to address both the houses of the state legislature on legal points but cannot vote in the proceedings of the state legislature ?
   (a) Advocate General of state
   (b) Attorney General of India
   (c) Law Officer
   (d) None of the above.

9. Which of the following is not an example of social legislation?
   (a) Offences Act
   (b) Suppression of Immoral Traffice Act
   (c) Dowry Act
   (d) National Security Act.

10. The legislature of a state make laws for
   (a) the whole or any part of the state
   (b) any part of the state
   (c) the whole of the state
   (d) the whole of the territory of India.

11 Democratic socialism is in favour of
   (a) Controlling and regulating private enterprise under state direction
   (b) Abolishing private entrprise completely
   (c) Helping sick industries run by private individuals
   (d) Promoting the interests and welfare of the procedures only.

12. The State Council of Ministers is collectively responsible to the
   (a) Legislative Council of the State
   (b) Governor
   (c) Chief Minister
   (d) Legislative Assembly of the State.

13. "A money bill shall not be introduced in a financial power of state council as per article
   (a) 196 (b) 197
   (c) 198 (d) 200.

14. Power of legislature of state to make provision with respect to elections to such legislature has been granted under article
    (a) 327 (b) 328
    (c) 331 (d) 350.

15. The salary and allowances of the members of the state council of ministers are
    (a) prescribed in the constitution
    (b) fixed by parliament
    (c) fixed by the Governor in consultation with president
    (d) fixed by the state legislature.

16. The ordinances promulgated by the Governor are subject to the approval of the
    (a) President (b) State Legislature
    (c) Vice President (d) Prime Minister.

17. The members of the state legislature exercise control over the State Council of Ministers through
    (a) questions and supplementary questions
    (b) criticism of its policies
    (c) adjournment motion
    (d) all of the above.

18. The Speaker of the legislative assembly can be removed from the office before his normal term by
    (a) The Chief minister
    (b) The Governor
    (c) The legislative assembly by passing a resolution by majority of its total membership
    (d) None of the above.

19. For the union territories that do not have legislative assemblies laws are passed by
    (a) the Union Cabinet
    (b) the President of India
    (c) the Parliament
    (d) the administration of the respective union territories.

20. The Governor of which of the following states has been vested with special power regarding schedule tribe areas ?
    (a) Bihar
    (b) Arunachal Pradesh
    (c) Assam
    (d) Madhya Pradesh.

21. The quorum of the legislative council is
    (a) one fourth of its total membership
    (b) one fourth of its membership
    (c) one fifth of its membership as
    (d) none of these.

22. The members of the Legislative Assembly are
    (a) elected by the local self governing bodies
    (b) directly elected by the people
    (c) nominated by the Governor
    (d) none of the above.

23. When a Governor reserves a bill passed by the state legislature?
    (a) He may be impeached
    (b) He sends it to the President
    (c) He may keep the bill pending indefinitely
    (d) He may give assent to the bill later.

24. In matter of ordinary legislation for the state
    (a) the legislative assembly has been given more powers
    (b) the legislative council has been given more powers
    (c) both the Houses have been given equal powers
    (d) none of these.

25. The recommendation for the creation or abolition of the Upper House of a state legislature can be made by the
    (a) Governor
    (b) State Legislative Assembly
    (c) Chief Minister
    (d) Parliament.

26. The members of the Council of Ministers in a state must
    (a) be members of either Houses of state legislature
    (b) be members of the legislature assembly
    (c) be eminent citizens of the state
    (d) be members of legislature council.

27. What is the maximum period upto which the legislative council of a state can delay the consideration of a bill that has been already passed once by the legislative assembly of the state?
    (a) one month (b) two months
    (c) three months (d) six months.

28. The name of the presiding officer of the legislative council is
    (a) Chairman (b) Vice-Chairman
    (c) President (d) Speaker.

29. The name of the presiding officer of the legislative assembly is
    (a) Speaker (b) President
    (c) Chairman (d) Vice President.

30. In which of the following articles have salaries and allowances of the Speaker, Dy. Speaker, the Chairman been mentioned
    (a) Act 136 (b) Act 156
    (c) Act 186 (d) Act 196.

31. Under which article has this been mentioned that the Speaker or the Deputy Speaker of the legislative assembly shall not preside while a resolution for his removal from office is under consideration?
    (a) 181 (b) 180
    (c) 179 (d) 178.

32. The provision for the Speaker and Deputy Speaker of the legislative assembly has been made
    (a) 177 (b) 178
    (c) 179 (d) 180.

33. Right of Governor to address and send messages to the House or Houses has been provided under article

(a) 175 (b) 275
(c) 250 (d) 150.

34. What is the maximum period which should not intervence between two sessions of the state legislature ?

(a) Two months (b) Four months
(c) Six months (d) One month.

35. The term of legislative council of a state is

(a) nine years (b) six years
(c) eight years (d) four years.

36. The term of the legislative assembly can be increased by the

(a) Governor
(b) President
(c) Chief Minister
(d) Parliament by law for a period of one year at a time during the emergency.

37. The duration of the state legislative assembly is

(a) five years (b) six years
(c) seven years (d) four years.

38. Which of the following person are not entitled to elect members of legislative council?

(a) Members of legislative assembly
(b) Members of district boards
(c) Teachers and Graduates
(d) Registered Medical Practitioners.

39. Which one of the following legislative assemblies has maximum strength ?

(a) Andhra Pradesh
(b) Uttar Pradesh
(c) Madhya Pradesh
(d) West Bengal.

40. Legislative Council of which one of the following states has less than the required number of members?
    (a) Jammu and Kashmir (b) Bihar
    (c) Tamil Nadu (d) Karnataka.

41. Which of the following states had legislative council before but now it has been abolished by an act of Parliament?
    (a) Bihar and Karnataka
    (b) Andhra Pradesh and Tamil Nadu
    (c) Bihar and Maharashtra
    (d) None of the above.

42. In which one of the following states has a legislative assembly with a strength of only 32 members ?
    (a) Tripura (b) Arunachal Pradesh
    (c) Sikkim (d) Nagaland.

43. Legislative Assembly of which one of the following states has minimum number of members?
    (a) Jammu and Kashmir (b) Manipur
    (c) Meghalaya (d) Goa.

44. In the states with bi-cameral legislature the Upper House is known as
    (a) Vidhan Parishad
    (b) Vidhan Sabha
    (c) Council of States
    (d) Council of Representatives.

45. Which Union Territory has a legislature Chief Minister and ministers?
    (a) Andaman & Nicobar
    (b) Chandigarh
    (c) Pondicherry
    (d) None of the above.

46. In which article has this been stated"The total number of members in the legislative council of a state having such a council shall not exceed one third of the total number of

members in the legislative assembly of that state

(a) 151 (b) 161
(c) 171 (d) 181.

47. Which one of the following is not a qualification for a member of the state legislative assembly?
   (a) He should be a citizen of India
   (b) He should not be less than twenty five years of age
   (c) He should not hold any office of profit under the government
   (d) He should be atleast a matriculate.

48. In which one of the following states is it constitutionally obligatory for the state to have a separate minister for the tribal welfare?
   (a) Bihar (b) Madhya Pradesh
   (c) Orissa (d) All of the above.

ANSWERS

1.	(c)	2.	(d)	3.	(c)	4.	(a)
5.	(a)	6.	(c)	7.	(a)	8.	(a)
9.	(d)	10.	(a)	11.	(a)	12.	(d)
13.	(c)	14.	(b)	15.	(d)	16.	(b)
17.	(d)	18.	(c)	19.	(c)	20.	(b)
21.	(c)	22.	(b)	23.	(b)	24.	(a)
25.	(b)	26.	(a)	27.	(a)	28.	(a)
29.	(a)	30.	(c)	31.	(a)	32.	(b)
33.	(a)	34.	(c)	35.	(b)	36.	(d)
37.	(a)	38.	(d)	39.	(b)	40.	(a)
41.	(b)	42.	(c)	43.	(d)	44.	(a)
45.	(c)	46.	(c)	47.	(d)	48.	(d)

10
STATE JUDICIARY

The High Courts

1. The highest judicial court in a state is the
   (a) Supreme Court (b) District Court
   (c) High Court (d) Sessions court

2 The Constitution has
   (a) fixed the number of judges of high court at five
   (b) not laid down any fixed number of the judges of the high court
   (c) fixed the number of the high court at seven
   (d) none of the above.

3. The Chief Justice and other judges of the High Court are appointed by the
   (a) President (b) Chief Minister
   (c) Governor (d) Chief Justice of India.

4. The President appoints additional judges in high court to cope up with the increased work or arrears of work for a period not exceeding
   (a) 2 years (b) 1 year
   (c) 6 monts (d) 5 years.

5. Mark the true statement
   (a) the high court is the higest court of law and appeal in the state

(b) appeals from all the lower courts need not be taken to the high court but directly to the Supreme Court
(c) High Courts are not established in all the states
(d) all of the above.

6. In criminal matters the highest court in a district is the
(a) Court of First Class Magistrate
(b) Court of Second Class Magistrate
(c) Court of the Sessions Judge
(d) High Court.

7. In civil matters the highest court of appeal in a district is the
(a) court of senior sub judge
(b) small causes court
(c) high court
(d) district court.

8. A common high court for two or more states and or union territory may be established by
(a) The President
(b) The Chief Justice of India
(c) The Governor of the state
(d) A law by the Parliament.

9. A judge of the high court can be removed from his office on the ground of proved misbehaviour or incapacity by the
(a) Governor of the state
(b) Chief Minister of the state
(c) Chief Justice of India
(d) President of India on the recommendations of the Parliament.

10. There can be
(a) high court for one state
(b) high court for two states
(c) common high court for two or more states and or union territory
(d) none of these.

11. The expenses of high court including all salaries allowances etc are charged upon the
    (a) Consolidated Fund of India
    (b) Consolidated Fund of the State
    (c) Contingency Fund of the India
    (d) Contingency Fund of state.

12. The power to extend the jurisdiction of a high court to or exclude the jurisdiction of a high court from any union territory rests with
    (a) The President of India
    (b) The Parliament
    (c) The Supreme Court
    (d) The State Legislature.

13. When a high court certifies that a case involves a substantial question of law as to interpretation of the Constitution it can be brought to the Supreme Court under its
    (a) original jurisdiction
    (b) appellate jurisdiction
    (c) advisory jurisdiction
    (d) none of the above.

14. The power to decided an election petition is vested in the
    (a) Parliament
    (b) Supreme Court
    (c) High Court
    (d) Election Commission.

15. "Parliament may be law constitute a high court for an union territory or declare any court in any such territory to the high court for all or any of the purpose of this constitution" has been stated under the Article
    (a) 171 (b) 271
    (c) 241 (d) 141.

16. Under which of the following articles has high court control over subordinate courts?
    (a) 235 (b) 270
    (c) 150 (d) 370.

17. Recruitments of persons after that district judge to the judicial service are made under article
(a) 134 (b) 190
(c) 234 (d) 140.

18. Appointments of districts judges are made under articles
(a) 160 (b) 193
(c) 233 (d) 250.

19. Provision for establishment of a common high court for two more states have been made under article
(a) 231 (b) 131
(c) 331 (d) 171.

20. "Parliament may by law extend the jurisdiction of a high court to or exclude the jurisdiction of a high court from any union territory". In which of the following article has this been mentioned?
(a) 130 (b) 230
(c) 330 (d) 160.

21. Which of the following states/union territories have a common high court?
(a) Uttar Pradesh and Bihar
(b) Punjab and Jammu Kashmir
(c) Punjab, Haryana and Chandigarh
(d) Assam and Bengal.

22. The President is authorised to
(a) reduce the salaries of the judges of the high courts at his sweet will
(b) reduce the salaries of the judges of the high courts during the promulgation of Presidential rule
(c) reduce the salaries of the judges of the high courts during the promulgation of financial emergency
(d) none of the above is correct.

23. The other judges of the high court get a salary of
(a) Rs. 8,000 per month
(b) Rs. 7,000 per month

(c) Rs. 6,500 per month
(d) Rs. 5,000 per month.

24. Salary of the Chief Justice of a high court is
(a) Rs. 9,000 per month
(b) Rs. 8,000 per month
(c) Rs. 7000 per month
(d) Rs. 6000 per month.

25. After retirement a judge of high court
(a) cannot plead in any court in the territory of India
(b) can plead only in the Supreme Court
(c) can plead only in the high court
(d) can plead of act only in the Supreme Court and the other high courts.

26. Who administers the oath of office to the judges of high courts?
(a) Chief Minister
(b) President
(c) Chief Justice of India
(d) The Governor of the respective state.

27. "The administrative expenses of a hight court including all salaries, allowances and pensions payable to or in respect of the officers and servants of the court, shall be charged upon the consolidated fund of the state and any fees or other money taken by the court shall form part of that fund". This has been mentioned under article
(a) 229 (b) 129
(c) 329 (d) 139.

28. High Court has power to transfer certain cases to high court that are pending in a court subordinate to it and which involves a substantial question of law as to the interpretation of this constitution. In which of the following article has this power been granted?
(a) 228 (b) 239
(c) 230 (d) 240.

29. Every high court shall have superintence over all courts and all courts and tribunals throughout the territorries in relation to which in exercises jurisdiction this has been state under article
    (a) 250 (b) 260
    (c) 270 (d) 227.

30. Which of the following articles has given power to high courts to issue certain writs?
    (a) 226 (b) 126
    (c) 130 (d) 150.

31. Jurisdiction of existing high courts has been stated under article
    (a) 125 (b) 225
    (c) 137 (d) None of the above.

32. In which of the following articles is there a provision for appointment or acting chief justice of a high court?
    (a) 202 (b) 210
    (c) 223 (d) 240.

33. "The President may after consultation with the chief justice of India transfer a judge from one high court to any other high court". This has been provided under article
    (a) 220 (b) 222
    (c) 212 (d) 112.

34. "No person who after the commencement of this Constitution can hold office as a permanent judge of a high court shall plead or act in any court or before any authority in India except the Supreme Court and the other high courts", this has been stated under article
    (a) 220 (b) 218
    (c) 118 (d) 120.

35. Every person appointed to be judge of a high court shall, before he enters upon his office make and subscribe before the Governor of the state or same person appointed on the behalf by him an oath or affirmation", under which of the following article has this been stated?

(a) 195 (b) 210
(c) 119 (d) 219.

36. Under which article has this been stated that "Every high court shall consist of a Chief Justice and such other judges as the President may form time to time deem it necessary to appoint?

(a) 40 (b) 140
(c) 216 (d) 116.

37. Which of the following articles lays down that every high court shall be a court of record?

(a) 215 (b) 115
(c) 315 (d) None of the above.

38. "There shall be a high court for each state", this has been stated under article

(a) 102 (b) 202
(c) 214 (d) 114.

39. A judge of a high court may resign his office by writing under his hand addressed to be

(a) Chief Justice of India
(b) Chief Justice of High Court
(c) Governor of the State
(d) President of India.

40. The age of the retirement for the judges of the High Court is

(a) 60 years (b) 62 years
(c) 70 years (d) 80 years.

ANSWERS

1.	(c)	2.	(c)	3.	(a)	4.	(a)
5.	(a)	6.	(c)	7.	(d)	8.	(d)
9.	(d)	10.	(c)	11.	(b)	12.	(b)
13.	(b)	14.	(c)	15.	(c)	16.	(a)
17.	(c)	18.	(c)	19.	(a)	20.	(b)
21.	(c)	22.	(c)	23.	(a)	24.	(a)

25.	(d)	26.	(d)	27.	(a)	28.	(a)
29.	(d)	30.	(a)	31.	(b)	32.	(c)
33.	(b)	34.	(a)	35.	(d)	36.	(c)
37.	(a)	38.	(c)	39.	(d)	40.	(b)

Attorney General

1. Under which Article a provision for the appointment of Attorney General for India?
   (a) 76 (b) 77
   (c) 78 (d) 79.

2. The Attorney General of India holds his office during the session of the
   (a) Parliament
   (b) Union Public Service Commission
   (c) President
   (d) Union Law Minister.

3. The Attorney General of India is appointed by the
   (a) Home Minister
   (b) Prime Minister
   (c) Union Public Service Commission
   (d) President.

4. According to the Article 79, the Parliament does not consist of the
   (a) President
   (b) Lok Sabha
   (c) Rajya Sabha
   (d) Attorney General of India.

5. The Attorney General of India gets a salary of
   (a) Rs. 11,000 per month
   (b) Rs. 10,500 per month
   (c) Rs. 9,000 per month
   (d) Rs. 8,500 per month.

6. Which of the following qualifications should the Attorney General of India fulfil?

   (a) He must fulfil the qualifications to be eligible for the post of a judge of Supreme Court
   (b) He must fulfil the qualifications to be eligible for the post of a judge of a High Court
   (c) He must fulfil the qualifications to practise as an advocate in the Supreme Court
   (d) He must fulfil the qualifications to be eligible for the post of sessions judge.

7. The Attorney General of India has the right of audience in

   (a) any High Court
   (b) the Supreme Court
   (c) any Sessions Court
   (d) any court of law within the territory of India.

8. The Attorney General of India enjoys all the powers and immunities as enjoyed by the

   (a) President
   (b) Prime Minister
   (c) Minister of Law
   (d) Member of Parliament.

9. The Atorney General of India has the privilege to address

   (a) the Lok Sabha
   (b) the Rajya Sabha
   (c) both the Houses of Parliament
   (d) none of the above.

10. The Attorney General of India is

   (a) the highest financial officer of the Union Government
   (b) the highest legal officer of the Union Government
   (c) the highest financial as well as the legal oficer of the Union Government
   (d) none of the above.

11. If the Auditor-General wants to resign, he addresses his or resignation letter to
    (a) The President
    (b) The Prime Minister
    (c) The Speaker of the Lok Sabha
    (d) None of the above.

12. Which non-member can participate in either of the Houses of the Parliament?
    (a) The Vice-President
    (b) The Solicitor General
    (c) The Attorney General
    (d) The Chief Justice of India.

13. The Attorney General of India
    (a) has the right to vote in the proceedings of the Lok Sabha
    (b) has the right to vote in the proceedings of the Rajya Sabha
    (c) does not have the right to vote in the proceedings of the Parliament
    (d) has the right to vote in the proceedings of both the houses of the Parliament.

14. Which of the following is not true about the Attorney General of India?
    (a) He is not a member of the Cabinet
    (b) He has a right to speak in the House of Parliament
    (c) He has a right to vote in Parliament
    (d) He must have the same qualifications as required to be judge of the Supreme Court.

15. Which of the following is not a function of the Attorney General of India?
    (a) To give advice to the Government of India upon legal matters
    (b) To perform such duties of legal character, as may from time to time, be referred or assigned to him, by the President

(c) To appoint the public prosecutors in the lower court

(d) He must have the same qualifications conferred on him, by the Constitution or any other law for the time being in force.

ANSWERS

1.	(a)	2.	(c)	3.	(d)	4.	(d)
5.	(c)	6.	(a)	7.	(d)	8.	(d)
9.	(c)	10.	(b)	11.	(a)	12.	(c)
13.	(c)	14.	(c)	15.	(c)		

11
CENTRE-STATE RELATIONS

1. The Concurrent List originally contained
   (a) 97 subjects (b) 47 subjects
   (c) 66 subjects (d) 44 subjects.

2. Which of the following parts deals with the services under the union and the States?
   (a) Part XIII (b) Part X
   (c) Part XIV (d) Part XI.

3. The residuary powers have been given to the
   (a) State Legislature
   (b) Lok Sabha
   (c) Rajya Sabha
   (d) Union Parliament.

4. Which one of the following parts deals with the trade, commerce and intercourse within the territory of India
   (a) Part XIII (b) Part XII
   (c) Part X (d) None of these.

5. Which article of the constitution empowers Parliament to provide for the establishment of additional courts for the better administration of Union laws?
   (a) Art. 246 (b) Art. 247
   (c) Art. 248 (d) Art. 249.

6. The State list originally contained
   (a) 66 subjects (b) 56 subjects
   (c) 82 subjects (d) 44 subjects.

7. In the seventh amendment, which was passed in 1956, was concerned with the
   (a) Right to Freedom
   (b) Re-organisation of the states
   (c) Right to property
   (d) None of these.

8. Power of Parliament to provide for the establishment of certain additional courts, has been stated under Aticle
   (a) 247 (b) 248
   (c) 249 (d) 245.

9. The Sarkaria Commision was appointed to
   (a) find a solution to the Punjab crisis
   (b) examine the Centre and State relations
   (c) resolving the dispute, regarding sharing of Cauveri water
   (d) examine the working of public sector undertakings.

10. The residuary power means,
    (a) the power which relates to the international affairs
    (b) the power which is shared between the Union Government and the states
    (c) the power which relates to the international affairs of the country
    (d) the power which has been not included in any of three lists above i.e. the Union, the State and Concurrent List.

11. Which of the following part deals with finance, property contracts and suits ?
    (a) Part X (b) Part XII
    (c) Part XIII (d) None of the above.

12. The Union List orginally contained
    (a) 77 subjects
    (b) 87 subjects
    (c) 97 subjects
    (d) none of the above.

13. The Union Territories are administered by
    (a) The Prime Minister of India
    (b) The Union Executive
    (c) The President through the administrators appointed by him
    (d) The administrator(s) appointed by the Government of India.

14. In which year were the state recognised on a linguistic basis
    (a) 1947
    (b) 1958
    (c) 1961
    (d) None of the above.

15. Who was the Chairman of the Commission appointed by the Government of India to review the question of Centre-State relations?
    (a) R.S. Sarkaria (b) S.C. Sarkar
    (c) Manmohan Singh (d) Swarn Singh.

16. Power of Parliament to legislate with respect to a matter in the State List in the national interest has been mentioned under article
    (a) 149 (b) 259
    (c) 249 (d) 159.

17. The Punjab Reorganisation Act which created the state of Punjab and Haryana in 1966 was passed on the basis of the recommendation of the
    (a) Shah Commission
    (b) Dass Commission
    (c) Dhar Commission
    (d) Mahajan Commission.

18. Power of Parliament to lagislate with respect to any matter in the state list in the national interest has been mentioned under article
    (a) 249 (b) 250
    (c) 251 (d) 252.

19. What is the total number of law as on the Ist June 1996 relating to land reforms and abolition of the Zamindari system included in the Ninth Schedule that are protected from judicial scrutiny?

(a) 257 (b) 108
(c) 202 (d) 284.

20. If any state law is repugnant to the union law made under article 249 or 250 then the

(a) union law will prevail over the state law
(b) union law will not prevail over the state law
(c) state law will prevail over the Union law
(d) none of the above.

21. The Parliament has also power to make a law for the whole or any part of the Territory of India for implementing

(a) the five year plans
(b) its industrial policy
(c) its financial policy
(d) any treaty, agreement or convention with any other country or countries.

22. Power of the Union to confer power etc. on state in certain cases has been granted under article

(a) 261 (b) 258
(c) 262 (d) 265.

23. Provision with respect to an inter-state council have made under article

(a) 263 (b) 241
(c) 251 (d) 271.

24. The provision for grants from the Union to certain state has been made under article

(a) 75 (b) 175
(c) 275 (d) 375.

25. When the proclamation of emergency is in operation?

(a) The Parliament is authorised under Article 250 of the Constitution to legislate with respect to any matter included in the state list

(b) The Parliament is not authorised to legislate with respect to any mater in the state list
(c) The state legislature are authorised to legislate with respect to any matter in the state list
(d) None of the above.

26. The provision for prior recommendation of President require to bill affecting taxation in which states are interested has been made under article
(a) 205 (b) 217
(c) 224 (d) 274.

27. "Full faith and credit shall be given throughout the territory of India to public acts, records and judicial proceedings of the Union and of every state" this has been stated under article
(a) 190 (b) 195
(c) 261 (d) 262.

28. Taxes levied and collected by the Union and distributed between the Union and states have been covered under article
(a) 169 (b) 170
(c) 163 (d) 270.

29. The provision for taxes on professional trades, callings and employments has been made under article
(a) 175 (b) 196
(c) 263 (d) 276.

30. The administrative relations between the Centre and the State have been stated under
(a) Art. 256 to 263 (b) Art. 260 to 267
(c) Art. 276 to 283 (d) Art. 286 to 293.

31. "No tax shall be levied or collected except by authority of law" this has been stated under article
(a) 65 (b) 165
(c) 265 (d) 365.

32. The provision for exemption of property of the Union from state taxation has been made under article
   (a) 163 (b) 193
   (c) 190 (d) 285.

33. Duties levied by the Union but collected and appropriated by the states are covered under article
   (a) 249 (b) 251
   (c) 268 (d) 285.

34. The property and income of a state shall be exempted from union taxation has been made under article
   (a) 163 (b) 195
   (c) 172 (d) 285.

35. Taxes levied and collected by the union but assigned to the state have been covered under the article
   (a) 169 (b) 170
   (c) 247 (d) 269.

36. The financial relation between the Union Government and State Government discussed under
   (a) Art. 264 to 291 of the constitution
   (b) Art. 278 to 291 of the constitution
   (c) Art. 289 to 295 of the constitution
   (d) None of the above.

37. Which one of the following is levied and collected by the Union and distributed between the Union and States?
   (a) Taxes on income other than agricultural income
   (b) Taxes on the sale or purchase of newspaper and on advertisements published therein
   (c) Taxes other than stamp duties on transaction in stock exchange and future markets
   (d) Taxes on railway fares and freights.

38. Borrowing by the Government of India has been covered under article
   (a) 192 (b) 140
   (c) 292 (d) 392.

39. Borrowing by the States have been covered under article

(a) 273 (b) 283

(c) 293 (d) 295.

40. "All contracts made in the exercise of the executive power of the Union or of a State shall be expressed to be made by the President or by the Governor of the state, as the case may be, and all such contracts and all assurances of property made in the exercise of that power shall be executed on behalf of the President or the Governor by such person and in such manner as he may direct or authorise", this has been stated under article

(a) 146 (b) 179

(c) 263 (d) 299.

41. Which one of the following was a Union Territory before it was accorded the status of a full fledged state?

(a) Tripura

(b) Himachal Pradesh

(c) Manipur

(d) All of the above.

42. The first linguistic state set up on the basis of the Wancho Report was

(a) Andhra Pradesh in 1953

(b) Gujarat in 1956

(c) Andhra Pradesh in 1956

(d) Gujarat in 1960.

43. At present India consists of

(a) 22 states and 9 union territories

(b) 22 states and 7 union territories

(c) 25 states and 7 union territories

(d) 28 states and 7 union territories.

44. Which of the following is represented in the Rajya Sabha?

(a) Arunachal Pradesh

(b) Dadra and Nagar Haveli

(c) Andman and Nicobar Islands

(d) All of the above.

45. Which of the following gives the correct descending order of state in number of seats allotted to them in the council of state?
    (a) U.P, M.P. Bihar and Maharashtra
    (b) Bihar, M.P., Maharashtra and U.P
    (c) U.P. , Bihar, Maharashtra, Tamil Nadu
    (d) None of the above.

46. Sikkim is
    (a) The 21st state of Indian Union
    (b) Part of the Union Territory
    (c) A full fledged state of India
    (d) All of the above.

47. "No person shall be deprived of his property saved by authority of law". this has been stated under article
    (a) 29 (b) 297
    (c) 298 (d) 300 A.

48. Which of the following article deals with recruitment and condition of service of person serving the union or a state?
    (a) 309 (b) 310
    (c) 311 (d) 312.

49. All India Services has been stated under article
    (a) 309 (b) 285
    (c) 251 (d) 312.

50. Which one of the following has been wrongly listed as a union territory?
    (a) Pondicherry (b) Tripura
    (c) Chandigary (d) None of these.

51. Grants-in-aid given to states are meant
    (a) to maintain friendly relationship between Centre and State
    (b) for meeting state plan project
    (c) for use in Centrally sponsored schemes
    (d) to cover gaps on revenue account so that states can undertake various benefical activiies.

52. Which one of the following states is given a special grant-in aid under the Constitution of India, for raising the level of administration of tribal areas to that of the administration of the rest of the areas of that state ?
    (a) Nagaland
    (b) Arunachal Pradesh
    (c) Tripura
    (d) None of the above.

53. Match the following columns of states and their year coming into being as states

	I		II
(a)	Himachal Pradesh	1.	1971
(b)	Manipur	2.	1960
(c)	Kerala	3.	1970
(d)	Maharashtra	4.	1956

    (a) A-3, B-1, C-4, D-2
    (b) A-3, B-2, C-4, D-1
    (c) A-1, B-2,C-3, D-4
    (d) A-4, B-1, C-2, D-3.

54. Transitional provisions regarding public service have been stated under article
    (a) 313 (b) 314
    (c) 311 (d) 312.

55. Tenure of office of person serving the Union or a State has been stated under article
    (a) 309 (b) 310
    (c) 311 (d) 312.

56. The structure of administration in various union territories
    (a) has been prescribed in the Constitution
    (b) is determined by the Union Home Ministry
    (c) is determined by the President
    (d) is determined by the Parliament.

57. Which state enjoys the distinction of being the latest state of the Indian Union?
   (a) Mizoram
   (b) Arunachal Pradesh
   (c) Goa
   (d) Nagaland.

58. Which one of the following is a leading recommendation of the Sarkaria Commission?
   (a) Activation of zonal councils
   (b) Abolition of all India services
   (c) Abolition of zonal council
   (d) Drastic changes in the present division of function between the finance commission and planning commission.

59. The state recognition Act 1956, divided the entire country into
   (a) 17 states and 7 union territories
   (b) 22 states and 9 union territories
   (c) 14 states and 6 union territory
   (d) None of the above.

60. Estate duty in respect of property except agricultural land is a
   (a) source of not state revenue
   (b) source of state revenue
   (c) source of revenue for the Union territories
   (d) none of the above.

61. The first commission appointed by the Government in 1948 to examine the case for the reorganisation on a linguistic base was headed by
   (a) justice M.C. Mahajan
   (b) justice S.K.Dhar
   (c) justice Wanchoo
   (d) None of the above.

62. India the relation between the union and the state are regulated
    (a) according to the parliamentary laws
    (b) according to the direction of the president
    (c) according to the provision of the Constitution
    (d) according to the well established convention.

63. Which state spearheaded the demand for greater autonomy of states
    (a) Punjab
    (b) Andhra Pradesh
    (c) Jammu and Kashmir
    (d) All of the above.

64. Which schedule gives details regarding the subjects included in the three lists Union list, State list and Concurrent List?
    (a) Schedule I (b) Schedule VII
    (c) Schedule VI (d) Schedule V.

65. In which of the following list has the subject of insurance been included?
    (a) State list (b) Concurrent list
    (c) Union list (d) All the three above.

66. Which one of the following lists of subjects can the Parliament legislate?
    (a) Union list (b) Concurrent list
    (c) State list (d) All of the above.

67. The subject of diplomatic counsellor and trade representation has been included in
    (a) State list (b) Union list
    (c) Concurrent list (d) None of the above.

68. The subject of the people debt of the union has been included in
    (a) State list (b) Union list
    (c) Concurrenty list (d) None of the above.

69. The subject of Defence of India and every part thereof has been included in

(a) Union list (b) State List
(c) Concurrent list (d) None of the above.

70. The subject of Banking has been included in

(a) State list (b) Concurrent list
(c) Union list (d) None of the above.

71. The subject of maritime shipping and navigation, including shipping and navigation on tidal water has been included in

(a) State list (b) Concurrent list
(c) Union list (d) None of the above.

72. The subject of port declared by or under law made by parliament or existing law to be major parts has been included in

(a) State list (b) Union list
(c) Concurrent list (d) None of the above.

73. The subject of highway has been included in

(a) State list (b) Union list
(c) Concurrent list (d) All of the above.

74. The subject of carriage of passengers and goods by railway, sea or air or by national water way in mechanically propelled vessels have been included in

(a) State list (b) Concurrent list
(c) Union list (d) None of these.

75. In which of following lists has Central Bureau of Intelligence and Investigation been included?

(a) Union list (b) State list
(c) Concurrent list (d) All of the above.

76. In which of the following lists has the subject of arms, fireams, ammunition and explosive been included?

(a) State list (b) Concurrent list
(c) Union list (d) None of the above.

77. The subject of war and peace comes in
   (a) State list
   (b) Union list
   (c) Concurrent list
   (d) All of the above.

78. The subject of atomic energy and mineral resources has been included in
   (a) State list (b) Union list
   (c) Concurrent list (d) All of the these.

79. The subject of railway has been included in
   (a) State list (b) Union list
   (c) Concurrent list (d) None of these.

80. The subject of bills of exchange, cheques, promissing notes and other like instruments have been included in
   (a) State list (b) Union list
   (c) Concurrent list (d) None of these.

81. The subject of naval, military and air forces, any other armed forces of the union has been included in
   (a) State list (b) Union list
   (c) Concurrent list (d) None of these.

82. The subject of Inter-state trade and commerce has been included in
   (a) State list (b) Union list
   (c) Concurrent list (d) None of these.

83. The subject of coordination and determination of standards in instruction for higher education or research and scientific and technical instruction have been included in
   (a) State list (b) Union list
   (c) Concurrent list (d) None of these.

84. Which one of the following subjects is not contained in the Union list?
   (a) Currency (b) Foreign Affairs
   (c) Census (d) Agriculture.

85. The subject of corporation tax has been included in
(a) State list (b) Union list
(c) Concurrent list (d) None of these.

86. The subject of taxes on the sale or purchase of newspaper and on advertisement published therein has been included in
(a) State list (b) Union list
(c) Concurrent list (d) None of these.

87. The subject of currency, coinage and legal tender, foreign exhange have been included in
(a) State list (b) Union list
(c) Concurrent list (d) None of these.

88. In which of the following lists has Reserve Bank of India included ?
(a) State list (b) Union list
(c) Concurrent list (d) None of these.

89. The subject of duties of custom including export duties has been included in
(a) State list (b) Union list
(c) Concurrent list (d) None of these.

90. The subject of terminal taxes on goods or passengers, carried by railway sea or air taxes on railway fares and freights have been included in
(a) State list (b) Union list
(c) Concurrent list (d) None of these.

91. The subjects of elections to Parliament to the legislature of states and to the offices of President and Vice-President, the Election Commision all have been included in
(a) State list (b) Union list
(c) Concurrent list (d) None of these.

92. The subject of civilization manufacture and sale for export of opium have been included in
(a) State list (b) Union list
(c) Concurrent list (d) None of these.

93. The subject of Constitution, organisation, jurisdiction and power of the Supreme Court has been included in
(a) State list (b) Union list
(c) Concurrent list (d) None of these.

94. The subject of airways, aircraft and air navigation, provision of aerodromes have been included in
(a) State list (b) Union list
(c) Concurrent list (d) None of these.

95. The subject of Constitution and organisation including vacations of the High Court has been included in
(a) State list (b) Union list
(c) Concurrent list (d) None of these.

96. The subject of manufacture, supply and distribution of salt by Union agencies have been included in
(a) State List
(b) Union List
(c) Concurrent List
(d) All of the above.

97. The subject of regulation of mines and mineral development to the extent to which such regulation and development under the control of the Union is declared by Parliament by law to be expedient in the public interest has been included in
(a) State List (b) Union List
(c) Concurrent List (d) All of the above.

98. The subject of Union Public Services, All India Services, Union Public Service Commission all have been included in
(a) State List (b) Union List
(c) Concurrent List (d) All of the above.

99. The subject of United Nations organisation has been included in
(a) State list (b) Union list
(c) Concurrent list (d) All of the above.

100. The subject incorporation regulation and windings up of trading corporations, including banking, insurance and financial corporation but not including co-operative societies have been included in

(a) State list (b) Union list
(c) Concurrent list (d) All of the above .

101. The subject of posts and telegraphs, telephones, wireless, broadcasting and other like forms of communication have been included in

(a) State list (b) Union list
(c) Concurrent list (d) None of these.

102. The subject of Industries, the control of which by the Union is declared by parliament by law to be expedient in the public interest have been included in

(a) State list (b) Union list
(c) Concurrent list (d) None of these.

103. The subject of ancient and historical monuments and records, and archaeological sites and remains, declared by or under law made by parliament to be of national importance have been included in

(a) State list (b) Union list
(c) Concurrent list (d) None of these.

104. The subject of trade and commerce with foreign country has ben included in

(a) State list (b) Union list
(c) Concurrent list (d) None of these.

105. The subject of audit of the accounts of the union and of the states has been included in

(a) State list (b) Union list
(c) Concurrent list (d) None of these.

106. The subject of preventive detenntion for reason conected with defence foreign affairs or the security of India has been included in

(a) State list (b) Union list
(c) Concurrent list (d) None of these.

107. The subject of patents, invention and designs, copywright, trade marks and merchandise marks all have been included in

(a) State list (b) Union list
(c) Concurrent list (d) All of these.

108. The subject of stock exchange and future markets have been included in

(a) State list (b) Union list
(c) Concurrent list (d) None of these.

109. The subject of establishment of standards of quality for goods to be exported out of India has been included in

(a) State list (b) Union list
(c) Concurrent list (d) None of these.

110. The subject of regulation of labour and safety in mines and oil field have been included in

(a) State list (b) Union list
(c) Concurrent list (d) All of these.

111. The subject of industrial disputes concerning union, employees has been included in

(a) State list (b) Union list
(c) Concurrent list (d) All of the above.

112. The subject of Survey of India, the Geological, Botanical, Zoological and Anthropological Survey of India, Meteorological organisation all have been included in

(a) State list (b) Union list
(c) Concurrent list (d) None of these.

113. The subject of powers privileges and immunities of each House of Parliament have been included in

(a) State list (b) Union list
(c) Concurrent list (d) None of these.

114. The subject of public health and sanitation, hospitals and dispensaries all have been included in

(a) State list (b) Union list
(c) Concurrent list (d) None of these.

115. The subject of taxes on profession, trades, callings and employement has been included in

(a) State list (b) Union list

(c) Concurrent list (d) None of these.

116. Which one of the following is not a source of state revenue?

(a) Land revenue

(b) Excise duty in respect of agricultural land

(c) Duties on succession to agricultural land

(d) Corporate tax.

117. The subject of elections to the legislature of the state object to the provisions of any law made by parliament has been included in

(a) State list (b) Union list

(c) Concurrent list (d) All of these.

118. The subject of taxes on luxuries including taxes on entertainments amusements, betting and gambling has been included in.

(a) State list

(b) Union list

(c) Concurrent list

(d) None of these.

119. The subject of production, manufacture profession, transport, purchase and sale of intoxicating liquors has been included in

(a) State list (b) Union list

(c) Concurrent list (d) All of these.

120. The subject of taxes on the entry of goods into a local area for consumption has been included in

(a) State list (b) Union list

(c) Concurrent list (d) None of these.

121. The subject of prisons, reformatories borstal institutions and other institution of a like nature have been included in

(a) State list (b) Union list

(c) Concurrent list (d) None of these.

122. The subject of taxes on goods and passengers carried by road or on inland water ways has been included in

(a) State list (b) Union list
(c) Concurrent list (d) None of these.

123. The subject of theatres and dramatic performance, cinemas, sports, entertainments and amusements has been included in

(a) State list (b) Union list
(c) Concurrent list (d) None of these.

124. The subject of works, lands and buildings vested in or in the possession of the state have been included in

(a) State list (b) Union list
(c) Concurrent list (d) None of these.

125. The subject of libraries, museums and other similar institutions controlled or financed by the state, ancient and historical monument and records other than those declared by or under law made by parliament to be of national importance have been included in

(a) State list (b) Union list
(c) Concurrent list (d) All of these.

126. The subject of salaries and allowances of member of the legislature of the state, of the Speaker and Deputy Speaker of the legislative assembly and if there is a legislative council, of the chairman and deputy chairman thereof all has been included in

(a) State list (b) Union list
(c) Concurrent list (d) None of these.

127. The subject of university has been included in

(a) State list (b) Union list
(c) Concurrent list (d) None of these.

128. The subject of the legislative assembly and of the members and the committee thereof all has been included in

(a) State list (b) Union list
(c) Concurrent list (d) None of these.

129. The subject of money-lending and money-lenders relief of agricultural indebetedness have been included in

(a) State list (b) Union list
(c) Concurrent list (d) None of these.

130. The subject of officers and servant of high court, procedure in rent and revenue courts, fees taken in all courts except the Supreme Court has been included in

(a) State list (b) Union list
(c) Concurrent list (d) None of these.

131. The subject of pensions payable by the state or out of the consolidated fund of the state has been included in

(a) State list (b) Union list
(c) Concurrent list (d) None of these.

132. The subject of roads, bridge ferries and other means of communications have been included in

(a) State list (b) Union list
(c) Concurrent list (d) All of these.

133. The subject of taxes on mineral rights subject to any limitations imposed by parliament by law relating to mineral development has been included in

(a) State list (b) Union list
(c) Concurrent list (d) All of these.

134. The subject of trade unions, industrial and labour disputes has been included in

(a) State list (b) Union list
(c) Concurrent list (d) All of these.

135. The subjects of prevention, protection and improvement of stock and prevention of animal diseases, veterinary training and practice have been included in

(a) State list (b) Union list
(c) Concurrent list (d) All of these.

136. The subject of gas and gas works have been included in

(a) State list (b) Union list
(c) Concurrent list (d) All of these.

137. The Parliament can make laws even on a subject included in the state list under article 249 of the Constitution if the

(a) President gives the permission
(b) Vice President gives the permission
(c) Speaker gives the permission
(d) Council of State passes a resolution by a two-third majority of the members present and voting that that it is in the national interest that the parliament should make law on a particular matter contained in the state list

138. The subject of water supplies irrigation and canals, drainage and embankment have been included in

(a) State list (b) Union list
(c) Concurrent list (d) All of these.

139. The subject of forest has been included in

(a) State list (b) Union list
(c) Concurrent list (d) All of these.

140. The subject of population control and family planning have been included in

(a) State list (b) Union list
(c) Concurrent list (d) All of these.

141. The subject of markets and fairs have been included in

(a) State list (b) Union list
(c) Concurrent list (d) All of these.

142. The subject of criminal law and procedure is contained in

(a) State list (b) Union list
(c) Concurrent list (d) All of these.

143. The subject of commercial and industrial monopolies combines and trusts have been included in

(a) State list (b) Union list
(c) Concurrent list (d) All of these.

144. The subject of public order is contained in the

(a) State list (b) Union list
(c) Concurrent list (d) None of these.

145. The subject of marriage and divorce, infants and minor adoption, wills, intastacy and succession, joint family and partition have been included in
(a) State list
(b) Union list
(c) Concurrent list
(d) None of these.

146. The subject of social security and social insurance, employment and unemployement have been included in
(a) State list (b) Union list
(c) Concurrent list (d) All of these.

147. The subjects of legal, medical and other profession have been included in
(a) State list (b) Union list
(c) Concurrent list (d) All of these.

148. The subject of price control has been included in
(a) State list (b) Union list
(c) Concurrent list (d) None of these.

149. The subject of transfer of property other than agricultural land, registration of deeds and documents have been included in
(a) State list (b) Union list
(c) Concurrent list (d) None of these.

150. The subject of prevention of the extension from one state to another of infectious or contagious disease has been included in
(a) State list (b) Union list
(c) Concurrent list (d) All of these.

151. The subject of contract including partnership, agency, contract of carriage and other special form of contracts but not including contracts relating to agricultral land have been included in
(a) State list (b) Union list
(c) Concurrent list (d) None of these.

152. The subject of economic and social planning have been included in

(a) State list (b) Union list
(c) Concurrent list (d) All of these.

153. The subject of newspapers, books and printing prices all have been included in

(a) State list (b) Union list
(c) Concurrent list (d) All of these.

154. The subject of wild animals and birds has been included in

(a) State list (b) Union list
(c) Concurrent list (d) None of these.

155. The subject of welfare of labour including condition of work, provident fund and employer's liability has been included in

(a) State list (b) Union list
(c) Concurrent list (d) All of these.

156. The subject of Administrators-General and official trustees has been included in

(a) State list (b) Union list
(c) Concurrent list (d) All of these.

157. Both the Parliament and the Legislature of any state have the power to make laws with respect to any of the matters enumerated in the

(a) State list (b) Union list
(c) Concurrent list (d) All of these.

158. Which of the following is not included in the concurrent list of our Constitution

(a) Boilers (b) Electericity
(c) Factories (d) Markets and fairs.

ANSWERS

1.	(b)	2.	(c)	3.	(d)	4.	(a)
5.	(b)	6.	(a)	7.	(b)	8.	(a)
9.	(b)	10.	(d)	11.	(b)	12.	(a)

13.	(c)	14.	(b)	15.	(a)	16.	(c)
17.	(a)	18.	(b)	19.	(c)	20.	(a)
21.	(d)	22.	(b)	23.	(a)	24.	(c)
25.	(a)	26.	(d)	27.	(c)	28.	(b)
29.	(d)	30.	(a)	31.	(c)	32.	(d)
33.	(c)	34.	(a)	35.	(c)	36.	(a)
37.	(a)	38.	(c)	39.	(c)	40.	(d)
41.	(d)	42.	(a)	43.	(d)	44.	(a)
45.	(c)	46.	(c)	47.	(d)	48.	(a)
49.	(d)	50.	(b)	51.	(d)	52.	(c)
53.	(a)	54.	(a)	55.	(b)	56.	(b)
57.	(c)	58.	(a)	59.	(c)	60.	(b)
61.	(b)	62.	(c)	63.	(d)	64.	(b)
65.	(a)	66.	(d)	67.	(b)	68.	(b)
69.	(a)	70.	(c)	71.	(c)	72.	(b)
73.	(b)	74.	(c)	75.	(a)	76.	(c)
77.	(b)	78.	(a)	79.	(b)	80.	(b)
81.	(b)	82.	(c)	83.	(b)	84.	(d)
85.	(b)	86.	(b)	87.	(b)	88.	(a)
89.	(b)	90.	(b)	91.	(b)	92.	(b)
93.	(b)	94.	(b)	95.	(c)	96.	(b)
97.	(b)	98.	(b)	99.	(b)	100.	(b)
101.	(b)	102.	(b)	103.	(b)	104.	(b)
105.	(b)	106.	(b)	107.	(b)	108.	(b)
109.	(b)	110.	(b)	111.	(b)	112.	(b)
113.	(b)	114.	(a)	115.	(a)	116.	(d)
117.	(a)	118.	(a)	119.	(a)	120.	(a)
121.	(a)	122.	(a)	123.	(a)	124.	(a)
125.	(a)	126.	(a)	127.	(a)	128.	(a)
129.	(a)	130.	(a)	131.	(a)	132.	(a)
133.	(a)	134.	(a)	135.	(a)	136.	(a)
137.	(d)	138.	(a)	139.	(a)	140.	(a)
141.	(a)	142.	(a)	143.	(a)	144.	(a)
145.	(c)	146.	(c)	147.	(c)	148.	(c)
149.	(c)	150.	(c)	151.	(c)	152.	(c)
153.	(c)	154.	(c)	155.	(c)	156.	(c)
157.	(c)	158.	(d)				

12
AMENDING OUR CONSTITUTION

Important Amendments in the Indian Constitution

1. Under which Amendment, Right to property was first of all amended ?
   (a) Sixth amendment (b) Fourth amendment
   (c) Ninth amendment (d) None of the above.

2. Which amendment removed the prescribed limit of 750,000 of the population to return one member to the Lok Sabha?
   (a) Second amendment (b) Third amendment
   (c) First amendment (d) Fourth amendment.

3. When was the seventh amendment passed?
   (a) 1995 (b) 1994
   (c) 1993 (d) 1992.

4. Which amendment of 1992 has provided to set up state level rent tribunals?
   (a) 72nd (b) 71st
   (c) 74th (d) 75th.

5. Constitutional guaranttee for formation of the Panchayats at the village and other levels was provided by
   (a) the 57th amendment
   (b) the 44th amendment
   (c) the 73rd amendment
   (d) none of these.

6. When was the third amendment passed?
   (a) 1954 (b) 1951
   (c) 1963 (d) 1952.

7. Which of the following amendments reduced the representation of the union territories from 25 to 20 in Lok Sabha?
   (a) 31st (b) 32nd
   (c) 34th (d) 37th.

8. When was the 31st amendment passed?
   (a) 1972 (b) 1973
   (c) 1975 (d) 1974.

9. Which amendment abolished the condition of Rs. 20,000 for an appeal in the Supreme Court to civil cases?
   (a) 31st (b) 39th
   (c) 30th (d) None of these.

10. Under 36th amendment of the Constitution
    (a) Sikkim was made the 22nd state of the Indian Union
    (b) The state of Haryana were created
    (c) The right to property was amended
    (d) The right to freedom was amended.

11. The territories of Goa, Daman and Diu had become part of the territory of India by the
    (a) 12th amendment
    (b) 10th amendment
    (c) 15th amendment
    (d) None of the above.

12. When was the 12th amendment passed?
    (a) 1965 (b) 1966
    (c) 1962 (d) 1970.

13. Under which amendment was the inclusion of the former french territory of Pondicherry legalised?
    (a) 30th (b) 14th
    (c) 17th (d) None of the above.

14. When was the 15th amendment passed?
(a) 1960 (b) 1962
(c) 1961 (d) 1963.

15. Which of the following amendments changed of ninth schedule ?
(a) 17th (b) 15th
(c) 20th (d) None of these.

16. Which amendment recognised Sindhi as the 15th language of the Constitution?
(a) 21st (b) 23rd
(c) 22nd (d) 20th.

17. By which amendment, the power to amend the Constitution was specifically conferred upon the parliament?
(a) 42nd amendment
(b) 52nd amendment
(c) 24th amendment
(d) 56th amendmennt.

18. When was the 25th amendment passed?
(a) 1940 (b) 1972
(c) 1971 (d) 1973.

19. Under which amendment Article 31 was amended and a new article 31 C was added?
(a) Thirty (b) Twenty fifth
(c) Twenty fourth (d) None of these.

20. Which amendment was upheld by the supreme court in the Keshvananda Bharati's case in 1971?
(a) 20th (b) 26th
(c) 25th (d) 24th.

21. Which of the following amendment raised the age of retirement of a High Court judge from 60 to 62?
(a) 15th (b) 17th
(c) 16th (d) None of these.

22. Under which amendment a new article 233 A was inserted?
    (a) Thirtieth (b) Twentieth
    (c) Fourtieth (d) None of these.

23. Which amendment added a new article 363 A?
    (a) Thirty-fifth (b) Thirtieth
    (c) Twenth-sixth (d) Twenty-seven.

24. Thirty first amendment Act 1973 raised the total strength of Lok Sabha to
    (a) 550 (b) 525
    (c) 570 (d) 545.

25. Thirty-fifth amendment was passed in
    (a) 1974 (b) 1975
    (c) 1980 (d) 1985.

26. Which amendment provided for a legislative assembly and a Council of Ministers for the union territory of Arunachal Pradesh?
    (a) Thirty sixth (b) Thrity seven
    (c) Thirty fifth (d) None of these.

27. When was the fortieth amendment passed?
    (a) 1975 (b) 1976
    (c) 1978 (d) 1977.

28. Which was the lengthiest amendment to the Constitution?
    (a) 24th (b) 44th
    (c) 42nd (d) None of these.

29. Which of the following amendment established the supremacy of the parliament in place of supremacy of the constitution?
    (a) Fortieth (b) Fourty first
    (c) Fourty second (d) None of these.

30. When was the forty-first amendment passed?
    (a) 1980 (b) 1977
    (c) 1975 (d) 1976.

31. Which one of the following has been most drastice and the most controversial amendment?
   (a) Fortieth amendment
   (b) Forty first amendment
   (c) Forty second amendment
   (d) Forty third amendment.

32. When was the forty fifth amendment passed?
   (a) 1975 (b) 1978
   (c) 1981 (d) 1980.

33. Defections were outlawed by the amendment of Constitution by
   (a) 51st amendment
   (b) 52nd amendment
   (c) 53rd amendment
   (d) 54th amendment.

34. When was the fiftieth amendment passed?
   (a) 1984 (b) 1985
   (c) 1982 (d) 1980.

35. The right of the private property was dropped from the list of Fundamental Rights by the
   (a) 24th amendment (b) 44th amendment
   (c) 42nd amendment (d) 46th amendment.

36. When was the fifty-fifth amendment passed?
   (a) 1985 (b) 1986
   (c) 1987 (d) 1988.

37. Which of the following amendments enhanced the salaries of judges of the Supreme Court and the high court?
   (a) 51st (b) 52nd
   (c) 54th (d) 56th.

38. Forty sixth amendment passed in
   (a) 1980 (b) 1981
   (c) 1983 (d) 1982.

39. The life of the Lok Sabha and also of state assemblies was reduced from six years to five years by

(a) 44th amendment (b) 45th amendment
(c) 43rd amendment (d) 46th amendment.

40. Which amendment amended the article 269 so that the tax levied on the consignment of goods in the course of inter-state trade on commerce should be assigned to the state?

(a) Forty fifth (b) Forty sixth
(c) Forty fourth (d) forty seventh.

41. When was the sixtieth amendment passed?

(a) 1985 (b) 1986
(c) 1987 (d) 1988.

42. Which amendment conferred statehood on the union territory of Goa?

(a) 55th (b) 56th
(c) 57th (d) 58th.

43. Fifty-seventh amendment was passed in the year

(a) 1987 (b) 1985
(c) 1988 (d) 1990.

44. Which one of the following subjects was transferred by the sixty-first amendment carried out in March 1989 from the state list to the concurrent list?

(a) Education (b) Health
(c) Irrigation (d) All of the above.

45. When was the sixty-fifth amendment passed?

(a) 1987 (b) 1988
(c) 1989 (d) 1990.

46. The seventh sechdeule of the Constitution was amended by

(a) second amendment
(b) eleventh amendment
(c) sixth amendment
(d) fith amendment.

47. Which amendment authorised the President to publish an authoritative Hindi translation of the Constitution of India?
(a) 57th (b) 58th
(c) 59th (d) None of these.

48. Which of the following amendment crapped the 59th amendment which impowered the government to impose emergency in Punjab?
(a) 61st (b) 60th
(c) 63rd (d) 62nd.

49. When was the sixty-ninth amendment passed?
(a) 1990 (b) 1989
(c) 1988 (d) 1991.

50. How many New Land Reform Laws were added to the Ninth Schedule by the seventy-eighth amendment?
(a) 27th (b) 37th
(c) 47th (d) 57th.

51. When was the fifth amendment passed?
(a) 1952 (b) 1994
(c) 1955 (d) 1958.

52. What was the number of the schedule added by the 35 amendment in 1974
(a) Tenth (b) Twelth
(c) Ninth (d) Eleventh.

53. Which amendment gave Sikkim the status of associate state of India?
(a) Thirty sixth (b) Thirty fourth
(c) Thirty seventh (d) Thirty fifth.

54. The Thirtieth amendment was passed in
(a) 1965 (b) 1972
(c) 1970 (d) 1971.

55. The 42nd amendment introduced
(a) Schedule VII
(b) Fundamental Duties

(c) Directive Principles of State Policy
(d) None of these.

56. Which of the following amendment provides for reservation of seats for tribes men of the North-eastern states in the Lok Sabha and in the state assemblies in these seats ?
(a) Fifty second (b) Fifty
(c) Fifty first (d) Fifty four

57. Which amendment in 1992 has provided to add new part relating to urban local bodies?
(a) Seventy second (b) Seventy fourth
(c) Seventy first (d) Seventy third.

58. In 1990 , 55 new land reform laws were added to the ninth schedule by the
(a) 65th amendment (b) 62nd amendment
(c) 20th amendment (d) 66th amendment.

59. Fifty-fifth amendment conferred full statehood to
(a) Arunachal Pradesh (b) Goa
(c) Mizoram (d) Sikkim.

60. Mizoram was conferred upon the statehood by
(a) 55th amendment (b) 56th amendment
(c) 53rd amendment (d) 51st amendment.

61. When was the forty fourth amendment passed?
(a) 1977 (b) 1978
(c) 1976 (d) 1975.

62. When was the thirty ninth amendment passed?
(a) 1975 (b) 1974
(c) 1972 (d) 1973.

63. The reservation of seats and posts for the scheduled castes and scheduled tribes people have been extended upto 1990 under the
(a) 40th amendment (b) 42th amendment
(c) 41st amendment (d) 45th amendment.

64. Which of the following amendment raised the term of the Lok Sabha and State Assemblies from five years to six years?
(a) 43rd amendment (b) 41st amendment
(c) 42nd amendment (d) 40th amendment.

65. Which amendment made certain changes in the first schedule?
(a) 6th amendment (b) 9th amendment
(c) 11th amendment (d) 10th amendment.

66. When was the eleventh amendment passed?
(a) 1961 (b) 1962
(c) 1960 (d) 1965.

67. Which amendment created Nagaland as the sixteenth state of the Indian Union?
(a) 15th amendment (b) 10th amendment
(c) 12th amendment (d) 14th amendment.

68. Which amendment of 1992 has provided that the Konkani, Manipur and Nepali shall be included in the Eighth schedule of the Constitution?
(a) 73rd amendment (b) 70th amendment
(c) 72nd amendment (d) 71st amendment.

69. Which of the following amendments has added a number of land reform laws in the Ninth Schedule of the Constitution and thus placed them outside the jurisdiction of the courts?
(a) 65th amendment (b) 60th amendment
(c) 66th amendment (d) 64th amendment.

70. The reservation for the scheduled castes and scheduled tribes in the Parliament and State Assemblies was extended upto 2000 A.D by the
(a) 61st amendment (b) 62nd amendment
(c) 63rd amendment (d) 64th amendment.

71. Sixty-first amendment was passed in the year
(a) 1989 (b) 1985
(c) 1986 (d) 1987.

72. When was the fifty-fourth amendment passed?
(a) 1985 (b) 1984
(c) 1986 (d) 1987.

73. Which amendment empowered the Supreme Court to decide the disputes regarding the election of the President and the Vice President?
(a) 44th amendment (b) 42th amendment
(c) 41st amendment (d) 43th amendment.

74. When was the seventy second amendment passed?
(a) 1991 (b) 1993
(c) 1990 (d) 1992.

75. Which amendment of the Constitution lowered the voting age from 21 years to 18 years?
(a) sixtieth (b) sixty first
(c) sixty second (d) sixty third.

76. Which of the following amendment empowered the state government to increase the ceiling of professional tax from Rs. 250 to Rs. 2500 per person per year?
(a) sixtieth (b) fifty ninth
(c) fifty eighth (d) sixty first.

77. When was the sixty-fourth amendment passed?
(a) 1987 (b) 1986
(c) 1990 (d) 1988.

78. By which amendment was the age of retirement of the Chairman and members of the State Public Service Commission raised from 60 to 62?
(a) 40th amendment
(b) 41st amendment
(c) 42th amendment
(d) 45th amendment.

79. When was the forty-seventh amendment passed?
(a) 1982 (b) 1980
(c) 1983 (d) 1984.

80. Which of the following amendments transferred the subject of sports from the state list to the concurrent list

(a) 62nd amendment (b) 63rd amendment
(c) 61st amendment (d) 60th amendment .

81. Under which of the following amendments act was the reservation of seats for scheduled tribes in the state assemblies of Meghalaya, Mizoram, Nagaland and Arunachal Pradesh?

(a) 60th amendment (b) 62th amendment
(c) 61st amendment (d) 57th amendment.

82. When was the sixty-third amendment passed?

(a) 1989 (b) 1986
(c) 1987 (d) 1988.

83. Which of the following amendment has given statutory status to the national commission for schedule castes and scheduled tribes?

(a) 55th amendment (b) 65th amendment
(c) 60th amendment (d) 45th amendment. .

84. When was the fifty-third amendment passed?

(a) 1987 (b) 1984
(c) 1986 (d) 1990.

85. When was the tenth amendment passed?

(a) 1961 (b) 1960
(c) 1962 (d) 1965.

86. One of the following amendment imposed restriction on the fundamental rights of citizens with a view to protect the sovereignity and itegrity of India, it was the

(a) 15th amendment (b) 42nd amendment
(c) 20th amendment (d) 16th amendment.

87. The sixteenth amendment was passed in

(a) 1964 (b) 1966
(c) 1963 (d) 1965.

88. Which amendment provided for the creation of an autonomous State known as Meghalaya comprising hill areas within the state of Assam?

(a) 52nd amendment (b) 22nd amendment
(c) 42nd amendment (d) 32nd amendment.

89. Under which amendment was the representation of the states in the Lok Sabha raised from 500 to 525?

(a) Thirty-third (b) Thirtieth
(c) Thirty second (d) Thirty first.

90. The twenty-sixth amendment was passed in

(a) 1971 (b) 1970
(c) 1975 (d) 1972.

91. When was the twenty-second amendment passed?

(a) 1969 (b) 1968
(c) 1965 (d) 1970.

92. When amendment extended the concession given to scheduled castes and scheduled tribes up to 1980?

(a) 25th amendment (b) 23rd amendment
(c) 20th amendment (d) 29th amendment.

93. When was the thirty-third amendment passed?

(a) 1976 (b) 1974
(c) 1975 (d) 1978.

94. Sikkim became a new State in the Union by the Amendment Act in

(a) 1974 (b) 1975
(c) 1974 (d) None of these.

95. Which amendment abolished the titles and special privileges of the former rulers of princely states?

(a) 26th Amendment
(b) 44th Amendment
(c) 41st Amendment
(d) 24th Amendment.

96. Which amendment provided for promulgation of emergency in Punjab on account of internal distrubances and extension of President's rule upto 3 years?

(a) sixtieth (b) fifty-eighth
(c) fifty-seventh (d) fifty-nineth.

97. The 52nd Amendment to the constitution

(a) provided an autonomous District Council in Tripura
(b) seeks to curb political defections
(c) extended reservation for scheduled castes and scheduled tribes till 1990
(d) brought person working in certain organisations whose character of duties as akin to the armed forces within the ambit of Article 33 of the Constitution.

98. Which amendment laid down that the general emergency could not be declared by the President unless it was advised by the decision in the Cabinet meeting and not by the Prime Minister alone?

(a) 44th amendment (b) 42nd amendment
(c) 41st amendment (d) 43rd amendment.

99. When was the fifty-second amendment passed?

(a) 1984 (b) 1985
(c) 1986 (d) 1983.

100. Which amendment gave power to the Parliament to form a new State of Union Territory by uniting a part of any state or Union Territory to any other state of Union Territory?

(a) 30th amendment (b) 29th amendment
(c) 17th amendment (d) 18th amendment.

ANSWERS

1.	(b)	2.	(a)	3.	(a)	4.	(d)
5.	(c)	6.	(a)	7.	(a)	8.	(b)
9.	(c)	10.	(a)	11.	(a)	12.	(c)
13.	(b)	14.	(d)	15.	(a)	16.	(a)
17.	(c)	18.	(c)	19.	(b)	20.	(d)

21.	(a)	22.	(b)	23.	(c)	24.	(d)
25.	(a)	26.	(b)	27.	(b)	28.	(c)
29.	(c)	30.	(b)	31.	(c)	32.	(d)
33.	(b)	34.	(a)	35.	(b)	36.	(b)
37.	(c)	38.	(d)	39.	(a)	40.	(b)
41.	(d)	42.	(b)	43.	(a)	44.	(b)
45.	(d)	46.	(c)	47.	(b)	48.	(c)
49.	(d)	50.	(a)	51.	(c)	52.	(a)
53.	(d)	54.	(b)	55.	(b)	56.	(c)
57.	(b)	58.	(d)	59.	(a)	60.	(c)
61.	(b)	62.	(a)	63.	(d)	64.	(c)
65.	(b)	66.	(a)	67.	(a)	68.	(d)
69.	(c)	70.	(b)	71.	(a)	72.	(c)
73.	(a)	74.	(d)	75.	(b)	76.	(a)
77.	(c)	78.	(b)	79.	(d)	80.	(c)
81.	(d)	82.	(a)	83.	(b)	84.	(c)
85.	(a)	86.	(a)	87.	(c)	88.	(b)
89.	(d)	90.	(a)	91.	(a)	92.	(b)
93.	(b)	94.	(d)	95.	(a)	96.	(d)
97.	(b)	98.	(a)	99.	(b)	100.	(d)

13
HUMAN RIGHTS

1. United Nations Organisation was established on
   (a) January 26, 1950 (b) December 26, 1945
   (c) October 24,1945 (d) August 15, 1947.
2. The Concept of U.N. was of
   (a) President Eison Hower
   (b) President Abraham Lincoln
   (c) President Roozevelt
   (d) President Trueman.
3. The main parts of U.N.O are
   (a) 4 (b) 5
   (c) 6 (d) 1.
4. Total number of members in Security Council is
   (a) 180 (b) 185
   (c) 25 (d) 15.
5. At present U.N.O consists of
   (a) 185 members
   (b) 188 members
   (c) 85 members
   (d) 285 members.
6. International Human Rights Day is
   (a) December 20th (b) December 10th
   (c) January 26th (d) August 15th.

7. Universal Declaration of Human Rights consists
   (a) 30 articles (b) 20 articles
   (c) 56 articles (d) 156 articles.

8. The General Assembly proclaimed the Universal Declaration of Human Rights on
   (a) 26th Nov. 1945 (b) 26th Jan. 1950
   (c) 15th August 1947 (d) 10th Dec. 1948.

9. The agreement of five permanent members of Defence council is
   (a) agreement of all (b) general acceptance
   (c) veto (d) universal offer.

10. The most powerful part of UNO is
    (a) General Assembly (b) International court
    (c) Every Council (d) Security Council.

11. First time how many states signed on the draft of univesal declaration for the
    (a) 50 (b) 60
    (c) 59 (d) 54.

12. Commission of Human Rights presents its reports to
    (a) General Assembly (b) International Court
    (c) Defence Council (d) Councils.

13. International convenant regarding economic, social and cultural rights as apply on
    (a) 20 June 1966 (b) 26 October 1966
    (c) 26 February 1970 (d) 3 Janaury 1976.

14. The General Assembly of UNO was agreed upon International Convenant on Economic, Social and Cultured Rights on
    (a) 26 Dec. 1966 (b) 16 Dec. 1966
    (c) 15th Aug. 1947 (d) 26 Jan. 1950.

15. How many convenants are proclaimed on Human Right
    (a) 6 (b) 2
    (c) 3 (d) 5.

16. The right guaranteed in the Convenant but have no place in universal declaration is
    (a) Right to Education
    (b) Right to self-determination
    (c) Right to marry
    (d) Freedom to assembly.

17. The main aim of International Convenant on Human Right is to give them
    (a) Political form (b) Legal form
    (c) Model form (d) Moral form.

18. The commission of Human Rights consist
    (a) 54 members
    (b) 5 members
    (c) 53 members
    (d) 63 members.

19. An important platform of United Nations Orgaisation regarding Human Rights is
    (a) Commission for Human Rights
    (b) Human Right Commission
    (c) Human Right Committee
    (d) None of these.

20. The post of U.N Commissioner of Human Rights was made in
    (a) 1995 (b) 1999
    (c) 1990 (d) 1993.

21. International conference on Human Rights was organised in Tehran is
    (a) 1988 (b) 1978
    (c) 1998 (d) 1968.

22. Which year of the following was declared as International Human Rights year
    (a) 1971 (b) 1980
    (c) 1968 (d) 1985.

23. In 1993 Ali world conference on human rights was organised is

(a) Tehran (b) Vienna
(c) London (d) New York.

24. How many specialists consists in sub-commission for Human Rights?

(a) 54 (b) 53
(c) 26 (d) 15.

25. Sub-commission was formed to help the commission for Human Rights

(a) 1986 (b) 1948
(c) 1946 (d) 1950.

26. The meeting of the commission for Human Rights held every year in

(a) Geneva (b) New Delhi
(c) New York (d) Paris.

27. What is the main work of sub-commission of Human Rights?

(a) To prevent discrimination with minors
(b) To prevent discrimination with children
(c) To prevent discrimination with women
(d) To prevent discrimination with olds.

28. Which organisation of the following is not related to Human Rights?

(a) Commission for Human Rights
(b) Committee for Human Rights
(c) U.N. Child Fund
(d) Sub-commission for human rights.

29. Centre for Human Rights is situated in

(a) Geneva
(b) New Delhi
(c) New York
(d) London.

30. The main gain of Vienna conference of Human Rights is
    (a) suggestion for formation of a commission for Human Rights
    (b) formation of a sub commission on Human Rights
    (c) formation of the commision for Human Rights
    (d) all the above.

31. The members of the commission for Human Rights are elected for a period of
    (a) 3 years (b) 5 years
    (c) 4 years (d) 6 years.

32. How many countries participate in world conference on Human Rights organised in Vienna?
    (a) 171 (b) 480
    (c) 71 (d) 841.

33. Liability of supervise the centre for Human Rights is of
    (a) Commission for Human Rights
    (b) Human Rights Committee
    (c) Commissioner for Human Rights
    (d) Defence Council.

34. The main function of centre for Human Rights is
    (a) help the parts of UNO to protect and promote Human Rights
    (b) inquiry regarding informations related to insulting Human Rights
    (c) to publish information related to Human Rights
    (d) all the above.

35. Which was not a recommendation fo Vienna Conference?
    (a) Force to promote socialism
    (b) Activities of terrorism are hurts on Human Rights
    (c) Treat democracy a human right
    (d) Universal acceptance that Right to development is a continuing right.

36. Which was not forced in Vienna Conference in 1993?
    (a) Right to development
    (b) Political Justice
    (c) Against Terrorism
    (d) Right to self determination.

37. The point related to Human Rights is
    (a)
    (b) Promotion
    (c) Prevention the discrimination
    (d) All the above.

38. Which is wrong regarding vienna conference 1993?
    (a) Common exception among developing and industrial countries on Human Rights
    (b) Fractions among developing and Industrial countries on Human Rights
    (c) Disputes on interdependence of Right of development and political rights with Human rights
    (d) Consideration on University of Human Rights is reference of special state.

39. What is compulsory to be conscious towards Human Rights?
    (a) Law (b) Right
    (c) Duty (d) Education.

40. Which is point related Human Rights?
    (a) Child Labour
    (b) Child prostitution
    (c) Police encounter
    (d) All the above.

41. National commission for Human Rights was formed in India in
    (a) 1994 (b) 1991
    (c) 1995 (d) 1993.

42. The first Chairman of National Commission for Human Rights of India was
   (a) Justice Rangnath Mishra
   (b) N.A. Palkiwala
   (c) Justice P.N. Bhagwati
   (d) Dr. Luxmimal Singhwi.

43. General Assembly of UNO proclaimed the declaration on Right to development in
   (a) 1976 (b) 1974
   (c) 1986 (d) 1998.

44. General Assembly of UNO accept the declaration on the right of minors
   (a) 1992 (b) 1996
   (c) 1999 (d) 1994.

45. National Commission for Human Rights in India is formed under
   (a) Part four of Constitution of India
   (b) Part three of Constitution of India
   (c) Under Human Rights Protection Act 1993
   (d) None of these.

46. Only Ex Judge of Supreme Court of India can be Chairman of
   (a) National Commission for Women
   (b) National Commission for Minors
   (c) National Commission for Human Rights
   (d) National Commission for SC/STs.

47. National Commission for Human Rights presents its report before
   (a) Parliament of India
   (b) Chief Justice of India
   (c) United Nations Organisation
   (d) None of these.

48. Which point is related to Human Rights?
    (a) Discrimination
    (b) Death in police lock up
    (c) Terriorism
    (d) All the above.

49. What is compulsory to apply Human Rights in India
    (a) Active Education system
    (b) Human Right Education to Para military forces
    (c) Human Right Education to police officials
    (d) All the above.

50. Which point is related to Human Rights
    (a) Discrimination
    (b) Rape
    (c) Persons neglecting by huge plane
    (d) All the above.

ANSWERS

1.	(c)	2.	(c)	3.	(c)	4.	(d)
5.	(a)	6.	(b)	7.	(a)	8.	(d)
9.	(c)	10.	(d)	11.	(a)	12.	(a)
13.	(d)	14.	(b)	15.	(b)	16.	(b)
17.	(b)	18.	(c)	19.	(b)	20.	(d)
21.	(d)	22.	(b)	23.	(a)	24.	(b)
25.	(c)	26.	(a)	27.	(a)	28.	(c)
29.	(a)	30.	(a)	31.	(a)	32.	(d)
33.	(d)	34.	(d)	35.	(a)	36.	(b)
37.	(a)	38.	(a)	39.	(d)	40.	(d)
41.	(d)	42.	(a)	43.	(b)	44.	(a)
45.	(c)	46.	(c)	47.	(a)	48.	(d)
49.	(d)	50.	(d)				

14
CONSUMER PROTECTION ACT 1986

1. The Consumer Protection Act came into force on
   (a) 23 December 1986
   (b) 16 December 1986
   (c) 24 November 1986
   (d) 28 December 1986.
2. The Consumer Protection Act 1986 is applicable in
   (a) matters of electricity consumer only
   (b) marketing matters only
   (c) each type of consumer matters
   (d) none of these.
3. The Consumer Protection Act 1986 does not apply in
   (a) Nagaland (b) Uttar Pradesh
   (c) Jammu and Kashmir (d) Meghalaya.
4. The Consumer Protection Act is based on
   (a) the consumer
   (b) the setters
   (c) the basic right of consumers
   (d) industries.
5. Which is not the basic right of consumer?
   (a) of choice (b) information
   (c) to purchase credit (d) to be heard.

6. A consumer is

(a) a person who buys any goods for a consideration

(b) a person who hires or avails for a consideration

(c) both

(d) none of these.

7. Complaint means

(a) A complaint of unsocials

(b) Any physical problem

(c) Any defect in goods

(d) allegation in writing.

8. Consumer dispute means

(a) A dispute between state and person

(b) A dispute between buyer and purchaser

(c) A dispute betwen two consumers

(d) A dispute among four consumer.

9. The main object of Consumer Protection Act is

(a) To increase consumer disputes

(b) To earn more revenue

(c) To protect the interests of consumers

(d) To develop co-operation between buyers and purchaser.

10. How many member forms the central consumers council

(a) Three

(b) Four

(c) Nine

(d) as may be prescribed by the Central Government.

11. The Chairman of the Central Consumer Protections Council is

(a) Retired Judicial officer

(b) A judge of High court

(c) Minister incharge of the consumer affairs

(d) A senior Indian civil servant.

12. How many meetings of the central consumer protection council are compulsory in a year
    (a) Four (b) Two
    (c) One (d) None of these.

13. The procedure for meeting of the Central Consumer Protection Council depends on
    (a) The Central Government
    (b) The Supreme Court of India
    (c) The Chairman of the Central Consumer Protection Council
    (d) None of these.

14. Which is not a object of Central Consumer Protection Council
    (a) To promote the consumer rights
    (b) To protect the consumer rights
    (c) To consumer education
    (d) To avail a loan to consumer.

15. Who is liable to establish a State Consumer Protection Council?
    (a) Governor
    (b) Chairman of state Consumer Protection Council
    (c) State Government
    (d) None of these.

16. Who can be Chairman of State Consumer Protection Council?
    (a) Any Minister of State Government
    (b) Any Senior IAS
    (c) Any senior public servant
    (d) Minister Incharge of Consumer affairs in state Government.

17. State Council consist of the members
    (a) Four (b) Five
    (c) Three (d) None of these.

18. How many meetings are conpulsory of state council in a year?

(a) Two (b) One

(c) Nine (d) Seven.

19. The object of state council is to promote and to protect the right of consumer within the

(a) particular district

(b) particular market

(c) state

(d) none of these.

20. District Forum consists

(a) two members (b) three members

(c) five members (d) none of these.

21. Which is corret?

(a) All members should be judges

(b) All members should be women

(c) All members should be men

(d) One member should be a women.

22. The members of District Forum are appointed by

(a) State Government (b) High Court

(c) District Civil Court (d) State Commission.

23. The members of District Forum can work for a maximum period of

(a) 10 years (b) 5 years

(c) 15 years (d) one year.

24. Salary of the members of the District Forum prescribes

(a) State Government (b) High Court

(c) District Civil Court (d) None of these.

25. Pecriary limit of District Forum is

(a) 10 lakhs (b) 5 lakhs

(c) 2 lakhs (d) 1 lakhs.

26. Territorial limit of District Forum is
    (a) in Districts only
    (b) in state only
    (c) within local limits where cause of action arises
    (d) None of these

27. During proceeding of District court of opposite party have to give version within
    (a) 10 days (b) 5 days
    (c) 20 days (d) 30 days.

28. Appropriate laboratories are establish to
    (a) fund error
    (b) analysis
    (c) produce medicine
    (d) No (a) and (b) above.

29. District Forum can direct to appropriate laborotory to send its findings within
    (a) 15 days (b) 10 days
    (c) 45 days (d) 30 days.

30. The burden of expenses of laboratory analysis or test is on
    (a) District Forum (b) State Government
    (c) Complain (d) Opposite party.

31. Every order made by the District Forum shall be signed by
    (a) president (b) members only
    (c) president members (d) none of these.

32. In case no appeal against order the order made by the district forun shall be
    (a) rejected (b) final
    (c) to re-consideration (d) none of these.

33. Appeals against the orders to District Forum entertains
    (a) District Civil Court (b) High Court
    (c) State Commission (d) None of these.

34. Appeal against the order of District Forum should be made within

(a) 15 days (b) 20 days
(c) 17 days (d) 30 days.

35. State Commission consists of

(a) 9 persons (b) 15 persons
(c) 3 persons (d) None of these.

36. To appoint person as President of State Commission it is compulsory to consult with

(a) State Government
(b) Ex-President of State Commission
(c) Chief Justice of High Court
(d) None of these.

37. All members of the State Commission shall hold office for a term of

(a) Three years (b) Five years
(c) Seven years (d) Two years.

38. State commission have jurisdiction within

(a) the city where such commission is situated
(b) any particular district
(c) the state
(d) none of these.

39. Procedure for the disposal of complaints by the state commission is same as the procedure of

(a) High court (b) National Commission
(c) District Forum (d) None of these.

40. State Commission have the powers same as

(a) High Court (b) Session court
(c) District court (d) None of these.

41. Aggrieved person by an order made by state commission may prefer appeal in

(a) High Court (b) Supreme Court
(c) District Civil Court (d) National Commission.

42. National Commission can entertain the appeal against the order of the state commisssion within

(a) 15 days (b) 25 days

(c) 32 days (d) 45 days.

43. National Commission consists

(a) Two members

(b) Ten members

(c) Five members

(d) None of these.

44. To appoint a person as President of National Commission it is compulsory to consult with

(a) Cental Government

(b) president of State Commissions

(c) members of National Commissions

(d) Chief Justice of India.

45. The appointments of members of National Commission shall be made by

(a) Central Government

(b) President of State Commissions

(c) Ex-President of National Commission

(d) None of these.

46. The National Commission have the powers of

(a) Supreme Court of India

(b) A Session Court

(c) A Civil Court

(d) None of the above.

47. An appeal against the order made by the National Commission shall consider

(a) High Court

(b) President of India

(c) Supreme Court of India

(d) None of these.

48. The National Commission have administrative control over all the
    (a) members of State Commission
    (b) members of National Commission
    (c) the State Commission
    (d) all consumers.

49. Complaint, before District Forum or State Commission National Commission can be file within
    (a) 12 years of cause of Action
    (b) 1 year of cause of action
    (c) 5 years of cause of action
    (d) None of these.

50. To maintain a complaint in any consumer court
    (a) Court free is compulsory but Advocate court
    (b) Advocate is compulsory but court free not
    (c) Both are not compulsory
    (d) All are not correct

ANSWERS

1.	(b)	2.	(c)	3.	(c)	4.	(c)
5.	(c)	6.	(c)	7.	(d)	8.	(b)
9.	(c)	10.	(d)	11.	(c)	12.	(c)
13.	(c)	14.	(d)	15.	(c)	16.	(d)
17.	(d)	18.	(a)	19.	(c)	20.	(b)
21.	(d)	22.	(a)	23.	(b)	24.	(a)
25.	(b)	26.	(c)	27.	(d)	28.	(d)
29.	(c)	30.	(c)	31.	(c)	32.	(b)
33.	(c)	34.	(d)	35.	(c)	36.	(c)
37.	(b)	38.	(c)	39.	(c)	40.	(d)
41.	(d)	42.	(c)	43.	(c)	44.	(d)
45.	(a)	46.	(c)	47.	(b)	48.	(c)
49.	(b)	50.	(c)				

SET 1
ASSESS YOURSELF

1. Right to property is a
   (a) moral right (b) legal right
   (c) civil right (d) political right.

2. Which of the following rights has been the subject of controversy in recent years ?
   (a) Freedom of press (b) Right to equality
   (c) Right to property (d) Freedom of speech.

3. In democracy the final authority rests with
   (a) Parliament (b) People
   (c) Council of Ministers (d) Civil Servant.

4. Freedom of speech is a feature of
   (a) democratic constitutions
   (b) totalitarian constitutions
   (c) democratic and totalitarian constitution
   (d) none of the above.

5. The Concept of Constitution first originated in
   (a) Switzerland (b) Britain
   (c) U.S.A (d) Japan.

6. The method of the amending the constitution popular vote is found in
   (a) U.K (b) U.S.A
   (c) Switzerland (d) U.S.S.R.

7. A parliamentary form of Government first developed in
   (a) A written constitution
   (b) An Independent judiciary
   (c) Political parties
   (d) A rigid constitution.

8. Which one of the following is a feature of Presidential Government?
   (a) Instability (b) Stability
   (c) Irresponsibility (d) Inalienability.

9. Presidential system of Government is
   (a) Representative without being responsible
   (b) Responsible without being representative
   (c) Neither responsible nor representative
   (d) None of the above.

10. The Directive Principles of State Policy in Indian Constitution are ______ in their nature
    (a) non justiable (b) collectivist
    (c) democratic (d) Gandhian.

11. "I like the idea of making the Constitution begin with the village and group of the centre", whose words are these?
    (a) Jawahar Lal Nehru (b) Dr. Rajendra Prasad
    (c) B.N.Rau (d) Dr. Ambedkar.

12. Right to freedom is guarnteed by
    (a) 17th article (b) 18th article
    (c) 19th article (d) 20th article.

13. The members of Rajya Sabha are elected for a term of
    (a) six years (b) nine years
    (c) five years (d) three years.

14. The Rajya Sabha
    (a) is a permanent House
    (b) has a maximum life of 6 years
    (c) has no fixed life
    (d) has a maximum life of 5 years.

15. Which one of the following Lok Sabha was dissolved before the expiry of its normal term?
(a) First Lok Sabha (b) Fourth Lok Sabha
(c) Sixth Lok Sabha (d) None of the above.

16. Which one of the following is not essential qualification for contesting election to Lok Sabha?
(a) Citizenship of India (b) Age of 25 years
(c) Soundness of mind (d) Graduation.

17. How many seats have been reserved for the Union Territories in Lok Sabha?
(a) 20 (b) 25
(c) 30 (d) 50.

18. The first Indian was associated with the Executive Council for Legislative purpose under
(a) Act of 1858 (b) Act of 1861
(c) Act of 1892 (d) Act of 1909.

19. The Government of India was transferred from the Company to the Crown by the
(a) Act of 1858 (b) Act of 1861
(c) Act of 1892 (d) Act of 1909.

20. The amendment in Indian Constitution called 'a Mini Revision' was
(a) 24th amendment (b) 26th amendment
(c) 42nd amendment (d) 38th amendment.

21. 44th amendment in Indian Constitution curtails the freedom of
(a) Association
(b) Residence
(c) Movement
(d) Acquiring and disposing of property.

22. Directive principles of State policy are like "a cheque on a bank payable at the convenience of the bank" was said by
(a) Pt. Nehru (b) Dr. B.N.Rao
(c) Dr. Ambedkar (d) Prof. K.T.Shah.

23. 42nd amendment extended the term of the Lok Sabha to
    (a) 7 years (b) 6 years
    (c) 8 years (d) 9 years.

24. The Gap between two sessions of the Parliament could not be more than
    (a) 3 months (b) 6 months
    (c) one year (d) two years.

25. The Quorum for the meetings of the legislative Assemblies in India is
    (a) 1/10th of total membership or ten
    (b) 10
    (c) 20
    (d) decided by the Speaker.

26. The candidate for the Presidentship must be sponsored by
    (a) 25 electors (b) 10 electors
    (c) two ministers (d) none of these.

27. "Emergency powers of the President of India are a fraud on the Constitution" was said by
    (a) K.N. Nambiar (b) B.N. Rao
    (c) B.R. Ambedkar (d) K.M. Munshi.

28. Apart from the Chief Justice, the Supreme Court has
    (a) 7 judges (b) 10 judges
    (c) 15 judges (d) 17 judges.

29. The Governor of a state enjoys
    (a) no discretionary power
    (b) very extensive discretionary powers
    (c) discretionary power in certain matters
    (d) none of these.

30. The rule of law means
    (a) law is supreme
    (b) President is Supreme
    (c) parliament is Supreme
    (d) none of the above.

31. For which State the Constitution makes a special provision in regard to administration?

(a) Jammu and Kashmir (b) Nagaland
(c) Assam (d) None of these.

32. Which amendment transferred Education to the Concurrent list

(a) 24th (b) 25th
(c) 44th (d) 42nd.

33. Parliamentary form of Government in India is adopted from the Constitution of

(a) Britain (b) France
(c) U.S.S.R (d) Switzerland.

34. In India the Union Government is headed by

(a) President
(b) Parliament
(c) Cabinet
(d) Prime Minister.

35. In India the Parliament can not

(a) Propose new taxes
(b) Reduce taxes
(c) Refuse taxes
(d) Debate taxes proposed by Council of Minister.

36. Indian Federation is based on the pattern of

(a) Canada (b) U.S.A
(c) U.S.S.R (d) Britain.

37. Who of the following do not take part in the election of the President of India but take part in the election of Vice-President?

(a) Nominated members of Lok Sabha and Rajya Sabha
(b) Members of Rajya Sabha
(c) Elected members of Rajya Sabha
(d) None of these.

38. Indian President is
   (a) Titular head
   (b) A part of Union Legislature
   (c) Chief Executive
   (d) None of these.

39. Cabinet Minister are
   (a) members of Council of Ministers
   (b) not members of Council of Ministers
   (c) members of Rajya Sabha
   (d) None of these.

40. Cabinet is
   (a) smaller body in members than Council of Ministers
   (b) larger body in members than Council of Ministers
   (c) equal to Council of Ministers
   (d) none of these.

41. The term "Cabinet" is used only once in our Constitution in
   (a) Directive Principles
   (b) Preamble
   (c) Fundamental Rights
   (d) None of these.

42. Constitutional law means
   (a) administrative laws
   (b) law of political conduct
   (c) law made by parliament
   (d) none of these.

43. Which of the following is not correct about the Speaker of Lok Sabha?
   (a) Presiding over the meeting of Lok Sabha
   (b) Protective the privileges of member of Lok Sabha
   (c) He is Chief of Lok Sabha
   (d) None of these.

44. President nominates two members to Lok Sabha to
   (a) represent Anglo-Indian community
   (b) represent backward classes
   (c) represent general classes
   (d) None of these.

45. Who has the right to attend the meetings of Parliament but does not have the right to vote?
   (a) Attorney General
   (b) Auditor General
   (c) President
   (d) None of these.

46. Fundamental duties in Indian Constitution formed a part of
   (a) originally
   (b) by the 42nd amendment
   (c) by the 44th amendment
   (d) by Parliament.

47. The Directive Principles are contained in ______ of the Constitution of India
   (a) Part I
   (b) Part III
   (c) Part IV
   (d) None of these.

48. Which one of the Articles of the Indian Constitution is mainly associated with the principle of rule of law ?
   (a) Article 14 (b) Article 15
   (c) Article 16 (d) Article 17.

49. The Fundamental rights have been given in the Indian Constitution
   (a) from Article 12 to 35
   (b) from Article 13 to 36
   (c) from Article 15 to 39
   (d) from Article 36 to 51.

50. Which of the following articles of the Indian Constitution is related with the provision of the amendment of the Constitution
    (a) Article 19 (b) Article 226
    (c) Article 326 (d) Article 368.

ANSWERS

1.	(a)	2.	(c)	3.	(b)	4.	(a)
5.	(a)	6.	(c)	7.	(a)	8.	(b)
9.	(a)	10.	(d)	11.	(b)	12.	(c)
13.	(a)	14.	(a)	15.	(c)	16.	(d)
17.	(a)	18.	(d)	19.	(a)	20.	(c)
21.	(d)	22.	(d)	23.	(b)	24.	(b)
25.	(a)	26.	(d)	27.	(d)	28.	(d)
29.	(c)	30.	(a)	31.	(a)	32.	(d)
33.	(a)	34.	(a)	35.	(d)	36.	(b)
37.	(a)	38.	(c)	39.	(a)	40.	(a)
41.	(d)	42.	(c)	43.	(b)	44.	(a)
45.	(a)	46.	(c)	47.	(c)	48.	(a)
49.	(a)	50.	(d)				

SET 2
ASSESS YOURSELF

1. What is the main provision of 44th Amendment?
   (a) Empowered the administration of the Union Territory to promulgate ordinances when the legislature is not in a session
   (b) Abolished privy purses
   (c) Increases the total members of Lok Sabha from 425 to 545
   (d) Restores liberties curtailed under 42nd amendment.

2. Which of the following are the powers of the President with regard to the Parliament?
   (a) Summon or prorogue the session of Parliament
   (b) Address the Joint Sesssion of the two Houses
   (c) Can call a joint sitting of the two Houses
   (d) All of these.

3. How long can Vice-President act as President if the office of the President falls vacant?
   (a) For five years
   (b) For six month
   (c) For the remaining form
   (d) For two years.

4. How long will the Prime Minister remain in office?
   (a) Till the president wants him to remain so
   (b) Till he enjoys the confidence of the majority party in Lok Sabha

(c) Till the remain M.P and the Leader of the majority party in Lok Sabha
(d) Till he wishes to remain.

5. Who of the following was the permanent Chairman of the Constituent Assembly
(a) Dr. Rajendra Prasad
(b) Pt. Jawahar Lal Nehru
(c) Sardar patel
(d) B.R. Ambedkar.

6. The Rajya Sabha
(a) is a permanent House
(b) has a maximum life of 6 years
(c) has a maximum life of 5 years
(d) has no fixed life.

7. At present the maximum strength of Lok Sabha can be
(a) 500 members (b) 550 members
(c) 545 members (d) 552 members.

8. The major portion of the Indian Constitution can be amended by
(a) Parliament alone
(b) President alone
(c) The Parliament with the consent of the states
(d) The state Legislatures along.

9. The right to reshuffle to Council of Ministers rests with
(a) The President (b) The Cabinet
(c) The Prime Minister (d) The Speaker.

10. The meetings of the Council of Minister in India are presided over by
(a) The Prime Minister
(b) The President
(c) All the Ministers
(d) The Speaker by rotation.

11. The Government in India is known as 'Parliamentary' because
    (a) Parliament is elected by the poeple
    (b) Parliament consist of two Houses
    (c) Parliament is a sovereign body
    (d) The executive is accountable to the legislature.

12. Parliamentary Government was adopted in India
    (a) by sheer accident
    (b) because it was made obligatory to adopt this government under Indian Independence Act of 1947
    (c) because of historical consideration and practical necessities
    (d) on account of all the above reasons.

13. The Constitution of India is
    (a) One of the smallest constitutions in the world
    (b) a medium sized constitution
    (c) one of the most elaborated constitution of the world
    (d) None of these.

14. The Constitution of India is
    (a) Very rigid
    (b) Very flexible
    (c) A combination of rigidity and Flexibility
    (d) Neither rigid nor flexible.

15. The subject on which the Central Government enjoys exclusive power are contained in
    (a) The Union List
    (b) The Federal List
    (c) The Central List
    (d) Concurrent list.

16. The subject on which the State Government enjoys exclusive power are given in
    (a) Concurrent list (b) State list
    (c) Provisional list (d) None of the above.

17. The subordinate courts enjoys
    (a) only civil jurisdiction
    (b) only criminal jurisdiction
    (c) only revenue jurisdiction
    (d) all the above.
18. The subordinate Civil courts are headed by
    (a) District Court (b) Session Court
    (c) Board of Revenue (d) None of these.
19. At the apex of the sub-ordinate criminal court stands the
    (a) Court of Session Judge
    (b) Court of District Judge
    (c) The State of High Court
    (d) None of the above.
20. The judges of the Supreme court hold office till they reach the age of
    (a) 58 years (b) 60 years
    (c) 62 years (d) 65 years.
21. The real executive authority under Cabinet Government rests with
    (a) The Council of Ministers
    (b) The Prime Minister
    (c) The Legislature
    (d) The nominal Executive.
22. A person can be a member of Cabinet without being a member of Parliament for a maximum period of
    (a) three months (b) six months
    (c) one year (d) two years.
23. In Parliamentary system of Government, the bills are
    (a) preparaed by the civil servants but introduced by the Ministers
    (b) prepared as well as introduced by the civil servants
    (c) prepared as well as introduced by the ministers
    (d) None of the above.

24. The High Court consist of a Chief Justice and
   (a) 5 other judges
   (b) 7 other judges
   (c) such other judges as may be decided by the President from time to time
   (d) such other judges as may be decided by the Governor of the State.

25. The sub-ordinate courts enjoy
   (a) only civil jurisdiction
   (b) only criminal jurisdiction
   (c) only revenue jurisdiction
   (d) all of the above type.

26. The Fundamental Rights imply the rights
   (a) Which are indispensible for the growth of human personality
   (b) Where a man inherits from natural at the time of his birth
   (c) Which are enforced by the state
   (d) Which impose no obligation on the state.

27. Political justice is ensured by
   (a) Courts (b) Political parties
   (c) Constitution (d) All of these.

28. Political parties are
   (a) Essential for democracy
   (b) Not essential for democracy
   (c) Essential for totalitarian government
   (d) Not essential either for democracy or totalitarian government.

29. Constitution is an essential feature of
   (a) democratic government
   (b) desportic government
   (c) all government
   (d) non-monarchial states.

30. A Constitution is known as flexible
    (a) If it can be amended by the ordinary law making procedure
    (b) If the states alone can amend the constitution
    (c) If the amendment of constitution is simple than the ordinary law-making procedure
    (d) If it is difficult to amend.

31. The method of amending the constitution by popular vote is found in ____
    (a) U.K (b) U.S.A
    (c) Switzerland (d) U.S.S.R.

32. The cabinet under Parliamentary government is accountable to
    (a) The Council of Ministers
    (b) The President
    (c) The Prime Minister
    (d) The Legislature.

33. Judicial Review is a feature of
    (a) Parliamentary government
    (b) Presidential government
    (c) Unitary government
    (d) Federal government.

34. The Real Executive authority under Cabinet Government rests with
    (a) The Council of Minister
    (b) The Prime Minister
    (c) The Constitution
    (d) The Parliament.

35. The member of the Union Cabinet holds office
    (a) for a fixed term
    (b) during the pleasure of the prime minister
    (c) as long as it enjoys support to majority of the member of Parliament
    (d) None of the above.

36. Bureaucracy is an important feature of
   (a) democratic government
   (b) dictatorial system of government
   (c) All government
   (d) None of the above.

37. The Cabinet under Parliamentary Government is accountable to
   (a) The Council of Minister
   (b) The Prime Minister
   (c) The Legislature
   (d) The President.

38. The President of the Board of Control was made Minister for Indian affairs by
   (a) The Charter Act of 1833
   (b) The Charter Act of 1813
   (c) The Indian Council Act of 1861
   (d) The Charter Act of 1853.

39. Who of the following was the permanent Chairman of the Constituent Assembly?
   (a) Dr. Rajendra Prasad
   (b) Pt. Jawahar Lal Nehru
   (c) Sardar Patel
   (d) B.R. Ambedkar.

40. Which one of the following State/Union territory send only one representative to the Rajya Sabha
   (a) Pondicherry (b) Arunachal Pradesh
   (c) Mizoram (d) All the above.

41. Which one of the following qualification for office of the President has been wrongly listed?
   (a) He must be a citizen of India
   (b) He must be more than 35 years ofage
   (c) He must posses qualification laid down the election as member of the Lok Sabha
   (d) He must be a member of either House of Parliament.

42. Which one of the following statement regarding the Supreme Court of India is not correct?
    (a) It acts as the guardian of the liberties of the people of India
    (b) It acts as the guardian of the constitution
    (c) It acts as the protector of the Directive Principle of State Policy
    (d) It has final power to investigate disputes regarding election of the President and Vice-President of India.

43. Which one of the following statement is correct?
    (a) an individual has to be loyal to state
    (b) an individual may be disloyal to state but he has to be loyal to the government
    (c) an individual has to be loyal to the Supreme Court
    (d) an individual has to be loyal to the Parliament.

44. The Parliamentary government
    (a) leads to frequent conflicts between the legislature and the executive
    (b) secure Swiftness in decision and vigour in action
    (c) encourages dispotic tendencies of government
    (d) is not able to adopt itself according to changing requirements.

45. The member of Cabinet hold office
    (a) for a fixed term
    (b) during the pleasure of the head of the state
    (c) as long as it enjoy support to majority of the members of Parliament
    (d) None of the above.

46. Which one of the folowing judicial functions is performed by the civil servant
    (a) They assist the head of the state in appointment of judges
    (b) They ensure that rule of law prevails in the country
    (c) They take number of administrative and quasi-judicial decisions of final nature

(d) The take administrative and quasi-judicial decision which can be challlenged only in the court.

47. Article 370 of the Constitution of India deals with
(a) Emergency power of President
(b) Special status of Jammu and Kashmir
(c) Special provision for minorities
(d) Amendment procedure.

48. The Council of Minister consist of
(a) The Prime Minister, The President, the Vice President and other Ministers
(b) The Prime Minister, the President and other Minister
(c) The Prime Minister and other ministers
(d) None of the above.

49. In India the power of judicial review is enjoyed by
(a) The Supreme Court alone
(b) The Supreme Court as well as High Court
(c) All the courts
(d) None of the above.

ANSWERS

1.	(d)	2.	(d)	3.	(c)	4.	(b)
5.	(a)	6.	(a)	7.	(c)	8.	(c)
9.	(c)	10.	(a)	11.	(a)	12.	(b)
13.	(c)	14.	(c)	15.	(a)	16.	(b)
17.	(d)	18.	(b)	19.	(a)	20.	(d)
21.	(b)	22.	(b)	23.	(c)	24.	(c)
25.	(d)	26.	(a)	27.	(c)	28.	(a)
29.	(a)	30.	(a)	31.	(c)	32.	(d)
33.	(d)	34.	(b)	35.	(b)	36.	(b)
37.	(c)	38.	(a)	39.	(a)	40.	(d)
41.	(d)	42.	(c)	43.	(a)	44.	(b)
45.	(b)	46.	(d)	47.	(b)	48.	(c)
49.	(a)	50.	(b)				

SET 3
ASSESS YOURSELF

1. Which one of the following statements is not correct?
   (a) Political rights are available only in a democratic country
   (b) Political rights make the government responsible to public opinion
   (c) Political rights are granted only to the citizens
   (d) Political rights are available both to citizens as well as aliens.

2. Multiparty system means
   (a) government is formed by all the political parties present in the country
   (b) there are number of political parties but the government is formed by that single party which secures largest number of seats
   (c) that the country has more than two political parties which aim at capturing power
   (d) there is one dominant party which keeps the other political parties under the umbrella.

3. The member of the Cabinet under Presidential system are
   (a) accountable to the President
   (b) individually accountable to legislature
   (c) collectively accountable to legislature
   (d) accountable to the electorate.

4. Which one of the following provisions can be amended by the Parliament by simple majority?
   (a) Provisions concerning the establishment of High Court
   (b) Provisions concerning Federal Judiciary
   (c) Provisions concerning representation of state in Parliament
   (d) None of the above.

5. The Parliament can legislate on the subject in the State List
   (a) if the President issues an order authorising it do so
   (b) if the Supreme Court of India gives authority to the Parliament of India in this regard
   (c) if the Rajya Sabha passes a resolution by two third of its members declaring it expedient to legislate on a State matter in the nation interest
   (d) none of the above.

6. The Office of the Prime Minister of India
   (a) has been created by the Constitution
   (b) rests on convention
   (c) has been created by the Parliamentary statute
   (d) is the result of the combination of all the above three factor.

7. Right to equality is a
   (a) Civil right (b) Moral right
   (c) Political right (d) Legal right.

8. Which one of the following immunities of the Governor of the state has been wrongly listed?
   (a) He is not answerable before any court for anything done in the exercise of his official duties
   (b) No criminal proceeding can be launched against Governor during his term of office
   (c) No legal proceedings can be launched against Governor during his term of office the last years of his term
   (d) The Governor is entitled to rent free official residence.

9. At the apex of the subordinate criminal courts stands the
   - (a) Court of Session Judge
   - (b) Court of District Judge
   - (c) The State High Court
   - (d) None of the above.

10. The Dyarchical System of Government was introduced in India under
    - (a) Act of 1858
    - (b) Act of 1909
    - (c) Act of 1919
    - (d) Act of 1892.

11. The Chief Minister stays in office
    - (a) for fixed term of 5 years
    - (b) as long as the Governor of the state wants
    - (c) as long as the Council of Minister wants him
    - (d) as long as he enjoys the confidence of the majority party in the Legislative Assembly.

12. During the recess of the Parliament the President can promulgate ordinances
    - (a) with the prior approval of the Parliament
    - (b) with the prior approval of the Supreme Court of India
    - (c) with the consent of the Council of Ministers
    - (d) on his own.

13. Which one of the following qualifications of the judges of the Supreme Court has been wrongly listed?
    - (a) He must be a citizen of India
    - (b) He has been an advocate of a High Court for at least ten years
    - (c) He has been judge of a High Court for at least five years
    - (d) He has either worked as Comptroller and Auditor General of India for at least three years.

14. The President of India, who is the head of the state under Parliamentary system prevailing in India
    (a) enjoys absolute power
    (b) enjoys limited but real powers
    (c) enjoys only nominal powers
    (d) enjoys no powers.

15. Though the Parliament seat of the Supreme Court is at Delhi, it can also meet at
    (a) Bombay
    (b) Madras
    (c) Calcutta
    (d) Any other place as decided by the Chief Justice of India in consultation with the President.

16. A member of Parliament or a state legislature can be elected as president by
    (a) He has to resign his seat before contesting election
    (b) He has to relinquish his seat as soon as he is selected
    (c) He has to relinquish his seat within six months of his election
    (d) A member of parliament can contest but a member of state legislature can not contest.

17. The Central Government can legislate on a subject in the State list
    (a) If the Parliament passes a resolution declaring that is essential to do so in national interest.
    (b) If the president issues an ordinance to this effect on the plea of national interest.
    (c) The Supreme Court grants necessary authority to the Parliament
    (d) The Rajya Sabha passes a resolution by two thirds majority declaring that particular subject in the state list to be of national importance.

18. The member of the Council of Ministers in India
    (a) Cannot be member of Parliament
    (b) Must be member of Parliament

(c) May or may not be member of Parliament

(d) None of the above.

19. In Rajya Sabha the Upper House of the Indian Parliament, the state have been given

(a) Equal representation

(b) Representation on the basis of population as well as economic position

(c) Representation on the basis of population

(d) None of the above.

20. With regard to the re-election of the Vice-President

(a) The Constitution is absolutely silent

(b) The Constitution places a clear ban

(c) The Constitution permits re-election for a maximum period of two terms

(d) The Constitution permits re-election only once.

21. It became imperative for the framers of the Constitution to adopt the doctrine of judicial review in India because of

(a) Her Republican Character

(b) Adoption of Parliamentary system of government

(c) Adoption of Federal system of government

(d) A written constitution.

22. Which one of the following statements is correct?

(a) Rule of law is a basic feature of the Constitution which cannot be amended under article 368 of the Constitution.

(b) Rule of law is an ordinary feature of the Indian Constitution which can be amended under article 368

(c) Rule of law is only an implied feature of the Indian Constitution

(d) All the above.

23. What is the impact of the financial emergency on the relations between the Centre and the States?

(a) The President can reduce the salaries of all state servants except the judges of High court

(b) The President can reduce the salaries of state civil servants including those of the judges of High Court
(c) The state legislature are deprived of the right to enact money bills
(d) None of the above.

24. Which one of the following is a feautre of Cabinet system in India
(a) Secret of proceedings
(b) Leadership of the President
(c) Separation of Legislature and Executive
(d) Dominance of Bureaucracy.

25. The 42nd amendment included addition to the directive principles related to three of the following matters
1. Participation of workers in the management of industry
2. Minimising inequality in income and status
3. Protection of the environment
4. Free legal aid to the poor.

Select the correct answer from the codes given below
(a) 1, 3 and 4 (b) 1,2 and 3
(c) 1, 2 and 4 (d) 2,3 and 4.

26. Which of the following are the types of authority attributed to the President of India
1. Real and popular
2. Titular and de jure
3. Political and nominal
4. Constitutional and nominal.

Choose the correct answer from the codes given below
(a) 1 and 3 (b) 2 and 4
(c) 1 and 4 (d) 2 and 4

27. Which of the following provision are not included in the Indian Constitution?
1. President can suspend any of the Fundamental Right during Emergency

2. Prime Minister can dismiss any Chief Minister
3. States have power to amend any law enacted by Parliament on a subject in the concurrent list with the President's assent
4. Governor can reserve any bill for consideration by the President.

Choose the correct answer from the codes given below

(a) 1 and 2 (b) 2 and 3
(c) 3 and 4 (d) 1 and 4

28. Which of the following are the exclusive powers of the Lok Sabha?

1. To introduce money bills
2. To rectify the declaration of emergency
3. To pass a motion of no-confidence against the Council of Ministers
4. To impeach the President.

Choose the correct answer from the codes given below

(a) 1 and 3 (b) 2 and 3
(c) 1 and 4 (d) 3 and 4

29. The Chief Minister of a state can be removed if

1. a no confidence motion is passed by the Legislative Assembly
2. a no confidence motion is passed by both Houses of the state legislature
3. a resolution is passed by a 2/3rd members of the Legislative Council or the Rajya Sabha
4. in the opinion of the Governor, there is a breakdown of the constitutional machinery in the state

Choose th correct answer from the codes given below

(a) 1 and 2 (b) 2 and 3
(c) 1, 2 and 4 (d) 1 and 4

30. Which of the following are not in harmony with the system of rule of law?

1. Independent Judiciary
2. Administrative courts

3. Administrative law
4. Discretionary powers of officers
5. Supremacy of Law.

Choose the correct answer from the codes given below
(a) 1, 3 and 5
(b) 2, 3 and 4
(c) 3, 4 and 5
(d) 2, 4 and 5

31. Which one of the following is not an indicator of public opinion?
(a) Result of by-elections
(b) Result of general elections
(c) Writ petitions before the courts of law
(d) Debates in the Legislature.

32. Which one of the following statement is not correct?
(a) Constitutional monarchy and democracy can go together
(b) Freedom of the Press is inconsequential to the success of democracy
(c) Social equality is necessary for the success of democracy
(d) All countries in the world today can be called democratic.

33. The Head of the state under a Parliamentary government
(a) is an elected representative
(b) is a hereditary person
(c) is a nominated person
(d) may be any one of the above.

34. The essence of the Presidential system of government is that, in such a system
(a) the executive is independent of the legislature
(b) the President is elected directly by the people
(c) it has a written and rigid constitution
(d) the Supreme Court has power of judicial review.

35. The most important characteristic of parliamentary government is
    (a) sovereignty of the Parliament
    (b) collective responsibility of executive to the Legislature
    (c) rule of Law
    (d) majority rule.

36. In which of the following conditions can Indian Parliament pass a bill on subjects mentioned in the State list.
    (a) When Rajya Sabha adopts a resolution by a simple majority to that effect
    (b) When Rajya Sabha adopts a resolution to that effect by two thirds majority
    (c) When the State assemblies adopt a resolution to the effect.
    (d) When Lok Sabha adopts a resolution by two third majority to that effect.

37. Which one of the following is not equally of the Indian Parliament committee
    (a) The Public Account Committee
    (b) The Estimates Committee
    (c) The Committee on Public Undertakings
    (d) The Committee on Subordinate legislation.

38. Which one of the following statements is correct?
    (a) The Chairman of Rajya Sabha is elected by the elected member of the Rajya Sabha
    (b) The Chairman of Rajya Sabha presides over the joint session of both the Houses of Parliament
    (c) The electoral college for the election of the Vice-President is the same as that for the election of the President
    (d) The nominated member of both the Houses of Parliament have voting right in the election of the Vice-President but not in the election of the President.

39. Who amongst the following acts as the presiding officer of the House without being its member?
    (a) Vice President of India
    (b) Speaker of the Lok Sabha
    (c) Chairman of the Legislative Council
    (d) Speaker of the Legislative Assembly.

40. Article 315 of our Constitution refers to
    (a) recruitment and conditions of service of persons
    (b) all India service rules and safeguards
    (c) public Service Commission for the union and a Public Service Commission for each state
    (d) tenure of office of person serving the union or a state.

41. The doctrine that fundamental right can not be amended under article 368 was profounded by the Indian Supreme Court in
    (a) Gopalan Vs. State of Madras
    (b) Keshvanand Vs. State of Kerala
    (c) Golak nath Vs. State of Punjab
    (d) Maneka Vs. Union of India.

42. Cabinet system of government leads to concentration of power in the executive because
    1. Parliamentary controls are rarely effective
    2. The Cabinet comprises of members of the majority party only
    3. The cabinet is appointed by the Head of the State.

    Select the correct answer from the codes given below
    (a) 1 and 2 (b) 1,2 and 3
    (c) 2 and 3 (d) only 1

43. In which one of the following lists of the Indian Constitution is the subject of 'Social Security Insurance' included?
    (a) Union list
    (b) Concurrent list
    (c) State list
    (d) Residuary powers.

44. Under which of the following circumstances can President declare an emergency?
    1. External aggression
    2. Internal disturbances
    3. Government instability
    4. Financial crisis.

    Choose the correct answer from the codes given below

    (a) 1, 2 and 3 (b) 1, 3 and 4
    (c) 2, 3 and 4 (d) 1, 2 and 4

45. Under which article of the Indian Constitution can the President of India be impeached?

    (a) Article 356 (b) Article 75
    (c) Article 76 (d) Article 61.

46. The source of all political power in India lies with

    (a) the Parliament
    (b) the Lok Sabha
    (c) the People
    (d) the Constitution.

47. The Constitution of India uses the expression 'the Union of States' following

    (a) Canada (b) U.S.A
    (c) erstwhile U.S.S.R (d) Germany.

48. The authority to alter the boundaries of states in India rests with the

    (a) State Government (b) Parliament
    (c) Prime Minister (d) President.

49. The Supreme Court of India enunciated the doctrine of 'Basic Structure of the Constitution' in

    (a) the Golaknath case in 1967
    (b) the Sajjan Singh case in 1965
    (c) the Shankari Prasad case in 1951
    (d) the Keshvannad Bharati case in 1973.

50. The authority empowered to make laws in respect of matters not enumerated in any of the three lists is
   (a) State Legislature
   (b) Union Parliament
   (c) Union Parliament and State Legislature
   (d) The advocates General of the states.

ANSWERS

1.	(d)	2.	(b)	3.	(b)	4.	(b)
5.	(c)	6.	(d)	7.	(d)	8.	(c)
9.	(a)	10.	(c)	11.	(d)	12.	(d)
13.	(d)	14.	(c)	15.	(d)	16.	(b)
17.	(d)	18.	(c)	19.	(c)	20.	(a)
21.	(b)	22.	(a)	23.	(a)	24.	(c)
25.	(a)	26.	(b)	27.	(b)	28.	(a)
29.	(d)	30.	(b)	31.	(c)	32.	(d)
33.	(a)	34.	(b)	35.	(b)	36.	(b)
37.	(d)	38.	(d)	39.	(a)	40.	(c)
41.	(c)	42.	(c)	43.	(d)	44.	(c)
45.	(d)	46.	(c)	47.	(b)	48.	(b)
49.	(d)	50.	(b)				

SET 4
ASSESS YOURSELF

1. The Central Government gives grant-in-aid to the states out of the Consolidated Fund of India on the basis of the recommendation of
   (a) the Planning Commission
   (b) the Finance Commission
   (c) the Public Accounts Committe
   (d) the Estimate Committee.
2. The distribution of powers between the Centre and the State in Indian Constitution is based on the scheme provided in
   (a) The Minto-Morley Reforms, 1909
   (b) Montague-Chelmsford Act, 1919
   (c) The Government of India Act, 1935
   (d) India Independence Act, 1947.
3. Sarkaria Commisssion was set up for reviewing the relations between
   (a) the Prime Minister and President
   (b) Legislature and the Executive
   (c) Judiciary and the Executive
   (d) Centre and the States.
4. Under which of the five year plans the introduction of Panchayati Raj in India was suggested?
   (a) First five year plan
   (b) Second five year plan

(c) Third five year plan
(d) Fourth five year plan.

5. The right to freedom under Article 19 of the Constitution of India may be suspended by the President of India
(a) At any time he desire so
(b) Under Article 356
(c) Under Article 352
(d) Under Article 360.

6. 'Writs'can be issued for the enforcement of fundamental right by
(a) the District Courts
(b) the President
(c) the Supreme Court only
(d) both Supreme and High Courts.

7. Under which of the following circumstances can the President of India exercise discretionary powers?
(a) When there is dispute between the Prime Minister and Cabinet Minister
(b) When there is no majority party in the Lok Sabha and he has to choose a Prime Minister
(c) When the ruling party loses its majority in the Lok Sabha
(d) When the President decided to refer the advice of the Union Cabinet back for reconsideration.

8. Which of the following is a Directive Principle of the State Policy?
(a) The state shall not deny to any person equality before the law
(b) The state shall not discriminate against any person on grounds of religion, race caste, sex or place of birth
(c) Untouchability is abolished and its practise in any form shall be punishable by law
(d) The state shall endeavour to protect and improve the environment.

9. Liberal Democracy means
   (a) Government by majority
   (b) Government by people
   (c) Government in the interest of the people
   (d) Limited majority rule.

10. Which one of the following categories of Fundamental Rights incorporates 'Abolition of Untouchability'?
   (a) The Right of Religion
   (b) The Right of Equality
   (c) The Right to Freedom
   (d) The Right against exploitation.

11. If the President is to resign from the office he should address his letter of resignation to
   (a) the Prime Minister (b) the Vice President
   (c) the Chief Justice (d) the Speaker.

12. Rajya Sabha can take initiative in
   (a) ensuring a Central Minister
   (b) creating a new all India Service
   (c) considering money bills
   (d) appointment of judges.

13. The joint sitting of Indian Parliament for transacting a legislative business is presided over by
   (a) the President of India
   (b) the seniormost member of Parliament
   (c) the Chairman of Rajya Sabha
   (d) the Speaker of the Lok Sabha.

14. Who among the following is considered to be the custodian of the Lok Sabha?
   (a) The Prime Minister
   (b) The Leader of the Opposition
   (c) The Chief whip of the ruling party
   (d) The Speaker.

15. The Speaker of the Lok Sabha has to address his letter of resignation to the
    - (a) Prime Minister of India
    - (b) President of India
    - (c) Vice President of India
    - (d) Deputy Speaker of India.

16. Which one of the following statement correctly describes "a hung Parliament"?
    - (a) The Parliament lacks the quorum to conduct business
    - (b) The Prime Minister has resigned but Parliament is not dissolved
    - (c) In Parliament no party has a clear majority
    - (d) A lame duck Parliament.

17. To which one of the following categories does the Right to property belong?
    - (a) Legal Right (b) Human Right
    - (c) Fundamental Right (d) Natural Right.

18. Who nominates the Chairman of the Lok Sabha
    - (a) Speaker
    - (b) Prime Minister
    - (c) Secretary to Parliament
    - (d) Deputy Speaker.

19. Seats in the Lok Sabha are not reserved for the
    - (a) Scheduled Castes
    - (b) Scheduled tribes
    - (c) Scheduled tribes in the autonomous districts of Assam
    - (d) Anglo-Indian.

20. The Fundamental Duties of the Indian citizen have been
    - (a) originally provided by the Constitution
    - (b) including in the Constitution by the 42nd amendment
    - (c) included in the Constitution by the 44th amendment
    - (d) inserted into the constitution by a judgement of the Supreme Court.

21. Which one of the following objectives is not embodied in the preamble to the Constitution of India
    (a) Liberty of thought (b) Liberty of Expression
    (c) Liberty of Beliefs (d) Economic Liberty.

22. Under which Article of the Indian Constitution can Parliament legislate on any subject in the State list
    (a) Article 229 (b) Article 239
    (c) Article 249 (d) Article 259.

23. Which one of the following cases is related to Fundament Rights?
    (a) State of Bombay Vs. Balsara (1951)
    (b) Sharma Vs. Krishna (1959)
    (c) State of West Bengal Vs. Union of India (1963)
    (d) Golak nath Vs. State of Punjab (1967).

24. The normal term of the Lok Sabha may be extended by
    (a) An act passed by the Parliament
    (b) An order of the Supreme Court
    (c) An order of the Prime Minister of India
    (d) An order of the President of India.

25. Freedom of speech under the Indian Constitution is subject to reasonable restriction on the grounds of protection of
    (a) sovereignity and integrity of the country
    (b) the dignity of the office of the Prime Minister
    (c) the dignity of the constitutional functioning
    (d) the dignity of the Council of Ministers of the Central Government.

26. Which one of the following pairs is not correctly matched?
    (a) Equality before law : Guaranteed to both citizen and non - citizens
    (b) Altering the name : Power of a state legislature of a state
    (c) Creating a new state : Power of Parliament
    (d) Equality of opportunity : Guaranteed only to the India Citizens.

27. Which of the following are not included in the right to freedom of religion in the Constitution of India?
    1. Freedom of conscience and the right to practice and propagate religion
    2. Lavying of taxes or use of funds of the Government for the promotion or maintenance of any religion
    3. Establishment and maintenance of religious and charitable institution
    4. Imparting of religious instruction in any Government maintained instruction.

    (a) 1 and 2 (b) 1, 2 and 3
    (c) 1, 3 and 4 (d) 2 and 4

28. Which one of the following is not a fundamental duty?
    (a) To respect the National Anthem
    (b) To safeguard public property
    (c) To protect monuments and places of national importance
    (d) To protect and improve the natural environment.

29. Which of the following statements about the changes made by the 42nd amendment to the Constitution relating to the Directive Principle of State Policy are correct?
    1. It enabled state to provide free legal aid to its citizens
    2. It provided to the state to secure the participation of workers in the management of undertakings
    3. It made dowry taking a culpable offence

    (a) 1 and 2 (b) 1 and 3
    (c) 2 and 3 (d) 1, 2 and 3

30. Which one of the following statements is correct?
    (a) Dogri is included in the 8th schedule of the constitution
    (b) Union Territories are represented in the Lok Sabha but not in the Rajya Sabha
    (c) Of late the Directive Principles of State Policy have been having precedence over the Fundamental Rights
    (d) Economic and social planning is in the Union List.

31. Which of the following is/are among Directive Principles of State Policy?
    1. The state shall strive to promote science and technology for development
    2. The state shall endeavour to secure for citizens a uniform Civil Code throughout India
    3. The state shall try to develop population policy and family planning programmes
    4. The state shall take steps to promote tourism

    (a) 1 and 3 (b) 2 and 4
    (c) only 2 (d) 1, 2, 3, and 4.

32. Which one of the following pairs is not correctly matched?
    (a) Protection of childhood and youth from exploitation: Article 39
    (b) Right to work, to education and to public assistance in certain cases: Article 41
    (c) Provision for free and compulsory education for Children below fourteen years: Article 45
    (d) Protection of Monuments and places and objects of national importance: Article 48 A.

33. Rajya Sabha has equal powers with Lok Sabha
    (a) in the matter of creating new all India Services
    (b) in amending the Constitution
    (c) in the removal of government
    (d) in making cut motions.

34. What is the correct sequence of the following?
    1. Scheduled Castes Order
    2. Untouchability Offences Act
    3. Protection of Civil Rights Act
    4. Communal Order of the Government of Madras

    (a) 3, 4, 1, 2
    (b) 1, 2, 3, 4
    (c) 2, 3, 4, 1
    (d) 4, 1, 2, 3.

35. Which of the following statements regarding the residuary power of legislature is correct in the context of India?
   1. The Lok Sabha has exclusive power to make law on any matter not enumerated in the concurrent list
   2. Residuary power of legislation is laid down in Article 248 of the Constitution
   3. Residuary power of legislation is laid down in Article 248 of the Constitution
   4. Article 248 of the Constitution provides for among other things, the power to establish additional courts

   (a) 1 and 2 (b) 1 and 3
   (c) 2 and 4 (d) 2 and 3.

36. Which of the following statements is correct regarding the procedure of passing of bills in parliament?
   (a) A bill pending in parliament shall not lapse because of the prerogation of the two Houses of Parliament
   (b) A billing pending in the Rajya Sabha which has not been passed by the Lok Sabha shall lapse on its dissolution
   (c) A bill pending in the Lok Sabha and pending in the Rajya Sabha shall not lapse on the dissociation of the Lok Sabha
   (d) A bill pending in the Rajya Sabha which has been passed by the Lok Sabha shall not lapse on the adjournment of the Rajya Sabha.

37. Which one of the following is constitutionally obligatory on the part of the Prime Minister of India?
   (a) As the President is the supreme commander of the defence forces, the Prime Minister has to take all major decisions regarding defence only after prior approval by the President
   (b) The Prime Minister has to communicate to the President all decisions of the Cabinet regarding to administration and proposals for legislation
   (c) As the ministers are appointed by the President ,the Prime Minister has to go by Presidential discretion in the allocation of business among the ministers

(d) The Prime Minister,if he happens to be the leader of a party not having the required majority, should prove his majority strength in both the houses of Parliament within the period stipulated by the President.

38. Which of the following statement regarding Judiciary in India are correct?

1. In India Judiciary is not a part of the state
2. In India the pattern and designation of subordinate courts in the state are not uniform
3. Munsiff's courts have both civil and criminal jurisdiction
4. The pattern of subordinate courts in metropolitan areas is the same as that in districts

(a) 1 and 2 (b) 1 and 3
(c) 2 and 3 (d) 3 and 4.

39. Which of the following statements regarding 'the advisory jurisdiction' of the Supreme Court are correct?

1. The opinion of the Supreme Court may be sought by the President on any question of law or Act
2. In case the opinion of the Supreme Court is sought it is bound to give it
3. The advice given by the Supreme Court on a matter referred to it is binding on the President since the 42nd amendment
4. Advisory jurisdiction of the Supreme Court can also be exercised over disputes arising out of references made over pre-constitutional treaties

(a) 1 and 3 (b) 2 and 3
(c) 1 and 4 (d) 1, 2 and 3.

40. Judge of the High Court can be removed from office during his tenure by

(a) The Governor, if the state Legislature passes a resolution to this effect by two third majority
(b) The President, on the basis of a resolution passed by the Parliament by two-third majority
(c) The Chief Justice of the Supreme Court on the recommendation of the Parliament

(d) The Chief Justice of the High Court on the recommendation of the State Leislature.

41. Restriction of the writ jurisdiction of the High Courts under Article 226 of the Constitution is only possible through
   (a) an amendment of the Constitution passed by two-third majority of members present and voting and a majority of the total membership of each House of Parliament
   (b) an amendment of the Constitution passed by a simple majority of members present and voting in both Houses of parliament
   (c) an amendment of the Constitution passed by two-third majority of members present and voting and a majority of the total membership of each House of Parliament together with the ratification of half of the State Legislature
   (d) an amendment of the Constitution passed by two-third majority of members present and voting and majority of a total number with the ratifiction of three quarters of the state legislature.

42. Judicial Review in the Indian Constitution is based on
   (a) Procedure established by law
   (b) Due process of law
   (c) Rule of law
   (d) Precedents and Conventions.

43. Which one of the following are matters on which the Indian Parliament has the power to modify provisions of the Constitutions by a simple majority?
   1. Alteration of names, boundaries and areas of states
   2. Appointment of additional judges
   3. Abolition of the second chamber of a state legislature
   4. Administration of Scheduled Areas
   (a) 1, 2 and 3 (b) 1, 2 and 4
   (c) 1, 3 and 4 (d) 2, 3 and 4.

44. Which of the following taxes are levied and collected by the Government of India and assigned to the states?
   1. Taxes on railway fares and freights

2. Taxes on the sale and purchase of newspapers and on advertisement published therein
3. Taxes on agricultural income
4. Taxes on professions, trades, callings and employments

(a) 1 and 2 (b) 1 and 4
(c) 2 and 4 (d) 3 and 4.

45. What is the procedure required to be followed for the abolition of an existing Legislative Council in a State
    1. The Rajya Sabha must pass a resolution to that effect.
    2. The State Legislature Assembly must pass a resolution to the effect by a special majority as prescribed in the Constitution
    3. Parliament must enact a law abolishing the legislative Council
    4. The State Legislative Assembly must pass a resolution by ordinary majority as in the case of a bill

    (a) 1 and 2 (b) 2 and 3
    (c) 1 and 3 (d) 1 and 4.

46. The area of a Lok Sabha Constituency for the purpose of general election is determined by the
    (a) Delimitation Commission
    (b) Election Commission of India
    (c) Census Commission
    (d) President.

47. The provision of providing identity cards to voters has been made in
    (a) the Constitution of India
    (b) the Representation of People Act, 1958
    (c) the Election Laws (Amendment) Act, 1975
    (d) the Criminal and Election Laws (Amendment) Act, 1969

48. Which one among the following is regarded as a civil right?
    (a) Right to public employment
    (b) Freedom of speech and expression

(c) Right to elect and to be elected
(d) Right to property.

49. Which one of the following freedoms is not guaranteed by the Constitution of India?
(a) Freedom to own, acquire and dispose of property
(b) Freedom to move freely throughout the country
(c) Freedom to assemble peaceful and without arms
(d) Freedom to practise any trade or profession.

50. Which of the following regarding the Rajya Sabha are correct?
1. It is not subject to dissolution
2. It has a term of six years
3. One third of its members retire after every two years
4. Its members shall not be less than 25 years of age
(a) 1, 2 and 3 (b) 2, 3 and 4
(c) 1 and 3 (d) 2 and 4.

ANSWERS

1.	(a)	2.	(c)	3.	(d)	4.	(c)
5.	(c)	6.	(c)	7.	(b)	8.	(d)
9.	(c)	10.	(c)	11.	(b)	12.	(d)
13.	(a)	14.	(d)	15.	(d)	16.	(c)
17.	(a)	18.	(b)	19.	(c)	20.	(b)
21.	(c)	22.	(c)	23.	(d)	24.	(d)
25.	(a)	26.	(a)	27.	(b)	28.	(b)
29.	(c)	30.	(c)	31.	(d)	32.	(d)
33.	(b)	34.	(d)	35.	(c)	36.	(c)
37.	(d)	38.	(d)	39.	(d)	40.	(b)
41.	(c)	42.	(c)	43.	(a)	44.	(c)
45.	(a)	46.	(b)	47.	(c)	48.	(d)
49.	(a)	50.	(c)				

SET 5
ASSESS YOURSELF

1. Who was the first Chief Justice of India?
   (a) H.J. Kania (b) M.P. Shastri
   (c) M.C Mahajan (d) B.K Mukherjee.
2. By which Act the British Crown assumed over India from East India Company?
   (a) Indian Council Act, 1861
   (b) Government of India Act, 1858
   (c) Indian Council Act, 1892
   (d) India Council Act, 1909.
3. How many Articles and Schedules the original Constitution of India contain?
   (a) 398 Articles and 8 Schedules
   (b) 396 Articles and 9 schedules
   (c) 395 Articles and 8 schedules
   (d) 396 Articles and 8 schedules.
4. Which amendment to the Constitution incorporated "Socialist Secular" words in the Preamble?
   (a) 42nd Amendment (b) 43rd Amendment
   (c) 45th Amendment (d) 44th Amendment.
5. Which date can be referred to as the passing of the Constitution?
   (a) 26 January, 1950 (b) 26 January 1949
   (c) 26 November 1950 (d) 26 January 1948.

6. Which Constitution of a Country inspired the founder to frame Directive Principles of the State Policy?
   (a) Constitution of Germany
   (b) Constitution of Ireland
   (c) Constitution of the U.S.A.
   (d) Constitution of the U.K.

7. From where did the framers incorporated 'Emergency provisions' in the Constitution of India?
   (a) Constitution of Germany
   (b) Constitution of Ireland
   (c) Constitution of the U.S.A.
   (d) Constitution of the U.K.

8. From which Constitution framers have taken the system of elected President
   (a) Constitution of Germany
   (b) Constitution of U.K.
   (c) Constitution of the U.S.A.
   (d) Constitution of the Ireland.

9. In addition to the Government of India Act, 1935, which Country inspired the framers in introducing federal system to the Constitution
   (a) Constitution of U.S.A.
   (b) Constitution of U.K.
   (c) Constitution of the Canada
   (d) Constitution of the France.

10. Which country inspired framers to incorporate fundamental duties
    (a) U.K. (b) Canada
    (c) France (d) Erstwhile U.S.S.R.

11. Identify the features which Indian Constitution had borrowed from the U.S. Constitution
    A. Equal protection of Law
    B. Equality before Law
    C. Fundamental Duties
    D. Fundamental rights

(a) A, B and D (b) A and D
(c) B and D (d) A and C.

12. The Parliament can legislate on any subject in the state list
A. for the implementation of international treaties or agreements
B. when Art. 356 is imposed in the state
C. if two or more states make a request to Parliament to do so
D. If the Rajya Sabha declares by a two-third majority resolution that it is expedient to do so in national interest
(a) B,C and D (b) A C and D
(c) A,C,B and D (d) A B and C.

13. Which of the following are a feature of the Indian Constitution?
A. It rests sovereignity in the Legislature
B. It declares India a secular state
C. It declares India to have socialistic pattern of society
D. It has introduced the principle of universal adult made suffrage
(a) A, C and D (b) A, B and D
(c) A and C (d) B and C.

14. A money bill and finance bill differ in that
(a) a finance bill is only an ordinary bill
(b) a finance bill can be introduced in the Rajya Sabha
(c) a finance bill can be effectively rejected by the Rajya Sabha whereas money bill can not
(d) There is no difference.

15. Vote on account is made by the Lok Sabha
(a) to meet expenditure for a period before the passing of the annual budget
(b) to meet the additional expenditure incurred by the government on any approved item of expenditure during the supplementary budget

(c) to meet expenditure on unexpected demand
(d) to meet expenditure on secret services.

16. Consider the following statement about the Attorney General of India
A. He is appointed by the President of India
B. He must have the same qualification as one required for a judge of the Supreme Court
C. He must be a member of either House of Parliament
D. He can be removed by impeachment by Parliament
Which of these statement are correct?
(a) B and D (b) A and C
(c) C and D (d) A and B.

17. Consider the following functionaries
A. Cabinet Secretary
B. Chief Election Commissioner
C. Union Cabinet Ministers
D. Chief Justice of India
The correct sequence, in the order of precedence is
(a) CDAB (b) CDBA
(c) DCBA (d) DCAB.

18. What was the exact constitutional status of the Indian Republic on January 26, 1950, when the constitution was inaugurated?
(a) a sovereign secular Democratic Republic
(b) a sovereign Democratic Republic
(c) a sovereign Socialist Secular Democratic Republic
(d) a Democratic Republic.

19. The Fundamental Rights of Indian citizens
(a) can be suspended by the President during national emergency
(b) can be suspended by the President during all type of emergencies
(c) can be suspended by the President with the prior approval of the Supreme Court at any time
(d) can not be suspended under any condition.

20. Which one of the following rights is available only to the citizens within the territory of India?

    A. Freedom of speech
    B. Right to form association or unions
    C. Equality before law
    D. Freedom to assemble peacefully without arms.

    Select the corrrect answer using the code given below

    (a) A, B and D (b) A, B and C
    (c) B, C and D (d) A, C and D.

21. Which one of the following writs literally means 'what is your authority'?

    (a) Habeas Corpus (b) Certio rari
    (c) Quo Warranto (d) Prohibition.

22. The Constitution has vested the executive power of the Union government in

    (a) The President
    (b) The Prime Minister
    (c) The Council of Ministers
    (d) All the above three.

23. The President can make use of his discretionary powers

    A. when there is a dispute between the Prime Minister and the Cabinet
    B. when there is no majority party in the Lok Sabha and he has to choose a Prime Minister
    C. when the ruling party loses its majority in the Lok Sabha
    D. when he decides to refer the advice of the Union Cabinet back for reconsideration.

    Select the correct answers from the codes given below

    (a) B, C and D (b) A, B and C
    (c) A and B (d) B and D.

24. The term of office, salaries and allowances of the Chairman and other members of the finance Commission are determined by

(a) The Union Finance Minister
(b) The Union Cabinet
(c) The President
(d) The Parliament.

25. Which of the following languages are in the VIII Schedule of the Indian State?
A. Sindhi
B. Sanskrit
C Kashmiri
D. Urdu
(a) A, B and C (b) A, C and D
(c) B, C and D (d) A, B and D.

26. In the Indian Budgetary system pending the passage of finance bill in the Parliament, the provisional collection under tax act 1931 empowers the government to collect taxes for a period of
(a) 50 days (b) 60 days
(c) 75 days (d) 30 days.

27. The Parliamentary Commissioner for Administration in U.K was set up on the recommendations of
(a) Fulton Committee Report
(b) Whgatt Report
(c) Plowden Committee Report
(d) Davies Report.

28. The Central Council of Local Self Government was set up by
(a) the provisions of the Constitution of India
(b) the executive order of President of India
(c) an enactment of Parliament
(d) the order of the Ministry of Agriculture and Rural Development.

29. Which of the following Committee first felt the need of giving constitutional status to Panchayati Raj Institution?
(a) Balwant Rai Mehta Committee
(b) Ashok Mehta Committee

(c) Gorwala Committee
(d) L.M. Singhwi Committee.

30. Some state governments have besides Cabinet Ministers and Ministers of State, Parliamentary Secretaries also. These Parliamentary Secretaries who are also member of the State legislature are appointed by
(a) The Chief Minister
(b) The Governor
(c) The Chief whip of the Ruling party
(d) The Speaker.

31. The Supreme Court propounded the theory of 'basic structure of the constitution' in the
(a) Gopalan Vs. State of Madras case
(b) Golak Nath case
(c) Keshavananda Bharti case
(d) Minerva Mills case.

32. The Pension of the judges of the High Court is charged to
(a) the consolidated fund of the state where he last served
(b) the contingency fund of India
(c) the consolidated fund of India
(d) the Reserve Bank of India.

33. Which one of the following enjoys the distinction of being the first recognised leader of opposition in the India Parliament?
(a) A.K. Gopalan
(b) Y.B. Chavan
(c) Shayama Prasad Mukherjee
(d) Indira Gandhi.

34. The President can proclain national emergency only on the written advice of
(a) The Prime Minister
(b) The Union Cabinet
(c) The Chief Justice of India
(d) The Speaker of the Lok Sabha.

35. The Central Governement gives grant-in-aid to the states out of the consolidated fund of India on the basis of the recommendation of
    (a) The Planning Commission
    (b) The Finance Commission
    (c) The Public Accounts Committee
    (d) None of these.

36. Who among the following is the Chief Justice of India?
    (a) A.M.Ahmadi
    (b) J.S Verma
    (c) Madan Moham Puchi
    (d) None of these.

37. The Chief Justice of a High Court in India is appointed by the
    (a) Governor of the State
    (b) Prime Minister of India
    (c) Chief Justice of the Supreme Court
    (d) President of India.

38. Who among the following has taken over as the Governor of the Reserve bank of India?
    (a) Bimal Jalan
    (b) M.S. Ahluwalia
    (c) Arjun Sengupta
    (d) C. Ranga Raja.

39. The Consumer Protection Act came in to being in the year
    (a) 1986 (b) 1996
    (c) 1987 (d) 1997.

40. The state which has registered largest number of consumer rights related cases
    (a) West Bengal
    (b) Maharashtra
    (c) Tamil Nadu
    (d) Gujarat.

41. Recently the Union Government has amended the ordinance constituting the Central Vigilance Commission to make it
    - (a) Three member body
    - (b) Four member body
    - (c) Five member body
    - (d) Six member body.

42. The Supreme Court tenders advice to the President on a matter of Law or Act
    - (a) on its own
    - (b) only if the matter relates to the fundametal rights of citizens
    - (c) only if he seeks such advice
    - (d) only if the issue poses a threat to the unity and integrity of the country.

43. The Committee, on whose recommendation Panchayati Raj was introduced in the Country was headed by
    - (a) Balwant Rai Mehta
    - (b) Jagjiwan Ram
    - (c) Jivaraj Mehta
    - (d) Shriman Narayan.

44. In which case did the Supreme Court hold that the Preamble was a part of the Constitution
    - (a) Golak Nath case
    - (b) Berubari case
    - (c) Keshavanada Bharati case
    - (d) All the above cases.

45. Which of the following political parties enjoys the distinction of having formed the first non-Congress government in an Indian state
    - (a) DMK in Tamil Nadu
    - (b) Akalis in Punjab
    - (c) Lok Dal in Uttar Pradesh
    - (d) Communist in Kerala.

46. Grants-in-aid is provided to the states by the Centre for
    (a) improving the development of rural areas
    (b) improving the Centre State relations
    (c) implementing various development programmes and rehabilitation
    (d) reducing the regional imbalances.

47. Which one of the following are financial committees of Parliament in India?
    A. Public Accounts Committee
    B. Estimates Committee
    C. Committee on Public Undertakings
    (a) A only (b) A and C
    (c) A and B (d) A, B and C.

48. The National Integration Council is chared by
    (a) The President of India
    (b) The Prime Minister
    (c) The Home Minister
    (d) The Deputy Chairman of the Planning Commission.

49. The maximum strength of the nominated members in both the houses of Parliament can be
    (a) 10 (b) 14
    (c) 18 (d) 20.

50. In which part of the Constitution the concept of welfare state finds elaboration?
    (a) Preamble
    (b) Fundamental Rights
    (c) Fundamental Duties
    (d) Directive Principles of State Policy.

ANSWERS

1.	(a)	2.	(b)	3.	(c)	4.	(a)
5.	(c)	6.	(b)	7.	(a)	8.	(d)
9.	(c)	10.	(d)	11.	(b)	12.	(c)

13.	(d)	14.	(c)	15.	(a)	16.	(d)
17.	(c)	18.	(b)	19.	(a)	20.	(a)
21.	(c)	22.	(a)	23.	(d)	24.	(d)
25.	(a)	26.	(c)	27.	(b)	28.	(d)
29.	(d)	30.	(b)	31.	(c)	32.	(c)
33.	(b)	34.	(b)	35.	(b)	36.	(c)
37.	(d)	38.	(a)	39.	(a)	40.	(b)
41.	(b)	42.	(c)	43.	(a)	44.	(c)
45.	(d)	46.	(c)	47.	(d)	48.	(b)
49.	(b)	50.	(b)				

SET 6
ASSESS YOURSELF

1. Which one of the following statements regarding the Fundamental Duties contained in the Indian Constitution are correct?
   1. Fundamental duties can be enforced through writ jurisdiction
   2. Fundamental duties have formed a part of the Indian Constitution since its adoption
   3. Fundamental duties became a part of the Constitution in accordance with the recommendation of the Swaran Singh Committee
   4. Fundamental duties are applicable only to citizen of India

   (a) 1, 2 and 3 (b) 1, 2 and 4
   (c) 2 and 3 (d) 3 and 4.

2. Which of the following statement about a uniform civil code is/are correct?
   1. It is binding on the State that a uniform civil code must be made applicable to all
   2. The provision regarding a uniform civil code is contained in Part III of the Constitution
   3. The provision regarding the uniform civil code is not applicable to the state of Jammu and Kashmir
   4. The Supreme Court of India has directed that a uniform civil code must be made applicable to all with in ten years

(a) 3 only (b) 3 and 4
(c) 1, 2 and 3 (d) 1, 2 and 4.

3. The authority to specify which castes shall be deemed to be Scheduled Castes rests with the
   (a) President
   (b) Governor
   (c) Prime Minister
   (d) Commission for Scheduled Castes and Tribes.

4. The question whether any and if so what advice was tendered by Council of Ministers to the President
   (a) shall not be inquired into in any court
   (b) may be inquired into by any of the high courts
   (c) shall be inquired into only by the Supreme Court
   (d) may be inquired into by either House of Parliament.

5. The constitutional amendment relating to the declaration of emergency (1978) requires the President of India to act in accordance with the
   (a) collective advice of the entire Council of Ministers
   (b) advice of the Union Cabinet
   (c) advice of the Attorney General of India
   (d) advice of the Supreme Court.

6. Decision on question as to disqualifications of membership of either Houses of Parliament rests with the
   (a) Election Commission
   (b) House of Parliament concerned
   (c) Chief Justice of India
   (d) President after consultation with the Election Commission.

7. What is the maximum permissible strength of the legislative assembly (Vidhan Sabha) of any state?
   (a) 400 members
   (b) 425 members
   (c) 500 members
   (d) 525 members.

8. Disqualification on grounds of defection for a member of Parliament will not apply
   (a) in case of the split in the original political party to which he is elected
   (b) if he has voluntarily given up his membership of a political party
   (c) if he abstains from voting in the House contrary to the direction of the political party
   (d) if a nominated member of a House joins a political party after six months.

9. The Rajya Sabha has exclusive jurisdiction in
   (a) approving a proclamation of emergency
   (b) the creation and abolition of states
   (c) the election of Vice-President
   (d) authority Parliament to legislate on a subject in the state list.

10. The quorum to laid a meeting of a House of a state legislature shall be
   (a) 30 members or one-tenth of total membership whichever is less
   (b) one half of the total membership of the House
   (c) one-tenth of the total membership of the House
   (d) ten members or one-tenth of total membership whichever is more.

11. Which one of the following is directly related to the Appelate Jurisdiction of the Supreme Court of India?
   (a) Appeals made in civil, criminal and constitutional cases
   (b) Appeals made in constitutional cases
   (c) Adjudication of disputes between the Union and states
   (d) Adjudication of disputes between the Union and the states.

12. Which one of the following statements regarding the exercise of judical review in India is not correct?
    (a) A case must be brought before the Supreme Court regarding the validity of a law
    (b) Unanimous opinion of all the judges is necessary for declaring a law null and void
    (c) Legislative enactment and executive orders may be struck down by the Supreme Court
    (d) The power is implicit in the provision of Article 13 of the Constitution.

13. The Supreme Court of India is different from its counterpart in the U.S.A.
    (a) in its role as the guardian of the constitution
    (b) in its advisory role
    (c) in its role as the supreme authority in the judicial field in the country
    (d) it its writ jurisdiction.

14. In which of the following categories of cases the Supreme Court of India has the power to decide?
    1. A reference made by the President on a question of law or fact
    2 A case involving interpretation of the Constitution
    3. A case involving a substantial question of law of general importance
    4. A case where the constitutionality of any law has been challenged

    (a) 1,2 and 3 (b) 1,3 and 4
    (c) 1,2 and 4 (d) 2,3 and 4.

15. Which one of the following items comes under the concurrent list of Indian Constitution?
    (a) Inter-State rivers
    (b) Trade Unions
    (c) Citizenship
    (d) Local Government.

16. Which of the following statements regarding the residuary powers in the Constitution of India are correct?
    1. Residuary powers have been given to the Union Parliament
    2. In the matter of residuary power of India
    3. The final authority to decide wheather a particular matter falls under the residuary power or not is to Parliament
    4. The Government of India Act, 1935 placed residuary powers in the hand of the Governor General

    (a) 1,2 and 3 (b) 2 and 3
    (c) 1 and 4 (d) 3 and 4.

17. An inter-state council may be established by
    (a) The Parliament
    (b) The President
    (c) The National Development Council
    (d) The Zonal Council.

18. Which of the following are the principles on the basis of which the Parliamentary system of government in India operates
    1. National Executive head
    2. Vice President as the Chairman of the Upper House
    3. Real executive authority with Council of Ministers
    4. Executive Responsibility to the lower house

    (a) 1,2 and 3 (b) 1,2 and 4
    (c) 1,3 and 4 (d) 2,3 and 4.

19. A rigid constitution is one which
    (a) cannot be amended
    (b) can be amended by a new constituent assembly
    (c) can be amended only by two third majority of the members present and voting
    (d) can be amended by any procedure other than ordinary law making process prescribed by the constitution.

20. In the Parliamentary form of government the members of the Council of Ministers are collectively responsible to
    (a) The Head of State
    (b) The Chairman of the Upper House and Speaker of the Lower House
    (c) The popular House of the Parliament
    (d) The Prime Minister.

21. Which one of the following is not included as a fundamental duty in the Constitution of India?
    (a) To cherish and follow the noble ideals which inspired our national struggle.
    (b) To develop the scientific temper, humanism and the spirit of inquiry and reform
    (c) To protect the minorities
    (d) To safeguard public property and to adjure violence.

22. Which one of the following Directive Principles was not originally provided for in the Constitution of India?
    (a) Citizen's right to an adequate means of livelihood
    (b) Free legal aid
    (c) Free and compulsory education to the children under 14 years of age
    (d) Prohibition of the slaughter of cows and calves.

23. If the President of India exercises his power provided under Art. 356 of the Constitution in respect of a particular state, than
    (a) The Assembly of the state is automatically dissolved
    (b) Article 19 is suspended in that state
    (c) Parliament assumes the power to legislate on the subject in the state list
    (d) The President can make laws relating to that state.

24. A non-money bill passed by the Parliament is returned by the President to Parliament for reconsideration. It is passed once again by the Parliament without any change. Now the
    (a) President can again withhold his assent
    (b) Bill will automatically lapse

(c) Bill will be referred to the Supreme Court
(d) President will give his assent.

25. According to the Constitution of India a new All India Service can be instituted with the initiative taken by
(a) more than two-third of the states
(b) the inter-state council
(c) the Lok Sabha
(d) the Rajya Sabha.

26. The Supreme Court of India declared by issuing a writ that"the respondent was not entitled to an office he was holding or a privilege he was exercise?" which writ is that?
(a) Habeas Corpus (b) Prohibition
(c) Quo Warranto (d) Certiorari.

27. Which of the following are the main jurisdiction of the High Court of a State?
(a) Original jurisdiction
(b) Appellate jurisdiction
(c) Supervisory jurisdiction
(d) Advisory jurisdiction.

28. The term 'Law' used in the phrase 'Rule of Law'refers to
(a) Positive law
(b) Natural law
(c) Common law
(d) Conventions of the Constitution.

29. Which of the following feature are present in the Indian Constitution
1. Multiple procedures for amendment
2. State not empowered to initiate amendment
3. Certain amendments have to be passsed just by state legislature
4. Joint sittings of Parliament to solve disputes regarding Constitutional amendments
(a) 1,2 and 4 (b) 1 and 2
(c) 2,3 and 4 (d) 1,3 and 4.

30. In India the Vice President is elected by an electoral college consisting of
    (a) members of both Houses of Parliament
    (b) elected members of both Houses of Parliament
    (c) elected members of both Houses of Parliament and the State Legislative Assemblies
    (d) members of both Houses of Parliament and the State Legislative Assemblies.

31. The Chief Election Commissioner of India can be removed from office during his tenure by
    (a) the Chief Justice of India if some charges are proved against him
    (b) by the President on the basis of a resolution of the Union Cabinet
    (c) by a committee consisting of Chief Justice of India, Law Minister of India and the Vice President of India
    (d) by the President on the basis of resolution passed by the Parliament by two third majority.

32. Which one of the following state has a seat reserved in the Legislative Assembly on the basis of religion
    (a) Goa
    (b) Sikkim
    (c) Mizoram
    (d) Jammu and Kashmir.

33. In India there is a single Constitution for the Union and the States with the exception of
    (a) Sikkim (b) J & K
    (c) Nagaland (d) Tamil Nadu.

34. Which Article of the Constitution empowers the Parliament to legislate on any matter of the state list?
    (a) Article 115
    (b) Article 183
    (c) Article 221
    (d) Article 226.

35. Which one of the following committees is not a Standing Committee of the Parliament?
(a) Public Account Committee
(b) Estimates Committee
(c) Committee on Public Undertakings
(d) Consultative Committee to the Ministry of Finance.

36. The authority to declare war or peace under the Indian Constitution is vested in
(a) the Prime Minister
(b) the Defence Minister
(c) the Parliament
(d) the President.

37. The members of the Constituent Asssembly were
(a) directly elected by the people
(b) nominated by the Governor General
(c) elected by the Legislature of various provinces and nominated by the rulers of the princely states
(d) nominated by the Congress and the Muslim League.

38. Between the 15th August, 1947 when the country became free and the 26th January 1950 when India declared itself a democratic sovereign republic the Governor of India functioned under the provision of
(a) the Government of India Act, 1935
(b) the Indian Independence Act, 1947
(c) the Indian (Provisional Constitution) Order, 1947
(d) None of the above.

39. Fundamental Rights guaranteed in the Indian Constitution can be suspended only by
(a) a proclamation of national emergency
(b) an act passed by the Parliament
(c) an amendement of the Constitution
(d) the judicial decisions of the Supreme Court.

40. Which one of the following is not a Constitutional prerogative of the President of India
    (a) Returning a Legislative Bill for reconsideration
    (b) Returning of financial bill for reconsideration
    (c) Dissolving the Lok Sabha
    (d) Summoning the Rajya Sabha.

41. The Chairman of Rajya Sabha is elected by
    (a) elected members of Rajya Sabha
    (b) all members of Rajya Sabha
    (c) eleected members of Parliament
    (d) all members of Parliament.

42. The Lok Sabha Secretariat comes under direct supervision of
    (a) Ministry of Home Affairs
    (b) Ministry of Parliament Affairs
    (c) Prime Minister's office
    (d) Speaker of the Lok Sabha.

43. There is a Constitutional requirement to have a Minister in charge of Tribal Welfare for the states of
    (a) Assam, Nagaland and Manipur
    (b) Himachal Pradesh, Haryana and Rajasthan
    (c) Bihar, M.P and Orissa
    (d) Manipur, Tripura and Meghalya.

44. A constitutional system with its basic principle to executive continuous responsibility to the legislature
    (a) People's Democracy
    (b) Parliament Democrary
    (c) Socialist Democracy
    (d) Direct Democracy.

45. Constitutional government stands for
    (a) limited government
    (b) a government limited by the desires and capacities of those who exercise power

(c) a government run according to general laws known to the people

(d) a government run by people's representatives.

46. Who among the following do not participate in the election of the President of India?

(a) Elected members of the Rajya Sabha

(b) Elected members of the Lok Sabha

(c) Elected members of the Vidhan Sabha

(d) Elected members of the Vidhan Parishads.

47. The accountability or responsibility of the Prime Minister and Cabinet to the Lok Sabha is

(a) intermittent

(b) indirect

(c) at the time of election

(d) direct continuous and collective.

48. The Chairman of Zonal Council is

(a) the Chief Minister and is nominated by the Prime Minister of India

(b) the Union Minister and is nominated by the President of India

(c) the Home Minister and is ex-officio

(d) the Vice-President of India.

49. The report of Public Accounts Committee is presented to the

(a) Prime Minister

(b) President

(c) Finance Minister

(d) Lok Sabha.

50. In the Constitution of India, the term'Federal'

(a) figure in the preamble

(b) figure in the Part III of the Constitution

(c) figure in Article 368

(d) does not figure anywhere.

ANSWERS

1.	(d)	2.	(b)	3.	(a)	4.	(a)
5.	(a)	6.	(d)	7.	(c)	8.	(d)
9.	(b)	10.	(c)	11.	(d)	12.	(a)
13.	(c)	14.	(d)	15.	(b)	16.	(a)
17.	(b)	18.	(c)	19.	(d)	20.	(c)
21.	(a)	22.	(b)	23.	(a)	24.	(d)
25.	(d)	26.	(c)	27.	(c)	28.	(c)
29.	(c)	30.	(a)	31.	(d)	32.	(d)
33.	(b)	34.	(b)	35.	(d)	36.	(d)
37.	(c)	38.	(a)	39.	(a)	40.	(c)
41.	(d)	42.	(d)	43.	(a)	44.	(b)
45.	(a)	46.	(d)	47.	(d)	48.	(a)
49.	(b)	50.	(c)				

ASSESS YOURSELF
SET 7

1. After a bill has been passed by Parliament and sent to the President for his consideration
   (a) He can refuse to sign it
   (b) He has to sign it
   (c) He can change certain clauses of the bill
   (d) He can send it back for reconsideration.

2. The Speaker of the Lok Sabha is
   (a) appointed by the President
   (b) appointed by the President on the recommendation of the Prime Minister
   (c) elected by the two Houses of Parliament at a joint sitting
   (d) elected by member of the Lok Sabha.

3. The Secretary-General of Lok Sabha, who is Chief of the Lok Sabha Secretariat, is appointed by
   (a) the President
   (b) the Speaker
   (c) the Minister of Parliamentary Affairs in consultation with the Speaker
   (d) a committee of the House especially constituted for this purpose.

4. If a 'no-confidence' motion is passed against a minister
   (a) he has to tender his resignation
   (b) the whole Council of Minister has to resign
   (c) the Minister as well as the Prime Minister have to resign
   (d) The Lok Sabha is dissolved.

5. A member of Parliament enjoys immunity from prosecution for having said anything
   (a) during the session of the Parliament anywhere
   (b) in the Parliament and its committees
   (c) at the press conference
   (d) on the floor of the parliament.

6. Which non-member can participate in the business of either House of the Parliament?
   (a) The Vice President
   (b) The Solicitor General
   (c) The Attorney General
   (d) The Chief Justice.

7. The electoral system of India is largely based on the pattern of
   (a) Britain (b) France
   (c) USA (d) Canada.

8. A motion for no-confidence against Council of Ministers can be moved in the Lok Sabha it is supported by at least
   (a) 50 members (b) 55 members
   (c) 60 members (d) 80 members.

9. Which one of the following enjoys the distinction of being the first recognised leader of Opposition in the Indian Parliament?
   (a) A.K. Gopalan
   (b) Y.B. Chavan
   (c) Syama Prasad Mukherjee
   (d) Indira Gandhi.

10. Which one of the following Indian states has the lowest population density?
    (a) Sikkim (b) Himachal Pradesh
    (c) Arunachal Pradesh (d) Rajasthan.

11. Which one of the following is not a statutory body?
    (a) The Planning Commission
    (b) The Election Commission
    (c) The Finance Commission
    (d) The Union Public Service Commission.

12. As per the recent announcement of Election Commission, Assembly Elections were held in which of the following states on November 25, 1998?
    (a) Madhya Pradesh, Gujarat, Delhi and Mizoram
    (b) Madhya Pradesh Rajasthan, Delhi and Mizoram
    (c) Madhya Pradesh, Bihar Delhi and Mizoram
    (d) Uttar Pradesh, Bihar, Delhi and Mizoram.

13. India's High commissioner in Pakistan Satish Chandra was appointed Chairman of the joint intellegence committee (JIC) which will be the secretariate of the high powered National Security Council (NSC) headed by
    (a) Finance Miniser (b) Defence Minister
    (c) President (d) Prime Minister.

14. Who of the following is charged with the delimitation of territorial constituencies for Lok Sabha election?
    (a) President of India
    (b) Lok Sabha
    (c) Election Commission of India
    (d) Supreme Court of India.

15. Shri K.R. Narayanan has been sworn in President of India, which of the statement related to his election is not true ?
    (a) He is the tenth President of India
    (b) He is fourth Vice President to be elected to the office of President
    (c) He is the fifth Head of the state from south
    (d) Mr. T.N. Seshan was his only rival.

16. To whom should be President of India address the letter of his resignation
    (a) The Prime Minister of India
    (b) The Chief Justice of India
    (c) The Speaker of Lok Sabha
    (d) The Vice President of India.

17. The formal announcement of the general election for the Lok Sabha is made by
    (a) The Joint Session of Parliament
    (b) The Election Commission
    (c) The President of India
    (d) The Prime Minister.

18. Who amongst the following has taken over as the Chairman of the newly constituted Disinvestment Commission?
    (a) Shri N. Vaghul
    (b) Shri G.V Rama Krishna
    (c) Shri D.Ghosh
    (d) Shri D.R. Mehta.

19. Recently with which country India has set up an Inter-Parliament committe to provide a permanent forum for expanding and connecting ties between the legislatures of two countries?
    (a) France (b) China
    (c) Canada (d) Russia.

20. Recently, which political party of India has decided to reserve thirty three per cent of seats in its all party committees for women?
    (a) Bhartiya Janta Party
    (b) Congress I
    (c) Janata Dal
    (d) Communist Party of India.

21. The proposed Vananchal State will be comprised
    (a) 24 districts (b) 26 districts
    (c) 25 districts (d) 28 districts.

22. Recently, a bill has been passed in the Lok Sabha, according to which those causing an explosion by special category explosives with an intent to endanger life or property will be awarded
    (a) 10 years rigorous imprisonment
    (b) 12 years rigorous imprisonment
    (c) 14 years rigorous imprisonment
    (d) Capital punishment.

23. Who was the Chairman of the Secret Committee?
    (a) Mr. W.E.M. Leckey
    (b) Mr. Dundas
    (c) Mr. Barwell
    (d) Lord Lamaister.

24. According to the provision of the Regulating Act of 1773, a Supreme Court was established at Fort William in 1974. Who was the first Chief Justice of the Supreme Court?
    (a) Justice Chambers (b) Justice Lemaister
    (c) Justice Hyde (d) Justice Sir. E, Impey.

25. How many councillors were there in Governor General in Council as per the provision of the Regulating Act?
    (a) Three (b) Four
    (c) Six (d) Eight.

26. The Supreme Court established under the Regulating Act of 1773, had
    (a) only original jurisdiction
    (b) only appellate jurisdiction
    (c) both original and appellate jurisdiction
    (d) only advisory role.

27. According to the provisions of the Regulating Act of 1773 the Presidency Government of Bombay and Madras were
    (a) abolished altogether
    (b) made subordinate to the Governor General of Bengal
    (c) made responsible to the Crown
    (d) given more autonomy.

28. The Regulating Act provided for liberal salaries to Governor General and other officials of the company. The salary of the Governor General was fixed at
    (a) £ 25000 per month
    (b) £ 20,200 per month
    (c) £ 25,000 per annum
    (d) £ 10,000 per annum.

29. India has a
    (a) Single, unified judicial system
    (b) Federal judicial system
    (c) Multiple Judicial system
    (d) Multiple unified judicial system.

30. The Governor of State is appointed by
    (a) the President
    (b) the Chief Justice of High Court on the advice of the Chief Minister
    (c) the Prime Minister
    (d) the President on the recommendation of the Prime Minister.

31. The Supreme Court tenders advice to the President on any legal matter
    (a) on regular intervals
    (b) only if the issue posed is related to the security of the nation
    (c) only if he seeks such advice
    (d) in a routine way.

32. In a state a money bill can be introduced
    (a) in any house
    (b) only in Legislative Council
    (c) only in Legislative Assembly
    (d) None of these.

33. The power of judicial Review is vested in the
    (a) Prime Minister
    (b) Parliament

(c) President
(d) Supreme Court and High Courts.

34. The functions of the state Legislature is
(a) mainly executive
(b) mainly legislative
(c) legislative as well as executive
(d) none of these.

35. Which Indian state has a seperate Constitution?
(a) Haryana (b) Punjab
(c) West Bengal (d) Jammu and Kashmir.

36. The use of English language has been permitted for official purposes
(a) Indefintely (b) till 1998
(c) till 2005 (d) till 2000.

37. The 'Contempt of Court' places a restriction on
(a) right to property
(b) right to freedom
(c) right to express opinion
(d) right to equality.

38. The first linguistic state is
(a) Jammu and Kashmir (b) Andhra Pradesh
(c) Tamil Nadu (d) karnataka.

39. The Attorney-General of India is appointed by
(a) The Union Law Minister
(b) The President
(c) The Chief Justice of Supreme Court
(d) None of these.

40. The status of the Attorney General is that of
(a) the Cabinet Secretary
(b) the Highest legal officer of the Government of India
(c) the legal advisor to the Prime Minister
(d) the Supreme legal authority in the country.

41. The member of Panchayat Samitis are
    (a) nominated by DRDAs
    (b) indirectly elected by the members of village panchayat
    (c) appointed by Sarpanch
    (d) none of these.

42. The Supreme Court is considered as
    (a) the guardian of the liberties and fundamental rights of the citizens of India
    (b) the court which has Supreme Court
    (c) the court having most impartial judges
    (d) none of these.

43. The Panchayati Raj is
    (a) a state structure
    (b) a financial structure
    (c) an administrative structure
    (d) a concurrent structure.

44. The decisions of the Supreme Court cannot be
    (a) challenged in any court
    (b) amended by the parliament
    (c) binding on the people of India
    (d) none of these.

45. The qualification for the Chairman and other members of the Finance Commission are
    (a) prescribed by the President
    (b) prescribed by the Council of Minister
    (c) prescribed by the parliament from time to time
    (d) none of these.

46. The framers of the constitution borrowed the idea of judicial review from
    (a) The Constitution of France
    (b) The Constitution of United States of America
    (c) The Constitution of Germany
    (d) None of these.

47. Which state enjoys the distinction of being the latest state of the Indian Union?

(a) Sikkim (b) Goa
(c) Arunachal Pradesh (d) Mizoram.

48. Who can approve the withdrawal of money from the consolidated fund of India?

(a) The President (b) The Prime Minister
(c) The Parliament (d) None of these.

49. The Constitution of India directs the States to establish Panchayat Raj institutions in the country under

(a) The Fundamental Rights
(b) The Directive Principles of State Policy
(c) The Fundamental Duties
(d) The Preamble.

50. The judicial appointment below those of judges of High court etc. is a state are made by

(a) The Governor
(b) The Chief Justice of High Court
(c) The State Law Minister
(d) The State Council of Ministers.

ANSWERS

1.	(d)	2.	(b)	3.	(a)	4.	(b)
5.	(b)	6.	(c)	7.	(d)	8.	(a)
9.	(b)	10.	(c)	11.	(a)	12.	(b)
13.	(d)	14.	(c)	15.	(b)	16.	(d)
17.	(d)	18.	(b)	19.	(d)	20.	(b)
21.	(c)	22.	(d)	23.	(b)	24.	(a)
25.	(b)	26.	(c)	27.	(c)	28.	(c)
29.	(d)	30.	(a)	31.	(c)	32.	(c)
33.	(d)	34.	(c)	35.	(d)	36.	(c)
37.	(a)	38.	(b)	39.	(b)	40.	(b)
41.	(b)	42.	(a)	43.	(c)	44.	(a)
45.	(c)	46.	(b)	47.	(b)	48.	(a)
49.	(b)	50.	(a)				

SET 8
ASSESS YOURSELF

1. Languages have been included under schedule
   (a) Seventh (b) Sixth
   (c) Eighth (d) None of the above.
2. An emergency due to internal disturbances underArticle 352 was first of all proclaimed in the country in the year
   (a) 1975 (b) 1976
   (c) 1977 (d) 1978.
3. What is Article 370?
   (a) It ensures the special status of Nagaland
   (b) It ensures the special status of Assam
   (c) It ensures the special status of Sikkim
   (d) It ensures the special status of Jammu and Kashmir.
4. A writ is a
   (a) proposal for a bill
   (b) law passed by the Parliament
   (c) formal order under seal issued in the name of a sovereign government or by a superior court enjoining the officer or other person to whom it is issued to do or refrain from doing some spcified act
   (d) none of these.
5. The Party system in India can be described as
   (a) single party
   (b) bi-party

(c) multi-party
(d) a mixture of all the above.

6. Panchayati Raj is
(a) Administrative Structure
(b) Financial Structure
(c) Physical Structure
(d) State of Strucutre.

7. How many languages were originally recognised by the constitution as regional languages?
(a) 14 (b) 15
(c) 16 (d) None.

8. How many times has a national emergency been declared so far by the President?
(a) Only once (b) Twice
(c) Thrice (d) Never.

9. The Jammu and Kashmir Resettlement Bill is associated with the
(a) resettlement of Muslims from Pakistan in Jammu and Kashmir
(b) resettlement of Kashmiris from other parts of the country in Jammu and Kashmir
(c) acquisition of the property of non-residents in the state
(d) (b) and (c).

10. Habeas Corpus means
(a). an order from a court to free a person who has been illegally detained by the police or any other person
(b) an order from the superior court to any official to show his right to the office
(c) an order from the superior court to any official to show his right to confine any person
(d) an order from a higher court to stop proceedings in the certain case.

11. A sound two-party system means
    (a) that both have been functioning for a considerable period
    (b) that both have clearcut ideologies but their difference are marginal
    (c) that the third party if any is only nominal
    (d) the two parties which are mentioned in the constitution.

12. In which part of the Constitution is the state enjoined to establish Panchayati Raj institutions?
    (a) Preamble
    (b) Directive Principles of State Policy
    (c) Fundamental Rights
    (d) Seventh Schedule.

13. "The official languages of the Union shall be Hindi in Devanagari script", this has been stated under article
    (a) 306 (b) 310
    (c) 323 (d) 343.

14. Duty of the Union to protect states against external aggression and internal disturbances has been laid down under article
    (a) 345 (b) 355
    (c) 365 (d) 375.

15. Sepcial status was accorded to Jammu and Kashmir in terms of
    (a) an assurance given to the state government at the time of its accession
    (b) the Independence Act, 1947
    (c) the cease fire agreeement concluded with Pakistan in 1948
    (d) all of the above.

16. Writ of Quo Warranto means
    (a) a writ from superior court commanding some officer or particular authority to do a specific act

(b) an order from a higher court to stop proceeding in a certain case
(c) an order from the superior court to any official to show his right to the office
(d) to produce the body of a person.

17. The most important feature of the political party system in India is
(a) the multiplicity of Political parties
(b) the overlapping in programmes of different parties
(c) the presence of regional or local parties
(d) voting for a particular candidate not a party.

18. Panchayati Raj was started in the country in
(a) 1957 (b) 1952
(c) 1959 (d) 1951.

19. Which of the following articles deals with the official language or languages?
(a) 344 (b) 345
(c) 346 (d) 347.

20. Which of the following articles deals with suspension of provisions of article 19 during emergencies?
(a) 358 (b) 352
(c) 356 (d) 370.

21. The constitution of Jammu and Kashmir was framed by
(a) the same constituent assembly which framed the Constitution of India
(b) a special constituent assembly set up by the parliament
(c) a special constituent assembly set up by the state
(d) none of the above.

22. Writ of Mandamus means
(a) produce the body of a person
(b) an order from a superior court to any official to show his right to the office
(c) an order from a higher court to stop proceedings in a certain case

(d) a writ from a superior court commanding some officer or particular authority to do a specific act.

23. Who accords recognition to various political parties as national or regional parties?

(a) The President
(b) The Election ommission
(c) The Parliament
(d) The President in consultation with the election commission.

24. The commitee upon whose recommendation Panchayati Raj was introduced in the country was headed by

(a) Jagjiwan Ram
(b) Jiraj Mehta
(c) Balwant Rai Mehta
(d) Shriman Narayan.

25. How many languages have been recognised by the Constitution of India?

(a) 20 (b) 17
(c) 16 (d) 18.

26. The provision for suspension of the enforcement of the rights conferred by Part III during emergencies has been made under article

(a) 356 (b) 357
(c) 358 (d) 359.

27. The head of the state of Jammu and Kashmir who was initially known as Sadar-i-Riyasat, was redesignated Governor in

(a) 1970 (b) 1960
(c) 1977 (d) 1965.

28. Which of the following writs literally means to produce the body of a person?

(a) Habeas Corpus (b) Ertiorari
(c) Quo Warranto (d) Prohibition.

29. A party can get recognition as a regional party if it secures
    (a) 10% of the valid votes in any one state
    (b) 5% of the valid votes in any one state
    (c) 25% of the valid votes in any one state
    (d) 4% of the valid votes in any one state.

30. The original scheme of Panchayati Raj, introduced in 1959, operates at
    (a) Zila Parishad Samiti, Gram Sabha
    (b) Panchayat Samiti, Gram Panchayat, Zila Parishad
    (c) Gram Sabha, Village Panchayat, Zila Parishad
    (d) Zila Parishad, Panchayat Samiti, Village Panchayat.

31. Which is the offical language of India?
    (a) Sanskri
    (b) Hindi in Devanagari script
    (c) Bengali
    (d) Urdu.

32. "If the President is satisfied that a situation has arisen where by the financial stability or credit of India or of any part of the territory thereof is threatened, he may by a proclamation make a declaration to that effect", this has been stated under article
    (a) 350 (b) 352
    (c) 356 (d) 360.

33. Which one of the following states has a separate constitution?
    (a) Jammu and Kashmir
    (b) Nagaland
    (c) West Bengal
    (d) (a) and (b).

34. Which one of the following writs literally means " we command"?
    (a) Certiorari (b) Quo Warranto
    (c) Mandamus (d) Habeas Corpus.

35. Which one of the following is the major advantage of the bi-party system over the multiparty system?
    (a) The opinion of soceity is better reflected
    (b) It is free from the weakness of a government elected on a simple majority which might actually be a minority
    (c) The election expenses are less
    (d) Voters know in advance what policies they are voting for.

36. A committee under the chairmanship of Ashok Mehta to review the working of Panchayati Raj Institution was appointed by
    (a) Indira Gandhi during emergency
    (b) The Janata Party when it come to power at the centre
    (c) Indira Gandhi after she staged a come back
    (d) None of these.

37. Originally it was laid down in the Constitution that English language shall continue to be used for all the official purposes at the Union for a period of
    (a) 30 years (b) 25 years
    (c) 20 years (d) 15 years.

38. The constitution of Jammu and Kashmir came into force
    (a) on January 26,1950 alongwith the Indian Constitution
    (b) on January 26, 1952
    (c) on August 15, 1952
    (d) on January 26, 1957.

39. Which of the following attributes is not a must for a political party in a democracy?
    (a) A cadre (b) An organisation
    (c) Leadership (d) Finances.

40. In the three-tier Panchayati Raj structure the block is
    (a) the lowest structure
    (b) the intermediary structure
    (c) the highest structure
    (d) none of the above.

41. Which of the following languages has not been recognised by the Constitution?
(a) Bengali (b) Tamil
(c) Rajasthani (d) Urdu.

42. The head of the government of Jammu and Kashmir is known as
(a) The Chief Minister (b) The Premier
(c) The Prime Minister (d) Sadar-i-Riyasat.

43. In which election was these a virtual straight fight between the Congress and Janata Party ?
(a) 1967 (b) 1977
(c) 1981 (d) 1977 & 1981.

44. Panchayati Raj came in the
(a) Union list (b) State list
(c) Concurrent list (d) Residual list.

45. Special procedure for enactment of certain laws relating to langauge has been made under article
(a) 250 (b) 290
(c) 329 (d) 349.

46. Which one of the following party/parties is/are a strong exponent of doing away with special status of Jammu and Kashmir by abrogating Article 370 of the Constitution?
(a) B.J.P
(b) Janata Dal
(c) National Conference
(d) Both (a) and (b).

47. Which one of the following was not a constituent of the Janata Party framed in 1977?
(a) Bhartiya Jan Sangh
(b) Bharitya Lok Dal
(c) Socialist Party
(d) Swatantra Party.

48. One of the following is not a part of Panchayati Raj
   (a) District Board
   (b) Town Area Committees
   (c) Village Block
   (d) Panchayat Boards.

49. Which language was added to the first of regional languages by the 21st amendement?
   (a) Oriya (b) Kashmiri
   (c) Sindhi (d) Assames.

50. Which of the following languages is not mentioned in the Eighth Schedule of our constitution?
   (a) Sanskrit (b) Sindhi
   (c) Urdu (d) Maithili.

ANSWERS

1.	(c)	2.	(a)	3.	(a)	4.	(c)
5.	(c)	6.	(a)	7.	(a)	8.	(c)
9.	(d)	10.	(a)	11.	(b)	12.	(b)
13.	(d)	14.	(b)	15.	(a)	16.	(c)
17.	(a)	18.	(c)	19.	(b)	20.	(a)
21.	(c)	22.	(d)	23.	(b)	24.	(c)
25.	(d)	26.	(d)	27.	(d)	28.	(a)
29.	(d)	30.	(d)	31.	(b)	32.	(d)
33.	(a)	34.	(c)	35.	(b)	36.	(b)
37.	(d)	38.	(d)	39.	(a)	40.	(b)
41.	(c)	42.	(a)	43.	(b)	44.	(b)
45.	(d)	46.	(a)	47.	(d)	48.	(c)
49.	(c)	50.	(d)				

SET 9
ASSESS YOURSELF

1. The Supreme Court of India, was set up
   (a) under the Indian Independence Act, 1948
   (b) under the Government of India Act 1930
   (c) by the Constitution
   (d) through the Parliament Act 1952.

2. The Panchayat is accountable for all its action to the
   (a) DRDA
   (b) Sarpanch
   (c) Panchayat Samiti
   (d) Gram Sabha.

3. Who can participate in the proceedings of Parliament even without being a member of Parliament?
   (a) The Cabinet Secretary
   (b) The Vice-President
   (c) The Attorney General
   (d) None of these.

4. The money flows in to the Consolidated Fund of India from
   (a) revenue collection (b) repayment of loans
   (c) fresh loans (d) all the above.

5. In India the party system can be described as
   (a) double party (b) single party
   (c) multi-party (d) none of these.

6. The power to review any judgements or order made by Supreme Court earlier is vested in
   (a) The Supreme Court itself
   (b) The President
   (c) The Council of Ministers
   (d) The Parliament.
7. In India the Panchayati Raj was started in
   (a) 1962 (b) 1950
   (c) 1952 (d) 1959.
8. Presently the Union Public Service Commission consists of a Chairman and
   (a) eight members
   (b) ten members
   (c) nine members
   (d) twelve members.
9. A constitutional bench of the Supreme Court consists of
   (a) 7 judges (b) 3 judges
   (c) 9 judges (d) 5 judges.
10. How many finance commissions have been appointed by the President so far?
    (a) Ten (b) Eight
    (c) Five (d) Fourteen.
11. The Constitution of India has created
    (a) a very weak Centre
    (b) a very strong Centre
    (c) a neutral Centre
    (d) none of these.
12. The Contingency Fund of India was
    (a) created by a parliamentary Act
    (b) created by the constitution amendment Act
    (c) created by a decisions of the Supreme Court
    (d) none of these.

13. The Annual Report of the Comptroller and Auditor General in respect of the Centre is submitted to
    (a) The President
    (b) The Public Accounts Committee
    (c) The Parliament
    (d) None of these.

14. The statutory status was given to the minorities Commission in
    (a) 1990 (b) 1992
    (c) 1979 (d) 1989.

15. The programme launched on October 2 was
    (a) The Panchayati Raj
    (b) The National Extension Service
    (c) The Community Development Programme
    (d) All the above programme.

16. The writ issued to courts, corporation or a persons enjoining to do its public duty is the
    (a) Writ of Prohibition
    (b) Writ of Quo Warranto
    (c) Habeas Corpus
    (d) Writ of Mandamus.

17. The executive head of a state is
    (a) The Chief Secretary
    (b) The Chief Minister
    (c) The Chief Justice of High Court
    (d) The Governor.

18. A person who is not a member of state legislature may be appointed a minister, but he ceases to hold office
    (a) if he is found guilty of corruption charges
    (b) if he is not found competent enough
    (c) if he is not elected to the state legislature within six months
    (d) none of the above.

19. Special status under article 370 of the Constitution was accorded to Jammu and Kashmir in terms of
    (a) the Government of India Act, 1947
    (b) an assurance given to the State Government at the time of its accession
    (c) the ceasefire agreeement concluded with Pakistan in 1948
    (d) none of these.

20. The Union list of the Constitution of India contains
    (a) 97 items (b) 74 items
    (c) 64 items (d) 54 items.

21. The Comptroller and Auditor General can be removed from office before expiry of his term by
    (a) The Parliament
    (b) The President on the advice of the Prime Minister
    (c) The Council of Ministers
    (d) The President on the recommendation of the Parliament.

22. The minorities commission comprises
    (a) six members (b) four members
    (c) seven members (d) nine members.

23. For meeting unforeseen expenses, the authority to advance money out of the contingency fund of India is vested in
    (a) The Prime Minister (b) The President
    (c) The Parliament (d) None of these.

24. The Panchayat Raj was first introduced in
    (a) Rajasthan (b) Kerala
    (c) Uttar Pradesh (d) Gujarat.

25. Which jurisdiction of the Supreme Court has been wrongly listed?
    (a) Original jurisdiction
    (b) Appellate jurisdiction
    (c) Advisory jurisdiction
    (d) None of the these.

26. The Ashok Mehta Committee on Panchayat Raj had recommended the
    (a) replacement of three -tier system by single -tier system
    (b) replacement of three -tier system by two-tier system
    (c) Continuation of Three-tier system
    (d) None of these.

27. The Judges of Supreme Court hold office till they attain the age of
    (a) 60 years (b) 65 years
    (c) 58 years (d) 62 years.

28. The Governor generally belongs to
    (a) the same state
    (b) some other state
    (c) the neighbouring state
    (d) any regular service.

29. The money bills can be introduced in the state legislature with prior consent by
    (a) The Chief Minister
    (b) The Governor
    (c) The Speaker, State Legislative Assembly
    (d) None of these.

30. The demand for ending the special status of Jammu and Kashmir gained momentum after
    (a) The end of terrorism in Punjab
    (b) The Indo Pak War in 1971
    (c) The enactment of Jammu and Kashir settlement Bill, 1982
    (d) None of these.

31. The Annual Report of the Union Public Service Commission is submitted to
    (a) The Union Home Secretary
    (b) The Parliament
    (c) The Minister of personnel, Government of India
    (d) The President.

32. India has been divided in to
    (a) Five Zonal Councils
    (b) Eight Zonal Councils
    (c) Six Zonal Councils
    (d) Ten Zonal Councils.

33. Originally how many Schedules were there in the Constitution?
    (a) 6 (b) 5
    (c) 9 (d) 8.

34. The Community Development Programme was launched on
    (a) August 15, 1952 (b) October 2, 1952
    (c) January 26, 1950 (d) None of these.

35. The Panchayat samities exist at
    (a) the village level
    (b) the block level
    (c) the district level
    (d) the taluka level.

36. The Supreme Court of India consist of a Chief Justice India and not more than
    (a) 18 other judges (b) 11 other judges
    (c) 15 other judges (d) 25 other judges.

37. The member of state legislature can draw the attention of government on matters of public importance through
    (a) Adjournment Motion
    (b) No-confidence motion
    (c) Cut motion
    (d) None of these.

38. The Constitutional Head of a state is
    (a) The Governor
    (b) The Chief Minister
    (c) The Chief Justice of High Court
    (d) The Chief Secretary.

39. The Union Public Service Commission can be assigned additional duties on the recommendation of

(a) The Prime Minister (b) The President

(c) The Parliament (d) None of these.

40. The Panchayat Raj institutions depends for funds mainly on

(a) Levy from farmers
(b) Government Finances
(c) Revenue Collection
(d) None of these.

41. The Attorney General holds office

(a) for a term of five years
(b) his post is coterminus with the Union Council of Ministers
(c) at the pleasure of the President
(d) None of these.

42. A judge of the Supreme Court can be removed from office by

(a) the parliament
(b) the President on the advice of parliament
(c) the Chief Justice of Supreme court on corruption charges
(d) the constitutional bench of the Supreme Court judges.

43. The Legislative Council in a state can be abolished by parliament on the recommendation of

(a) The State Legislative Assembly
(b) The Governor
(c) The Speaker, State Legislative Assembly
(d) The Prime Minister.

44. The Election Commission enjoys

(a) a Constitutional basis
(b) a statutory basis
(c) neither statutory nor constitutional basis
(d) none of these.

45. For the protection of minorities, The Minorities Commission was set up in

(a) January, 1979 (b) March, 1988
(c) February, 1987 (d) January, 1989.

46. The details of territories of the States and Union Territories are given in

(a) Schedule I
(b) Schedule II
(c) Schedule IV
(d) Schedule XI.

47. The Panchayati Raj is based on the ideology of

(a) democratic decentralisation
(b) people's participation in local administration
(c) rural people's awareness of political activities
(d) none of these.

48. The Judicial Review means

(a) the review of the judicial power of the judges
(b) the power of the courts to try cases
(c) the powers of the courts to declare null and void the powers enjoyed by any organ of the government beyond the power granted by the Constitution
(d) the review of the working of the judiciary.

49. The members of Legislative Assembly are elected for a term of

(a) Four years (b) Five years
(c) Four and half years (d) Six years.

50. The main advantage of Panchayati Raj is that

(a) it gives a sense of political awareness to the rural masses
(b) it creates more jobs under Panchayats
(c) it educates the rural masses
(d) it runs a parallel government in rural areas.

ANSWERS

1.	(c)	2.	(c)	3.	(c)	4.	(d)
5.	(c)	6.	(b)	7.	(b)	8.	(d)
9.	(a)	10.	(a)	11.	(b)	12.	(a)
13.	(a)	14.	(c)	15.	(c)	16.	(d)
17.	(d)	18.	(c)	19.	(b)	20.	(a)
21.	(b)	22.	(d)	23.	(b)	24.	(d)
25.	(d)	26.	(b)	27.	(b)	28.	(b)
29.	(b)	30.	(c)	31.	(d)	32.	(b)
33.	(c)	34.	(b)	35.	(a)	36.	(d)
37.	(a)	38.	(a)	39.	(b)	40.	(b)
41.	(c)	42.	(b)	43.	(b)	44.	(a)
45.	(c)	46.	(c)	47.	(a)	48.	(c)
49.	(b)	50.	(d)				

SET 10
ASSESS YOURSELF

1. Which one of the following is not a statutory body?
   (a) The Election Commission
   (b) The Planning Commission
   (c) The Union Public Service Commission
   (d) The Finance Commission.

2. Which of the following articles deals with appointment and term of office of members of Public Service Commission for the Union and for the States?
   (a) 304 (b) 315
   (c) 316 (d) 195.

3. The provision for a Consolidated Fund of India and consolidated fund for each state has been made under
   (a) Article 266 (b) Article 376
   (c) Article 166 (d) Article 366.

4. The Advocate General of each state receives a salary of
   (a) Rs. 8,000 per month
   (b) Rs. 7,000 per month
   (c) Rs. 6,500 per month
   (d) Rs. 5,000 per month.

5. The Zonal Councils were set up as a result of
   (a) Government of India Act 1935
   (b) Indian Indepedence Act 1947
   (c) State Reorganisation Act of 1956
   (d) None of these.

6. The provision for the establishment of the Inter-state Council has been made by the
   (a) Parliament (b) Cabinet
   (c) Constitution (d) None of these.

7. The Prime Minister is the Chairman of the
   (a) Planning Commission
   (b) Minorities Commission
   (c) Finance Commission
   (d) None of the above.

8. "Subject to the provisions of this article, there shall be a Public Service Commission for the Union and a Public Service Commission for each State", this has been stated under Article
   (a) 309 (b) 313
   (c) 315 (d) 115.

9. The provision for the Consolidated Fund of India has been made by the
   (a) President (b) Prime Minister
   (c) Constitution (d) Finance Ministry.

10. Which of the following articles deals with the appointment, duty and tenure of the Advocate General for the State?
    (a) 155 (b) 165
    (c) 175 (d) 185.

11. The meetings of the Zonal Council are presided over by the
    (a) President (b) Prime Minister
    (c) Chairman (d) None of these.

12. The Inter-state Councils are appointed by the
    (a) President
    (b) Prime Minister
    (c) Chief Justice of India
    (d) Vice President.

13. The Chief Election Commissioner is appointed by the
    (a) Prime Minister
    (b) Home Minister
    (c) Chairman, Union Public Service Commission
    (d) President.

14. "The President shall cause every recommendation made by the Finance Commission under the provision of this Constitution together with an explanatory memorandum as to the action taken thereon to be laid before each House of Parliament" this has been stated under article
    (a) 281 (b) 206
    (c) 217 (d) 280.

15. The Planning Commission was set upon
    (a) March 1950
    (b) March 1951
    (c) April 1951
    (d) April 1952.

16. Which of the following articles deals with removal and suspension of a member of a Public Service Commission
    (a) 317 (b) 305
    (c) 316 (d) 112.

17. Which one of the following is correct?
    (a) Each state has a seperate consolidated fund
    (b) All states have a common consolidated fund
    (c) Two or three states have a common consolidated fund
    (d) None of these.

18. Which of the following functionaries has the right to participate in the proceedings of State Legislature?
    (a) Chairman, State Public Service Commission
    (b) Chief Justice of High Court
    (c) Advocate General
    (d) Chief of Police Force in the State.

19. Which one of the following Zonal Council was created later on in 1972?
    (a) Northern Zonal Council
    (b) North Eastern Council
    (c) Central Zonal Council
    (d) Western Zonal Council.

20. Which of the following is the function of an Inter-state Council?
    (a) Inquiring into and advising upon disputes which may have arisen between states
    (b) Investigating and discussing subjects in which some or all of the states or the Union and one or more of the states, have a common interest
    (c) Making recommendations upon any subject and in particular, reconsideration for the better co-ordination of policy and action with respect to that subject
    (d) All the above.

21. The Chief Election Commissioner can be removed by the
    (a) Prime Minister
    (b) Parliament
    (c) President at his sweet will
    (d) None of these.

22. The Chairman and other members of the Finance Commission are appointed by the
    (a) President
    (b) Union Government
    (c) Chief Justice of India
    (d) State Governors.

23. Who was the first Chairman of the Planning Commission?
    (a) Jawaharlal Nehru
    (b) Gulzari Lal Nanda
    (c) K.C Neogy
    (d) Jivraj Mehra.

24. The Chairman and other members of the Union Public Service Commission are appointed by the
    (a) Prime Minister
    (b) President
    (c) Vice President
    (d) Home Minister.

25. The subjects of State Public Services and State Public Service Commission have been included in
    (a) Union List (b) State list
    (c) Concurrent list (d) None of the above.

26. All other public moneys received by or on behalf of the Government of India shall be credited to the
    (a) Contingency Fund of India
    (b) Consolidated Fund of India
    (c) Public Account of India
    (d) None of these.

27. Provision for the contingency Fund of India and a contingency fund for each state has ben made under
    (a) Article 267 (b) Article 268
    (c) Article 269 (d) Article 270.

28. The Advocate General of the State holds his office during the pleasure of the
    (a) Chief Minister
    (b) Prime Minister
    (c) Governor
    (d) Chief Justice of the High Court.

29. Which of the following regions does not have a Zonal Council?
    (a) Northern Zone
    (b) Southern Zone
    (c) Central Zone
    (d) North Western Zone.

30. The zonal councils discuss matters relating to
    (a) economic and social planning
    (b) border disputes
    (c) inter-state transport
    (d) all the above matter.

31. When can the President establish an Inter-state Council?
    (a) During an emergency
    (b) At his sweet will
    (c) If at any time it appears to the President that the public interest would be served by the establishment of an inter-state council he can establish the same
    (d) When the Governor of a state asks for it.

32. Who can recommend to President of India to waive the punishment awarded to a person by the Supreme Court due to the charge of use of corrupt practices in the election?
    (a) Prime Minister
    (b) Chief Election Commissioner
    (c) Chief Justice of India
    (d) Speaker of the Lok Sabha.

33. Who is responsible for keeping the voter's list up to date at all times?
    (a) The Home Ministry
    (b) The concerned states
    (c) The Election Commission
    (d) The parliamentary secretariat.

34. Who was the Chairman of the first Finance Commission?
    (a) K.Santhanm (b) Sri Niyogi
    (c) Sri A.K.Chanda (d) Dr. Rajamanner.

35. The recommendations of the Finance Commission are
    (a) not binding on the President
    (b) binding on the President
    (c) binding on the state
    (d) to be accepted by the Union Government.

36. Functions of Public Service Commissions have been stated under article
    (a) 303 (b) 310
    (c) 308 (d) 320.

37. The provision for the expenses of Public Service Commissions both of a union or states has been made under article
    (a) 322 (b) 323
    (c) 324 (d) 325.

38. All other public moneys received by or on behalf of the Government of a state shall be credited to the
    (a) Contingency Fund of the state
    (b) Public Account of the state
    (c) Consolidated Fund of the state
    (d) None of these.

39. From which source does money flow into the Consolidated Fund of India?
    (a) Revenues
    (b) Fresh holds
    (c) Repayments of loans
    (d) All these.

40. Advocate-General of a state is appointed by the
    (a) Chief Minister (b) Prime Minister
    (c) President (d) Governor.

41. How many Zonal Councils were originally constitutted?
    (a) Five (b) Six
    (c) Seven (d) Eight.

42. Zonal Councils are
    (a) Advisory bodies
    (b) Actually working bodies
    (c) Law making bodies
    (d) Administrative bodies.

43. Under which of the following articles the provision Inter-state Councils has been made?

(a) Art. 263 (b) Art. 363

(c) Art. 163 (d) Art. 170.

44. The Finance Commission consists of the

(a) Chairman and five other members

(b) Chairman and four other members

(c) Chairman and three other members

(d) Chairman and two other members.

45. The recommendations made by the Finance Commission are

(a) submitted to the Supreme Court

(b) submitted to the State Governor

(c) laid before the each house of Parliament by the President

(d) None of the above.

46. The members of the UPSC hold office

(a) for a term of six years or till they attain the age of 65 years

(b) for a term of five years irrespective of the upper age limit

(c) for a term of six years or till they attain the age of 62 years

(d) owing the pleasure of the President.

47. Which one of the following is not a function of the Union Public Service Commission?

(a) It conducts examinations for appointment to the service of the Union

(b) It shall be consulted on all matters relating to methods of requiretment to civil services and for civil posts

(c) Shall be consulted on all disciplinary matters affecting a person serving under the Government of India

(d) It also give suggestions regarding maintaining the accounts of the Union Government.

48. A State PSC member resigns by writing a letter addressed to the

(a) President (b) UPSC Chairman

(c) Governor (d) Chief Minister.

49. Provision for the Contingency Fund of India as well as a contingency fund for each state has been made by the

(a) President (b) Parliament

(c) Constitution (d) None of the above.

50. The contingency fund of the state is operated by

(a) The Governor

(b) The Chief Minister

(c) The State Finance Minister

(d) By all three jointly.

ANSWERS

1.	(b)	2.	(c)	3.	(a)	4.	(a)
5.	(c)	6.	(c)	7.	(a)	8.	(c)
9.	(c)	10.	(b)	11.	(c)	12.	(a)
13.	(d)	14.	(a)	15.	(a)	16.	(a)
17.	(a)	18.	(c)	19.	(b)	20.	(d)
21.	(d)	22.	(a)	23.	(a)	24.	(b)
25.	(b)	26.	(c)	27.	(a)	28.	(c)
29.	(d)	30.	(d)	31.	(c)	32.	(b)
33.	(c)	34.	(b)	35.	(a)	36.	(d)
37.	(a)	38.	(b)	39.	(d)	40.	(d)
41.	(a)	42.	(a)	43.	(a)	44.	(b)
45.	(c)	46.	(a)	47.	(d)	48.	(c)
49.	(c)	50.	(a)				

SET 11
ASSESS YOURSELF

1. Which of the following schedules deals with the provisions as to the Administration and control of Scheduled areas and Scheduled tribes?
   (a) Fifth (b) Sixth
   (c) Seventh (d) Eight.

2. Reservation of seats for scheduled castes and scheduled tribes in the legislative assemblies of the states have been mentioned under article
   (a) 330 (b) 331
   (c) 332 (d) 333.

3. Which of the following has not been correctly placed as power the Warrant of Precedence?
   (a) Ex-Presidents and Ex-Governor Generals
   (b) Lieutenant Governors within their respective charge
   (c) Chief Justice of India and Speaker of the Lok Sabha
   (d) None of these.

4. The words "Satyamave Jayte" are inscribed below the emblem in the
   (a) Roman script
   (b) Devanagri script
   (c) Arabic script
   (d) None of these.

5. Our National Flag was adopted by the
   (a) British Parliament
   (b) Our Parliament
   (c) Constituent Assembly
   (d) None of these.
6. A Schedule is a
   (a) syllabus of a college
   (b) law
   (c) written supplementary explanatory, or appended document, it is an appendix to a bill or an act of Parliament
   (d) none of these.
7. How many schedules are there in the Indian Constituion?
   (a) Nine (b) Ten
   (c) Eleven (d) Twelve.
8. Which Schedule details the territories of the states and Union territories?
   (a) Schedule I
   (b) Schedule VII
   (c) Schedule VIII
   (d) None of the above.
9. Provisions as to the judges of the Supreme Court and of the High Courts have been included under schedule
   (a) first (b) second
   (c) third (d) none of the above.
10. Provisions as to disqualification on ground of defection have been made under schedule
   (a) Tenth (b) Seventh
   (c) Sixth (d) Eighth.
11. Ninth Schedule of the Indian Constitution is associated with Article _______ of the Indian Constitution
   (a) 344 (b) 346
   (c) 318 (d) 224.

12. Which one of the following is wrong?
    (a) The first Schedule contains the name of the states of the Indian Union
    (b) The second schedule contains the details regarding he salaries and allowances for the President, Governor, Speaker and the Deputy Speaker, of the House of the People etc
    (c) The Third Schedule contains the forms of oaths and affirmations
    (d) None of these.

13. The Ninth Schedule
    (a) formed part of the original Constitution
    (b) was added to the Constitution by the first amendment
    (c) was added to the Constitution by the 24th amendment
    (d) was added to the Constitution by the 42nd amendment.

14. Which of the following parts deals with special provisions relating to certain?
    (a) Part XV (b) Part XVI
    (c) Part XI (d) None of the above.

15. Which one of the following has been wrongly placed as per the warrant of precedence?
    (a) President (b) Vice President
    (c) Governors (d) Prime Minister.

16. The National Emblem and the Seal of the Government of India is a replica of the Capital of Ashoka's pillar at
    (a) Delhi (b) Kangra
    (c) Sarnath (d) Ambala.

17. The design of the Dharma Chakra is the wheel which appears on the abacus of the Sarnath Lion Capital. The Dharma Chakra has
    (a) 12 spokes (b) 16 spokes
    (c) 20 spokes (d) 24 spokes.

18. Which one of the following is correct?
    (a) The fourth schedule gives the allocation of seats in the Council of States Councils
    (b) The fifth schedule gives provisions for the administration and control of scheduled areas and scheduled tribes
    (c) The sixth schedule gives provisions for the administration and control of scheduled areas and scheduled tribes
    (d) All the above.

19. In which of the following articles has the provisions for reservations of seats for scheduled castes and scheduled tribes in the House of the People been made
    (a) 330 (b) 331
    (c) 332 (d) 333.

20. Which one of the following has been correctly placed as per the warrant of precedence
    (a) Cabinet Ministers of the Union
    (b) Holders of the Bharat Ratna Decoration
    (c) Ambassadors Extra ordinaryand plenipotentiary accredited to India and High Commissioner of Commonwealth Government in India
    (d) All the above.

21. The pillar from where the emblem has been adopted was raised by emperor Ashoka between 242-232 B.C to mark the spot
    (a) Where Lord Buddha dies
    (b) Where Lord Buddha was born
    (c) Where Lord Buddha was married
    (d) Lord Buddha first initiated his disciples in the Eight fold path of Salvation

22. Which one of the following is wrong?
    (a) The National Flag of India consists of three horizontal tricolour
    (b) The saffron is at the top, dark green in the middle and white at the bottom

(c) All strips are equal in breadth

(d) The ratio of the width to the length of the Flag is two to three

23. Match the following columns of Schedules and their contents

A.	Fourth	1.	Allocation of seats in the Council of States
B.	Second	2.	Emoluments, Allowances and service conditions of President and to the Governors of the States
C.	Seventh	3.	Three lists
D.	Sixth	4.	Provisions relating to administration of tribal areas

Select the correct answer using the codes given below

(a) A-1,B-3,C-2, D-4

(b) A-1, B-2, C-4,D-3

(c) A-1, B-2, C-3, D 4

(d) A-4, B-3, C-1, D-2.

24. Representation of the Anglo-Indian Community in the Legislative Assemblies of the states has been made under article

(a) 333 (b) 350

(c) 370 (d) 380.

25. Which one of the following has been wrongly placed as per the Warrant of Precedence?

(a) Governors outside their respective charges

(b) Lieutenant-Governor outside their respective charges

(c) Chief Minister of State

(d) None of these.

26. The National Emblem and Seal was adopted on

(a) January 26,1949

(b) January 26,1952

(c) January 26, 1950 by the Government of India

(d) None of these.

27. Our National Flag was adopted by the Constituent Assembly of India on July 22, 1947 and it was presented to the nation at the mid night session of the Assembly on
    (a) January 26,1950
    (b) January 26,1947
    (c) August 14,1947
    (d) August 15,1947.

28. Which one of the following is wrong?
    (a) The seventh schedule gives three lists of subjects, the Union list, the state list and concurrent list
    (b) The Eighth schedule gives description of eighteen languages
    (c) The Ninth Schedule includes certain Acts regarding land ceiling and Abolition of Zamindari passed by the State Government which have been given protection under the Cabinet Union
    (d) None of these.

29. "Reservation of seats and special representation of cease after fifty years" This has been stated under article
    (a) 330 (b) 331
    (c) 333 (d) 334.

30. The administrators of Union Territories are designated as
    (a) Lieutenant Governors
    (b) Chief Commissioners
    (c) Administrators
    (d) All the above.

31. Which one of the following is wrong?
    (a) The dipping of the National Flag before any person or thing is prohibited
    (b) No other flag should be placed above the National Flag or to its right
    (c) All the other flags are only placed to the left of the National Flag if they are hung in a line
    (d) None of these.

32. Which amendment added the Tenth Schedule to the Constitution?

(a) 48th (b) 52nd
(c) 53rd (d) None of these.

33. Special provision with respect to educational grants for the benefit of Anglo-Indian Community has been made under article

(a) 303 (b) 315
(c) 327 (d) 337.

34. Which one of the following is correct?

(a) When other flags are flown alongwith the National Flag then the National Flag should be at the top
(b) The National Flag should always be carried a left and free
(c) If carried in a procession, the National Flag must be borne high on the right shoulder of the standard bearer and carried in front of the procession
(d) All the above.

35. The Tenth Schedule contains

(a) Details regarding the teritories of the newly created state of Mizoram and speical provisions in respect of that state
(b) Provisions regarding disqualifications on grounds of defection
(c) Terms and conditions of the associate status of Sikkim
(d) None of these.

36. "National Commission for Scheduled Castes and Scheduled Tribes" this has been stated under article

(a) 326 (b) 327
(c) 338 (d) 340.

37. Which one of the following is not correct?

(a) The National Flag is flown on all important government buildings, such as the Supreme Court, High Courts, Secretariat, Collectorates etc.

(b) In the frontier areas the National Flag can be flown on special points

(c) The use of the National Flag is unrestricted on certain special occasions such as Independence Day, Republic Day etc

(d) None of these.

38. The provision for control of the Union over the administration of Scheduled areas and the welfare of scheduled tribes has been made under article

(a) 239 (b) 339

(c) 350 (d) 370.

39. Special provision to Backward classes and minority communities have been made by the

(a) President

(b) Cabinet

(c) Constitution

(d) Parliament.

40. In which of the following articles has the provision for appointment of a commission to investigate the conditions of backward classes been made?

(a) 140 (b) 240

(c) 340 (d) 360.

41. Which one of the following provisions has been made regarding the protection of Linguistic Minorities?

(a) Certain provisions for the protection of Linguistic Minorities were added by the seventh amendment Act of 1956

(b) Provisions for adequate facilities for instruction in the mother tongue at the primary stage to the children of the minority groups have been made

(c) The President of India has been given the powers to issue directives to the states in this regard as well as to appoint a special officer for linguistic minorities

(d) All the above.

42. Which of the following provisions has been made for the Anglo-Indian Community?
    (a) Special provisions for the adequate representation of the community in the House of the People and the State Legislative Assemblies have been made
    (b) The President of India can nominate two members belonging to the Anglo-Indian Community to the Legislative Assembly
    (c) Certain special provisions have also been made regarding the educational grants for the benefit of Anglo-Indian Community
    (d) All the above.

43. Which one of the following is not a provision for the backward classes?
    (a) The President may appoint a Commission to investigate the conditions of socially and educationally backward classes
    (b) The Commission will make recommendations to improve the conditions of the Backward classes
    (c) President will place a copy of the commission's report together with a memorandum explaining the action taken thereon to be laid before each House of Parliament
    (d) None of these.

44. The Minorities Commission was given Statutory status in
    (a) 1989 (b) 1990
    (c) 1991 (d) 1992.

45. The Minorities Commission for protection of the minorities was first set up in
    (a) August 1956
    (b) January 1979
    (c) November 1984
    (d) June 1992.

46. For the protection and promotion of the interests of the backward classes (SCs and STs) seats have been reserved for them

(a) in public servcies
(b) in the defence services
(c) in none of the above
(d) in public services as well as legislatives.

47. The special officer who looks into the working of the safeguards for scheduled castes/scheduled tribes is known as the
(a) commissioner for scheduled castes and tribes
(b) commissioner for welfare of backward classes
(c) commissioner for social welfare
(d) commissioner for social welfare and family planning.

48. There shall be a special officer for linguistic minorities to be appointed by the President", this has been stated under article
(a) 360 (b) 350 A
(c) 350 B (d) 310.

49. Which one of the following is not a Right listed in the Constitutions?
(a) Equality in matters of appointment under state
(b) Denial of special treatment for all sections including women, children and backward classes
(c) Abolition of titles other than academic and military distinctions
(d) All of the above are part of the Constitution.

50. What is the present number of seats allotted to schedule tribes in Lok Sabha
(a) 40 (b) 50
(c) 79 (d) 89.

ANSWERS

1.	(a)	2.	(d)	3.	(d)	4.	(b)
5.	(c)	6.	(c)	7.	(d)	8.	(a)
9.	(b)	10.	(a)	11.	(c)	12.	(d)

13.	(b)	14.	(b)	15.	(c)	16.	(c)
17.	(d)	18.	(d)	19.	(a)	20.	(d)
21.	(d)	22.	(b)	23.	(c)	24.	(a)
25.	(d)	26.	(c)	27.	(c)	28.	(d)
29.	(d)	30.	(d)	31.	(d)	32.	(b)
33.	(d)	38.	(b)	39.	(c)	40.	(c)
41.	(d)	42.	(d)	43.	(d)	44.	(d)
45.	(b)	46.	(d)	47.	(a)	48.	(c)
49.	(b)	50.	(a)				

SET 12
ASSESS YOURSELF

1. A rigid constitution is one
   (a) that is not written
   (b) that does not permit of amendment
   (c) that can be amended by 3/4 majority
   (d) that can be amended by a special procedure, different from that ordinary law making.

2. The most essential feature of Federal Government is
   (a) Supremacy of Parliament
   (b) Supremacy of Judiciary
   (c) Division of power between the Federal and the State Governments
   (d) Single citizenship.

3. Constitutional Government means
   (a) representative government
   (b) limited government
   (c) government according to the constitution
   (d) government by the consent of the poeple.

4. Which one of the following statement is wrong?
   (a) Under the parliamentary system there exists the leadership of the Prime Minister, but under the presidential system the President is the leader of the government
   (b) Under the parliamentary system there exists both

titular head and the actual head, but under the Presidential system there is only one head

(c) Under the Parliamentary system there is the integration between the legislature and the executive but under the Presidential system there is seperation between the legislature and the executive

(d) Under the parliamentary system sovereignity rests with parliament but under the Presidential system the President is a sovereign.

5. Which of the following is /are form or system in which the unitary system is compatible?

1. Presidential form of government
2. Parliamentary form of government
3. System of judicial review

Choose the correct answer from the codes given below

(a) 1 and 2 (b) 1,2 and 3
(c) 1 and 3 (d) None of these.

6. The cabinet form of government mean

(a) a system of government which is marked by the existence of a group which collectively decided on the policies of the government and which also collectively responsible to the parliament

(b) a form of government in which the cabinet is supreme and is not accountable to any other organ as the state

(c) a form of government in which alll the members of the cabinet are popularly elected on the basis of universal adult franchise

(d) a form of government in which it is the President and not the Prime Minister who presides over the cabinet meetings for the reason that he is directly elected by the people.

7. The impeachment of the President of India can be initiated in

(a) either House of Parliament
(b) in a joint sitting of both Houses of parliament
(c) the Lok Sabha
(d) the Rajya Sabha.

8. To function successfully, Panchayati Raj needs the full co-operation of the
   (a) Central Government (b) Bureaucracy
   (c) Politicians (d) Local People.

9. The Municipal corporation of which one of the following major cities is not set up under a specific act of the state legislature, but under an act of parliament?
   (a) Bombay (b) Delhi
   (c) Calcutta (d) Madras.

10. Who has representation in the Zila Parishad?
    (a) Women
    (b) Scheduled Castes & Scheduled Tribes
    (c) Representatives of co-operative societies
    (d) All of the above.

11. The local MPs and MLAs are ex-officio members of the
    (a) Zila Parishad
    (b) Panchayat Samiti
    (c) Gram Sabha
    (d) All these bodies.

12. What is the usual term in office of an elected Mayor
    (a) one year (b) two years
    (c) three years (d) five years.

13. The Panchayat is accountable for all its actions to the
    (a) Sarpanch
    (b) Panchayat Samiti
    (c) District Officer
    (d) Gram Sabha.

14. The officer of the Comptroller and Auditor General was created
    (a) under the Constitution
    (b) through a cabinet resolution
    (c) through an enactment of the parliament
    (d) none of the above.

15. The Comptroller and Auditor-General of India is appoined by the
    (a) Vice-President (b) President
    (c) Prime Minister (d) Chief Justice of India.

16. The Comptroller and Auditor-General of India can be removed from his office by the
    (a) Prime Minister
    (b) Chief Justice of India
    (c) President (on the recommendations of the Parliament)
    (d) Home Minister.

17. The salary of the Comptroller and Auditor-General of India is
    (a) Rs. 10,000 per month
    (b) Rs 9,000 per month
    (c) Rs. 8,500 per month
    (d) Rs. 7,000 per month.

18. Duties and powers of the Comptroller and Auditor-General have been stated under article
    (a) 149 (b) 150
    (c) 151 (d) 152.

19. The Comptroller and Auditor-General of India was relieved of his responsibilities of maintenance of accounts in
    (a) 1967 (b) 1976
    (c) 1981 (d) 1989.

20. "The reports of the Comptroller and Auditor General of India relating to the accounts of the Union shall be submitted to the President, who shall cause them to be laid before each Houses of Parliament" under article.
    (a) 150 (b) 151
    (c) 152 (d) 153.

21. In which State was Panchayati Raj first introduced?
    (a) Gujarat (b) Rajasthan
    (c) Bihar (d) Andhra Pradesh.

22. Which one of the following Union Territories has a two-tier system of Panchayati Raj?
    (a) Chandigarh
    (b) Delhi
    (c) Dadra and Nagar Haveli
    (d) Daman andDiu.

23. What is the main purpose of Panchayati Raj?
    (a) To increase agricultural production
    (b) To create employment
    (c) To make people politically conscious
    (d) To make people participate in development administration.

24. The Panchayat Samiti exists at
    (a) the village level
    (b) the block level
    (c) the Zila level
    (d) all these level.

25. The local self-governing institution for a medium sized town with a population of twenty thousand and above is known as a
    (a) Municipal Corporation
    (b) Municipal Committee
    (c) Zila Parishad
    (d) Panchayat Samiti.

26. The Zila Parishad is
    (a) A co-ordinating and supervisory body
    (b) An implementing body
    (c) A judicial body
    (d) A combination of all the above.

27. Which of the following is not one of the source of revenue of village panchayats?
    (a) Government Grants
    (b) House Tax

(c) Income Tax
(d) Local Taxes on land.

28. Which one of the following has been the major cause for the failure of the Panchayati Raj System?
(a) Illiteracy
(b) Poor implementation
(c) Non-cooperation of the people
(d) Political pressure.

29. Community development is organised on the basis of
(a) population
(b) area
(c) community
(d) none of the above.

30. A Community development block covers about
(a) 10 villages (b) 100 villages
(c) one village (d) 150 villages.

31. The Comptroller and Auditor-General is associated with
(a) Business Advisory Committee
(b) Committee on Public Undertakings
(c) Public Accounts Committee
(d) All of the above.

32. Who is known as the 'Watch dog" of the Public Finance?
(a) Finance Minister
(b) Chairman of the Finance Commission
(c) The Chief Justice of India
(d) Comptroller and Auditor-General of India.

33. The Comptroller and Auditor-General acts as the friend, philosopher and guide of
(a) The Estimates Committee
(b) The Committee on Public Undertakings
(c) The Public Accounts Committee
(d) All of the above.

34. The salary and allowances of the Comptroller and Auditor General
    (a) have been prescribed in the Constitution
    (b) are determined by president in consultation with the Chief Justice of India
    (c) are determined by the Parliament
    (d) are determined by the Union council of Ministers.

35. The Comptroller and Auditor-General acts as
    (a) the guardian of People's liberties
    (b) the guardian of public finances
    (c) the Chief legal adviser of the government
    (d) all of the above

36. The salary of the Comptroller and Auditor-General of India is
    (a) not charged upon the Cosolidated Fund of India
    (b) votable in the parliament
    (c) charged upon the Consolidated Fund of India
    (d) none of the above.

37. The Comptroller and Auditor-General submits his annual report in respect of the Centre to
    (a) The President
    (b) The Parliament
    (c) The Chairman of the Planning Commission
    (d) The Chief Justice of India.

38. The Comptroller and Auditor-General performs
    (a) only audit functions
    (b) only accounting functions
    (c) both accounting and audit functions
    (d) accounting auditing and judicial functions.

39. Panchayati Raj Institutions depend for funds mainly on
    (a) local taxes
    (b) property tax
    (c) government finances
    (d) special taxes.

40. A Panchayat Samiti at the block level is
    (a) an advisory body
    (b) an administrative authority
    (c) a consultant committee
    (d) a supervisory authority.

41. Pick out the statement which is not correct?
    (a) The Gram Panchayat is headed by the Sarpanch
    (b) The Panchayat Samiti is headed by the Chairman
    (c) The Zila Parishad is headed by the Chairman
    (d) The Sarpanch and the Chairman are elected directly by the people.

42. Who are generally the members of Gram Sabha?
    (a) All the heads of families of the respective villages
    (b) All the voters in the respective villages
    (c) All the adult males in the villages
    (d) Nominated members.

43. When was the Community Development Programme launched?
    (a) January 26, 1950
    (b) August 15,1952
    (c) October 2, 1952
    (d) June 1, 1975.

44. The community development programme was launched with a view to
    (a) overcoming the problem of unemployment
    (b) developing scientific outlook among rural folk
    (c) cultivating the spirit of self reliance and initiative among rural people
    (d) All the above.

45. In the Community Development Programme the government provides
    (a) only technical guidance
    (b) only financial assistance

(c) none of these
(d) both (a) and (b).

46. What programme was launched on the birth day of Mahatama Gandhi?
(a) Community Development Programme
(b) National Extension Service
(c) Panchayati Raj
(d) All the above programmes.

47. Who played a vital role in the integration of princely states?
(a) Jawahar Lal Nehru and Sardar Patel
(b) Mahatama Gandhi and Jawahar Lal Nehru
(c) Sardar Patel and G.B. Pant
(d) Sardar Patel and V.P. Menon.

48. Which one of the following recommended a change in the pattern of dyarchy introduced under the act of 1919?
(a) Muddiman Committee
(b) Sapru Committee
(c) Simon Committee
(d) Butter Commission.

49. The Act in which for the first time statutory rules were formed to separate provincial subjects form the Central subjects was the
(a) Government of India Act 1935
(b) Government of India Act 1919
(c) Indian Councils Act, 1909
(d) Indian Councils Act 1892.

50. Under which one of the following acts was to command Electorate system introduced by te British in India for the first time?
(a) Government of India Act 1909
(b) Government of India Act 1919
(c) Indian Councils Act, 1861
(d) Indian Councils Act 1862.

ANSWERS

1.	(d)	2.	(c)	3.	(c)	4.	(b)
5.	(c)	6.	(b)	7.	(a)	8.	(d)
9.	(b)	10.	(d)	11.	(a)	12.	(a)
13.	(d)	14.	(a)	15.	(b)	16.	(c)
17.	(b)	18.	(a)	19.	(d)	20.	(d)
21.	(b)	22.	(c)	23.	(d)	24.	(b)
25.	(b)	26.	(a)	27.	(c)	28.	(b)
29.	(b)	30.	(b)	31.	(c)	32.	(d)
33.	(c)	34.	(c)	35.	(b)	36.	(c)
37.	(a)	38.	(b)	39.	(c)	40.	(b)
41.	(d)	42.	(b)	43.	(c)	44.	(c)
45.	(d)	46.	(d)	47.	(d)	48.	(c)
49.	(b)	50.	(a)				